CIVIL WARS

CIVIL WARS

INTERNAL STRUGGLES, GLOBAL CONSEQUENCES

Marie Olson Lounsbery and Frederic Pearson

University of Toronto Press

Library and Archives Canada Cataloguing in Publication

Olson Lounsbery, Marie, 1970–
    Civil wars / Marie Olson Lounsbery and Frederic Pearson.

Includes bibliographical references and index.
ISBN 978-0-80209-072-2 (paperback)
ISBN 978-1-44260-132-1 (cloth)

    1. Civil war. 2. Insurgency. I. Pearson, Frederic, 1944– II. Title.

JC328.5.L68 2008   303.6'4   C2008-905650-7

We welcome comments and suggestions regarding any aspect of our publications —
please feel free to contact us at news@utphighereducation.com or visit our internet site
at www.utphighereducation.com.

North America
5201 Dufferin Street
Toronto, Ontario, Canada, M3H 5T8

2250 Military Road
Tonawanda, New York, USA, 14150

UK, Ireland, and continental Europe
NBN International
Estover Road, Plymouth, PL6 7PY, UK
tel: 44 (0) 1752 202301
fax order line: 44 (0) 1752 202333
enquiries@nbninternational.com

orders phone: 1-800-565-9523
orders fax: 1-800-221-9985
orders email: utpbooks@utpress.utoronto.ca

This book is printed on paper containing 100% post-consumer fibre.

The University of Toronto Press acknowledges the financial support for its publishing
activities of the Government of Canada through the Book Publishing Industry
Development Program (BPIDP).

Designed by Aldo Fierro

Printed in Canada

For Luke and his generation

Contents

PREFACE • vii

Chapter One
CIVIL WAR IN THE CONTEMPORARY ERA • 1

Chapter Two
THE CAUSES OF CIVIL WAR: INDIVIDUAL AND GROUP ANALYSIS • 25

Chapter Three
STATE-LEVEL FACTORS LEADING TO CIVIL WAR • 55

Chapter Four
INTERNATIONAL EFFECTS ON CIVIL WARS • 83

Chapter Five
CONFLICT PROCESSES DURING CIVIL WARS • 119

Chapter Six
THE RESOLUTION OF CIVIL WARS • 155

Chapter Seven
THE AFTERMATH OF CIVIL WAR • 197

Appendix
A LIST OF INTRASTATE CONFLICTS, 1946–2000 • 223

REFERENCES • 229

INDEX • 247

PREFACE

The debate over whether the Iraq War became a civil war sometime between 2003 and 2007 highlighted more than uncertainties over the use of terminology. It carried political as well as legal implications for US involvement, the future of the Iraqi people, and the future of the Middle East. Upheavals involving large-scale civil violence always do.

Terms such as "civil war" are prone to be thrown around by media and batted around for political advantage by politicians, not least to condemn the policies of opponents. Yet, civil war has more specific meaning in the annals of international law and in foreign policy and war studies. This book is an attempt to gauge those meanings.

Whether a situation is recognized formally as a civil war, or as organized political violence short of war, or as communal violence, or as riots and anarchy has implications for legal responsibilities, such as third parties' responsibilities to stay out of the fray or combatants' responsibilities to protect local populations. War's unofficial or official status can also legitimize or delegitimize calls for "defense of the homeland" or to put down an insurrection. For a government to recognize, or have others recognize, that it is in a situation of civil insurrection or war, that its opponents are other than "bandits" or "criminals" or "terrorists," is a political minefield. Interests ranging from staying in power to losing economic standing are at stake.

This book grew out of a course offering on civil war at both Wayne State and Nova Southeastern universities, and more recently at East Carolina University. In the process of organizing this course, whose materials and structure are online at http://www.ecu.edu/polsci/faculty/lounsbery.html, we realized that there was no existing comprehensive text on civil wars as a phenomenon. While excellent studies of the origins of specific wars or of wars in general, or their patterns of fighting or foreign intervention, or their outcomes or peacemaking processes existed, no single text approached all three phases: origin, process, and outcome.

Political scientists tend to consider phenomena such as civil wars as amenable to comparative analysis and generalizations. They also point to the underlying political disputes and gambits, and the decisional processes and policy enactments, that constitute the grievances or motivations for such wars. The roles of individual leaders and groups of followers interact to produce the dynamics of warfare. Historians tend to think of such wars as *sui generis*, requiring first and foremost in-depth case analysis.

We have attempted to combine both approaches in this study, by offering aggregate data and comparative commentary, by considering the policy-making that precedes and accompanies warfare, and by delving into the particulars of specific situations, regions, and cases to determine their unique flavor. This combination of approaches is especially important as we grapple with the ways that culture, identity, and historical experience play into the origin and outcome of wars, even as larger patterns of international and national power, institutions, and structure exert their influence. We strive to present the latest research findings in the literature and to synthesize these results as best we can into explanatory frameworks.

Given that it is only relatively recently that scholars have paid sustained, systematic attention to civil wars as a category, we are also intrigued to study the relevance of time-tested concepts of international warfare, such as power balances, arms races, and action-reaction cycles, in domestic settings. We do not yet know whether notions such as "enduring rivalries," "recurrent crises," "security dilemmas," and "democratic peace" apply in such settings, and whether they apply similarly to the way they do in international wars. In this book we take the first steps to answer such telling questions and to generate greater understanding of war. We also note the fuzzy boundaries between domestic and international war, and the intriguing influence one has on the other and on related phenomena, such as revolution.

International war obviously is tremendously disruptive, with profound and deadly impacts on people's lives. How much more intense is the fallout of civil war, bringing tragedy and terror to people's doorsteps, and embodying the famous adage of US Representative Thomas "Tip" O'Neill, that "all politics are local." In the case of civil war, the distinctions between military versus civilian killing become even less tenable than in international warfare; events all too frequently boil over into "ethnic cleansing" and genocide. It is therefore of utmost importance to gain insight into domestic warfare processes, so that perhaps in the future early warning and timely remedial action can spare people some of this trauma—so that children of the next generation do not have to lose their loved ones and their futures in the morass of bloodletting among neighbors.

As in any endeavor seeking to break new ground, we have benefited greatly from the advice and assistance of others. In our case this includes such colleagues as Patrick Regan, Jacob Bercovitch, J. David Singer, Sean Byrne, Andrea Talentino, Louis Kriesberg, Dennis Sandole, Suzanne Grillot, Brad Roth, Hamdesa Tuso, Otto Feinstein, Melvin Small, Abdullahi Osman, Jeffrey Pickering, David Kinsella, Nic Marsh, and those at the Peace Research Institute Oslo (PRIO). We have also learned a great deal from our students, including Susumu Suzuki, Loreta Costa, Kofi Nsia-Pepra, John Manza, and Piotr Zagorowski. We would further like to thank Ashvini Ambardekar, Lisa Snyder, and Katie Miller for their clerical assistance. Of course, the responsibility for the conclusions and assertions we have made remains ours alone.

We owe a debt of gratitude to Gregory Yantz, our editor, along with the staff at Broadview Press and University of Toronto Press, who indeed have taken the broad view with vision and encouragement about the potential impact of this volume, and with warmth and patience in its development. Our families, Thor Lounsbery, Mebby, Nathaniel, Helen and Emma Pearson, also have provided the needed space and support, while asking the "right questions" to make writing possible through the most hectic and demanding times.

A young member of one of our families wrote the following poem as a 10th grade class project. We feel that it captures the human concerns upon which civil war impinges so heavily:

I Hear Uganda Crying

I hear Uganda crying, suffering from the pain of being an invisible nation
The crying of the children being used as weapons and victims
The crying of the families that see conflict and injustice, thinking that they know although they do not

The crying of the children that are living their life in hiding
The never-ending war that takes children away, along with their potential
I see the tears of lost education, determination—creating frustration
The innocent people dying of disease and starvation or dying of the misery of being forced to be a soldier
I see the tears of young children continuing to be cautious during this time of confusion
I see the tears of the invisible children that have to whisper within walls so they will not be heard
I see the tears of the people piling into the army losing their hopes, dreams and losing most of their life
The parents crying when their children are being taken away, forced to run away, or lost away in the small, crowded cities in Uganda
The crying that deepens the thoughts in all of people's minds in America, unexpectedly feeling a loss
I hear Uganda crying

—Ashley Miller, April 2008

CHAPTER ONE

Civil War in the Contemporary Era

"Civil war? What does that mean? Is there any foreign war? Isn't every war fought between men, between brothers?"

—Victor Hugo

The end of the Cold War in 1990 brought with it a challenging international environment. Although great optimism existed at that time regarding the possibility of a more collaborative and peaceful international political system, what followed was anything but. Quickly the terror of nuclear annihilation between superpowers was replaced with a perplexing new set of worries. Instead of Cold War ideological conflicts, the world witnessed a series of, what was termed at the time, "ethnic conflicts." Optimism waned as we watched Somalia disintegrate into chaos, with the quick withdrawal of US Marines once they had become targets of violence in the midst of a supposedly humanitarian mission. Hopes for a more peaceful world were further shattered as 800,000 Rwandans were killed by their own countrymen in a period of three months (BBC, 1 April 2004) as the international "community" stood by. The carnage in the Balkan wars also dashed the hopes for a new era based on a progressive "new Europe."

At the time we knew relatively little about this type of conflict. We were startled by the intense hatred and the renewal of old grievances

1

and grudges, and stymied by our seeming inability to do anything about it. As striking as traditional, international, or interstate war is, the intensity and brutality of civil violence seemed to be in a different league. Certainly soldiers are sometimes trained to hate their enemies, using stereotypical names or distorted images when they prepare for combat in distant countries. What occurred in Somalia, Rwanda, Bosnia, and several other countries at the time appeared quite different, and seemed to reflect deeply held, even ingrained, hatred bred over decades if not centuries. And yet many of these disputes also presented an enigma, in that for long periods of time diverse peoples had lived together relatively peacefully and even harmoniously, especially in multi-ethnic areas such as Bosnia. It was too simple to dismiss these as merely ongoing age-old wars.

The prevalence of civil conflicts has continued throughout the post-Cold War period, and although some analysts have detected a downturn in the outbreak of new wars (Gurr, 2000a), there is little indication that they are going away. In fact, we continue to see the types of intrastate struggles that could erupt into civil violence and even full-blown civil wars in states such as Iraq, Afghanistan, Pakistan, and Lebanon, to name a few. Internal and civil wars seem to have devastating consequences in the lives of those touched by the violence, as well as threatening future prospects of states struggling to build institutions across divided societies. Civil wars also transcend boundaries, as weaponry, mercenaries, terrorists, refugees, epidemics, and environmental degradation flow freely across borders, destabilizing regions in the process.

As a result, although international war still occurs (e.g., two Gulf wars in 15 years), and while many international wars stem from or degenerate into civil violence (as in Iraq in 2004), many scholars and researchers have turned their attention from interstate violence to that occurring within states in an effort to better understand the underlying conflicts so that we might prevent further bloodshed. We now know quite a bit more about the various factors that contribute to the outbreak of violence within states, factors such as perceived discrimination and insecurity, belligerent leaders, and the effect of economic dislocation (see for example, Kaufman, 1996, 2001). Among the factors explored is the way that conflicts change or re-emerge over time, thereby making them more or less amenable to resolution. Given that so much of this work has been completed since the end of the Cold War, what is needed is a review that brings this research together and draws further conclusions, allowing students and scholars of intrastate violence to assess the field's progress. This book is designed to do just that.

DEFINING THE PROBLEM: A CHECKLIST FOR CIVIL WARS

To this point we have talked generally about internal violence. We have used several terms to interchangeably identify violence within states. Civil violence can take many forms, however. The various terms available, though sometimes confusing, distinguish one form from another. In a sense we can view the violence in Israel and the surrounding territories it has occupied since 1967 as a civil war, though of course there are international elements to the situation as well. We further know that the Palestinian-Israeli conflict involves elements of terrorism, but how does this dispute compare to the terror and civil violence in Northern Ireland, or that of Sri Lanka, where the first cases of "suicide bombing" actually originated? Indeed, does Israel's occupation policy and its erection of a barrier fence against Palestinian infiltrators constitute, as is sometimes charged by critics, a form of apartheid, as seen previously for decades in South Africa, or an attempt to establish separate national zones?

Defining typologies and relations among various forms of civil violence, therefore, can help to clarify and improve the chances for peaceful resolution and transitions away from war, as indeed was finally witnessed in South Africa after years of strife. Typologies help to inform those who would offer their services in facilitating negotiations and agreements to settle disputes about the best, most effective, and practical remedies that tend to work in certain circumstances. In order to compare wars and draw conclusions about expected patterns and remedies, both general statistical and more specific case study approaches are appropriate. We seek to generalize about what types of war tend to occur when, and also to distinguish carefully among the cases. We will include elements of both types of analysis in this book.

Thresholds and Criteria

As we consider the various definitional criteria for civil war, we should remember what nearly all analysts agree on, namely that war is a political act of organized violence to obtain some advantage or goal in terms of power, territory, or security. Thus, war is not an isolated act of random violence, but rather one entailing political goals and outcomes, a form of armed contest between and among governments, factions, and groups wanting to have it "their way" in political terms. "War" per se can be seen, therefore, at the upper end of a violence continuum that might include "force short of war" or lesser levels of political violence.

One of the most pressing questions concerning categories of civil violence, and one that helps distinguish war from lesser forms of political violence, deals with intensity of fighting. At what points do disputes and sporadic fighting erupt into full-fledged civil war? What is the magnitude of fighting that constitutes war? This is a relevant question from the point of view of avoiding massacres and genocides; international and domestic laws designed to restrain and temper combat also depend on such definitions.

Small and Singer (1982) in the Correlates of War (COW) project have defined a civil war as a conflict with sustained combat actively involving the national government and with active resistance by opposing sides in a nation-state with an annual average of 1,000 battle-related deaths (see also, Collier and Hoeffler, 2001). The Small-Singer definition, consistent with their international war definition, provides a clear-cut reference point for identifying, counting, and accounting for wars. However, this definition is also more stringent than those of other civil war analysts since it sets a rather high (1,000) battle death threshold and also excludes some quite significant pitched battles between groups in a society. One could argue that civil violence resulting in the death of 500, for example, would, if it showed patterns of recurrence and continuity, be devastating enough to be considered a war, and would likely result in lasting bitterness that might spur future revenge attacks by the victimized groups.

Thus, in the search for a comprehensive dataset from which to analyze civil war patterns, several scholars have modified the COW threshold level. Regan (2000) has defined civil wars as violence against the recognized government of a state involving 200 or more battle-related deaths during a given year. Bercovitch (1996), although primarily focusing on international conflict, maintains that an "internationalized civil war," i.e., one attracting significant outside intervention by regional or major powers, is one that reaches 100 battle-related deaths per year. In a more recent project coming from the International Peace Research Institute Oslo (PRIO) in Norway, armed internal conflicts and civil violence have been separated into two intensity categories: armed conflicts within states that result in 25 to 999 battle-related deaths in a given year are considered "minor conflicts"; and conflicts meeting the same 1,000 battle death threshold used by COW are considered "wars" (Uppsala Conflict Data Program [UCDP] and PRIO, 2007).[1]

In the midst of these somewhat confusing differences in definition, those wishing to analyze civil war data systematically might adopt the Small-Singer criteria if looking only at the most "deadly" wars, or they might take the broader approach of PRIO and distinguish various intensity categories, or alternately opt for Regan's summary "middle-of-the-road" approach to estimating overall civil war patterns at the level of 200 deaths or more. Either way, systematic study and statistical counts of the emerging patterns would be possible and would be likely to include most of the relevant conflicts.

Organized Resistance

One further element of the COW definition needs exploration. Civil war, as distinct from other types of internal political violence, involves *sustained combat* between relatively organized forces. Essentially, for a conflict to be considered a war, opposing parties must have the ability to engage in more than just sporadic fighting, though the actual tactics employed in sustained combat might range from pitched battles to guerrilla hit-and-run raids (hence the term "guerrilla war" as one potential form of civil war). This distinction, therefore, allows us to study the range of internal violence from war to skirmishes.

At a step somewhat below full-scale civil war, for example, one often finds uprisings and rebellions by disaffected groups. Frequently, such uprisings are referred to as "insurgencies," and if sustained regularly over time by organized forces, and reaching a certain level of lethality, they become a form of civil war. Insurgent groups might begin by attacking police stations or symbols of government power and authority to steal arms and undermine public confidence and support for existing regimes, or, in places such as Iraq in 2004, to undermine occupying authorities and foreign interveners. The attacks, if sustained and nurtured by local or outside supplies of arms and resources, might then escalate into full-fledged civil war as bands of fighters become organized into military, paramilitary, or militia formations. The Vietnam War, an "internationalized civil war" in Bercovitch's terminology—since it drew many outside interveners—did involve such a sustained insurgency by the Viet Cong forces against the government of the "Republic of South Vietnam," and eventually engaged the North Vietnamese army and the Americans and their allies as well.

War itself often involves other forms of social violence such as "genocide, politicide, or democide" (the wanton killing of ethno-cultural groups, the extermination of political groups and parties, or the wiping out of large segments of society or political movements from sections of the country, respectively—see Harff, 1994). Civil wars sometimes spawn or end in such bloodbaths, but these excesses can also arise without formal combat between government and opposition forces. Governments or armed groups themselves might simply engage in such attacks on civilians.

Actors and Warriors

Several terms are used to refer to those who have taken up arms or who promote the use of violence against a government. These terms can be interchangeable, but often are used for political purposes. A term that has been used rather generically to identify those engaged in any armed conflict is "belligerent," and the term "rebel," of course, is applied to armed opponents of governmental authorities. In a civil war, belligerents can refer either to the government that uses its military to maintain control and defeat the rebels or to the rebels who engage in sustained armed conflict against the government. Both the North and the South in the American Civil War were considered belligerents by their European observers at the time. If a government breaks down or ceases to exist, armed groups and militia can contend with each other in a civil war for control of the state, as in Somalia during the 1990s and on into the new millennium. Indeed, even while engaging a government, various rebellious groups might compete with and attack each other to gain advantages.

As noted, belligerent rebels opposing a government are often referred to as "insurgents." A less neutral term often assigned to insurgents by their admirers is "freedom fighters," in reference to their perceived pursuit of justice. By the same token, governments wishing to delegitimize their opponents are ever more frequently prone to refer to insurgents, especially if certain destructive tactics are used, as "terrorists" or "criminals."

Depending on their military tactics, insurgents or rebels might also be referred to as "guerrillas," a Spanish term used to identify any irregular band of warriors that operate primarily in the countryside in a rather dispersed fashion, utilizing hit-and-run tactics that make them difficult to defeat. Guerrilla warfare has been a factor in many civil conflicts and wars, going all the way back to biblical accounts of the Jewish Maccabee fighters resisting Greek-Assyrian authorities in a struggle commemorated at Chanukah time. Among the notable modern guerrilla wars are the Vietnamese revolt, led by Ho Chi Minh, against the French colonizers and later in the Vietnam War, as well as the Cuban Revolution during the mid- to late-1950s, led by Fidel Castro.

As mentioned, the term "terrorist" has become a preoccupation of many states, especially in the wake of the September 11, 2001, incidents in the United States. While not necessarily a form of civil violence (the so-called 9/11 attacks were undertaken by groups from outside the country), terrorism can also be a difficult term to define (see for example, Chasdi, 2002). The term usually connotes unconventional violence undertaken by a group or by governmental authorities, targeting civilian and non-military facilities with the purpose of instilling fear and dread and raising the cost of policies that the "terrorists" oppose. On the surface, at least, we can differentiate terrorist activity from other forms of international or civil violence because it tends to involve sensational incidents such as bombings, assassinations, suicide attacks, or aircraft hijacking.

It is not required that terrorists are a part of an armed insurgent group per se. In fact, the United States has experienced terrorist attacks by individuals acting primarily on their own in pursuit of political goals, such as the Oklahoma City bombing of the Alfred P. Murrah Federal Building by Timothy McVey and his accomplices in 1995, or the Atlanta Olympic bombings in 1996 by accused suspect Robert Rudolph. Tactics involving terrorism, "counterterrorism," or "state terrorism" (employed by governments) have also been used, as indicated earlier, by insurgent groups to destabilize governments, or, as with General William Tecumseh Sherman's ravaging march through the American South in 1864, by governmental authorities themselves as a tool to subdue their opponents in a civil war or insurgency.

Despite the variance among civil war threshold levels, characteristics, and parties, one factor remains consistent across the board. Civil wars generally involve either organized opposition to the government of a state or competition among groups for control of the state. Here the significance of the government's role in defining civil war is not lost. The "intercommunal" violence occurring among various clan and ethnicity groups in northern Ghana in February 1994, for example, was not considered a civil war by any of the projects or scholars mentioned above. Yet, it had political relevance because over 1,000 people were killed and more than 150,000, by some estimates, were displaced. The Ghanaian case, although not considered a civil war because the government was intact and was not a party to the fighting, certainly is of concern to those studying factors surrounding internal conflict. Although the government was involved in the resolution of the conflict, it was not known as a player in the violence.

As a result, we would classify the 1994 Ghanaian episode, and cases similar to it, as communal violence, i.e., politically related violence among groups in the society. According to an analyst specializing in the study of contending identity groups that are "at risk," such identity (ethnic, religious, or cultural) groups are constituted "not by the presence of a particular trait or combination of traits, but rather the shared perception that the defining traits, whatever they are, set the group apart" (Gurr, 1993: 3).

More common terms used to distinguish violence among various identity groups, therefore, are "ethnic," "identity," or "sectarian" violence. Although these terms frequently appear in the media, they can mislead observers into thinking that such disputes are necessarily mainly about ethnicity or religion. For example, although the violence in Ghana involved members of the Konkomba versus the members of the Namumba ethnic communities ("tribes"), it was actually triggered by a dispute in a marketplace that seemed to have more to do with property ownership, land acquisition, and political representation than differences in identity per se (University of Maryland, 2004). The same can be said for the so-called sectarian violence that has plagued Northern Ireland. From an outsider's perspective, that conflict might appear to be a religious-based dispute between the Catholics and the Protestants. Upon closer historical examination, however, resources, national identities ("nationalism"), and political loyalties are the main issues in the conflict, with religion used as a proxy for political affiliation (Protestant "Unionists" as adherents of Great Britain, Catholic "Republicans" as favoring the Irish Republic). This type of violence, in which wider political disputes are reduced to identity group conflict, has also been referred to variously as "ethno-political" or nationalist in nature.

When discussing definitions of communal violence and episodes of

8

fighting where the state may or may not be a party, we must also distinguish such conflict from acts of random or organized crime. The Hindu killing of a Muslim shop owner in India, for example, is criminal and might even be considered a "hate crime" involving issues of identity. In other words, the Hindu might or might not have killed the victim out of hatred for Muslims, but such an act would be distinct from communal violence itself. If, however, the particular criminal act resulted in rioting and destruction by Hindus against Muslims in the community, or by Muslims seeking revenge on Hindus, then we could consider the violence to be communal in nature. The distinction, of course, is both identity and numbers. Generally, nonpolitical crime involves an individual or small group, whereas communal violence, as a form of ethno-political fighting, is often mass-based (and certainly would also be "against the law").

Of course, this distinction between communal violence and criminal offenses can blur in specific cases, as when we consider the mass-based murderous record of Nazi Germany, or other governments or groups that have committed "crimes against humanity," as these acts became enunciated under international law at the Nuremberg and Hague war crimes tribunals and as they might be interpreted in the future by the International Criminal Court. Further, criminal syndicates in Colombia have, through their drug interests, interacted, collaborated, and fought with political factions, both governmental and antigovernmental.

As indicated above, communal violence often involves peoples' self-perceived identities. Thus, parties to a conflict might self-identify with a nationality, a religion, a language, or a racial, clan, family, or ethnic/cultural group. The civil violence in South Africa from the 1940s to the early '90s involved the majority black population, which was politically and economically subordinate to a white politically and economically dominant minority that used repression and violence to maintain its power until the transfer to black majority rule in 1994. The "blacks" themselves belonged to at least two main ethnic identity groups, the Zulu and the Bantu peoples, and they sometimes conflicted with each other, a fact often seized upon by the minority white government in attempting to "divide and rule." The "white" community was also split into English and Dutch ethnic factions, and there was a mixed race, or "colored" population, as well as ethnic South Asians, Jews, and others. Although the entire conflict reached at least minimum threshold levels to be considered a "civil war" between African National Congress forces and the government, sporadic communal and terrorist violence among black and white South Africans was also considered racial violence because the conflicting groups were defined largely through their racial identity.

We can also distinguish communal violence from other forms of political violence, particularly according to the affiliation of the actors involved. Whereas communal violence involves the identification of groups through some sort of cultural trait, more general forms of political violence involve politically identified groups, such as ideological movements, interest groups, or political parties. Colombia, for example, has been engaged in a civil war, according to COW, since 1948. The groups opposed to one another, for the most part, consider themselves Colombian, probably Spanish-speaking, as well as Roman Catholic; however, segments of indigenous tribal and Afro-Colombian groups are negatively affected by the fighting. For the most part, Colombia's warring factions are considered to be less "identity-based" than politically opposed to one another.

In fact, the original Colombian conflict stemmed from a political dispute between the Liberal and the Conservative parties and political blocs. Obviously, the war has changed over time to one involving additional parties and more radical ideological conflict, as well as criminal groups dealing in the drug trade, along with economically contending groups of peasants and landowners. This type of violence has been referred to as "ideological violence," particularly if the sides have well-developed philosophical positions and because of the oppositional political ideologies involved. However, even in ideological conflict, aspects of competition for power, resources, representation, wealth, territory, or security are prominent and may indeed be the driving goals.

Characterizing parties engaged in war is, therefore, complex (see Box 1.1). Kaldor (1999, 2006) has referred to the oncoming phenomenon of "new war" in world affairs. By this she means a form of warfare less easily categorized as international or domestic, but featuring new and varied actors in different combinations of cooperation and interaction. Failed or "frail" states may be unable to contain the rise of insurgents, terrorists, and criminal elements profiting through political warfare and foreign interveners, and all interacting for their own motives. These groups might attack or defend each other, the state, or foreign states in pursuit of greater power, influence, wealth, and more secure "identities." Standard territorial or sequential battles, of the type made famous during the American Civil War, may be rare in such circumstances.

Instead groups seek to demonstrate their own viability and staying power in segments of state territory, or neighborhoods and enclaves. "Ethnic cleansing" of various sorts is attempted, ranging from killing opponents, or those different in identity, to removing them to different areas (e.g., Baghdad or Bosnia). Thus, the rise of a group such as Hezbollah in Lebanon, partially to fight the Lebanese establishment on behalf of less privileged Shi'a Muslims, partially to join that government in electoral politics, partially to resist Israel's power on the borders, partially to link to Syria and Iran for arms and funding in a region-wide alliance against Western opponents, represents the essence of the "new war" that Kaldor identifies.[2]

BOX 1.1 "IS IRAQ A CIVIL WAR?"

When the United States-led coalition engaged militarily in Iraq in March 2003, the action resulted in a clear case of interstate war with the coalition forces pitted against the Iraqi military of President Saddam Hussein. US President George W. Bush claimed victory in May 2003, followed by the capture of Hussein in December. Despite these seeming victories, however, coalition forces continued to find themselves under attack, and violence continued for years with expanding targets and thousands of victims, including Iraqis against Iraqis.

By 2004 questions began to arise as to whether or not Iraq was sliding into a civil war. The debate emerged in the political arena and the press but also found its way into academic circles. The case of Iraq demonstrates the difficulty that can emerge when one is seeking to apply operational definitions of war. Although conflict involving Iraq and the United States began much earlier, the interstate phase of war in Iraq began when the coalition forces, a group of states willing to team up with the US to topple the Ba'athist regime, intervened militarily in March 2003. By COW criteria, in order to be classified as an international war, the conflict must exhibit sustained organized political violence involving at least one state recognized as a member of the international system and resulting in at least 1,000 battle-related deaths, with at least 100 occurring at the hands of both parties involved.

The coalition versus Iraqi military conflict did indeed meet these criteria. Parties to the conflict remained actively involved in fighting, with members of the coalition (Poland, Spain, and others) gradually leaving the fight after the Iraqi government was defeated and as they themselves encountered domestic opposition or terrorism. The fighting continued as an insurgency against both the occupying coalition forces and the newly installed and elected Iraqi government, which largely reflected Shi'a and, to a lesser degree, Kurdish as opposed to Sunni, political forces. The conflict also became an intercommunal war between Iraqi sectarian militia and insurgents.

The essence of the definitional and political debate surrounding the conflict tends to concern whether or not the Iraqi War became a civil as well as an international war. It is clear that parties to the conflict changed over time, including the addition of so-called al-Qaeda in Mesopotamia elements that have either come from or have ties to Islamist or nationalist groups throughout the Middle East. The parties involved are integral to the identifying and categorizing the war. As a result, it is important to approach this conflict recognizing its dynamic nature.

The intrastate violence does appear to have been organized by the coalition forces and by the opposition. As of February 2007, the United States alone had experienced 3,122 battle-related deaths during both phases of the war, and, according to a United Nations envoy, at least 34,452 Iraqi civilians had been killed as a result of the conflict. Based on this assessment, the conflict in Iraq appears to meet the definition of an intrastate war.[3] For the most part, this assessment is not one that is debated in either the political or the academic arena.

Thus, the war seems to have shifted from a war between states or groups of states to one of the US-led coalition, including a re-established Iraqi state, fighting one or more nonstate insurgencies. In other words, the war has evolved to become both civil and extrastate in nature.[4]

By the time the first permanent and recognized government of Iraq was created in late 2005, multiple actors had emerged in the Iraqi conflict, with the newly formed government as a target of opposition (attacks on army and police recruits, government facilities, assassinations, etc.). It is at this point that the conflict appears to have met the definition of an internationalized civil war. The newly formed Iraqi government remained fairly weak and continued to require assistance from the United States. The Iraqi police and armed forces, as well as members of the US-led coalition, continued to find themselves under attack.

Militia and insurgents sought to stir the pot and increase the level of chaos in Iraqi society by targeting social groups across the ethnic divide, such as in attacks on revered mosques and religious leaders. This chaos would serve both to weaken and discredit the new government and the occupation coalition forces and to spark counterattacks that would further weaken the new state. Thus, neighborhoods would eventually be carved up along ethnic lines, populations expelled, and an uneasy cultural divide would prevail in the country until perceived disadvantages for minority groups and parties could be redressed. This too constituted a form of civil violence adding to the overall effects of a civil war.

The conflict in Iraq demonstrates exactly how complex wars can become. What began as an interstate war developed into an insurgency aimed primarily at the United States, and continued in attacks on institutions put in place during the coalition occupation. Once the Iraqi government was re-established, it too became a target of those attacks, mainly by Sunni groups who saw their power waning. As the situation deteriorated even further, violence then expanded to intercommunal attacks. Transnational elements appear to have introduced themselves to the conflict. Sectarian violence has emerged as a significant issue in the form of Shi'a versus Sunni fighting, and even Shi'a versus Shi'a fighting in the south, as well as against the government. In 2007, Washington devised a "surge" strategy aligned with Sunni tribal leaders against other militias. Kurdish "peshmerga" militia also held their territorial stronghold in the north, attracting concern and occasional cross-border raids from the Turks (who feared Kurdish uprisings within Turkey). In the midst of this complexity and chaos, the definition of a civil war appears to have been met in this case.

GOALS

The various types and thresholds of civil violence can thus be categorized by the goals of the insurgent group or groups when one of the actors is the state government. Goals help define civil violence, but they also help determine how a war will be waged, as well as the response by both the government facing the insurgency and by the international community.

A "revolution," for example, is an attempt by an insurgent group to overthrow the government and fundamentally change or reorient the political system. This was the case in the Russian Revolution following World War I and the Russian Civil War in 1918, as well as the Cuban Revolution and civil war of the 1950s. During the Russian Revolution the Bolshevik party engineered the Red Army victory over both the czar's forces and, subsequently, the republican "White Russian" army, despite an attempted foreign military intervention by European powers, Japan, and the United States. In Cuba insurgents led by Fidel Castro, Che Guevara, and others successfully overthrew the dictatorial Batista regime, which they viewed as corrupt and inconsiderate of Cuban peasants. The revolution also became increasingly ideological in nature, given the growing confrontation with the United States over the expropriation of private property in Cuba and Castro's subsequent adoption of revolutionary communist goals. Ironically, some revolutions begin as popular movements for reform and change, as when Mao Zedong led the People's Army in China against the nationalist forces of General Chiang Kai-shek in the 1930s and '40s, only to revert later to forms of repression and terror to hold on to power. Thus, the term "revolution" can entail both new departures and complete turnabouts back to "politics as usual."

A coup d'état is a military takeover that seeks to replace a government and/or its leaders, but coups generally entail less thorough societal and constitutional reforms than full-fledged revolutions. Revolutionary movements are often mass-based, even if led by elite "cadres" such as the Bolsheviks in Russia, and therefore fall within the realm of this book in relating more directly to civil wars. Coups, on the other hand, involve the often violent toppling of elites by other elites within the system, and hence a much narrower band of social or political changes than the thorough upheaval of a revolution. Unfortunately, some countries routinely experience coups d'état as a form of power transfer. However it is important to recognize that not all coups involve much violence, and that some mass-based revolutions, such as Czechoslovakia's "velvet revolution" of 1991, may essentially be carried out peacefully because of a lack of effective resistance.

Some wars and episodes of civil violence are aimed not at changing a state's leadership or government but rather at establishing political representation or self-government in a geographically distinct area within the sovereign nation-state. These can be wars pursuing local autonomy, or more extreme efforts at secession (as in the US "war between the states"). Secessionists seek to split from the main body of the country and become an independent state or territory of their own, as did former Soviet republics in the Baltic region in 1990. The government might or might not move forcefully to put down these movements, an option briefly tried and then abandoned at the time by Soviet President Mikhail Gorbachev as civil war in the Baltics was averted. Finally, so-called wars of national liberation can involve either antigovernment or secessionist struggles designed to put a new "national" grouping in power or to end a foreign territorial occupation (as in Vietnam).

Political autonomy allows minority groups to remain within a state but have some level of self-rule and protection against majority dominance. Autonomy movements are often met with initial government resistance rather than negotiation and reform efforts, so that by the time the government accepts the validity of the autonomy demands, the insurgents may be so disillusioned that they turn to secession. Ethnic Albanians of Kosovo province in Serbia enjoyed political autonomy within the former Yugoslavia prior to that privilege being revoked in 1991 in an ultranationalist move by then Yugoslav (Serbian) President Slobodan Milosevic. The result was the organization and mobilization of the Kosovo Liberation Army (KLA). Having had its autonomy revoked, however, the KLA was no longer satisfied with mere autonomy. Thus, the international community witnessed, and eventually became involved in, the Kosovar war of secession.

Originally, the right of national self-determination, a right endorsed by the United Nations, was designed to apply to colonies in their struggles for independence from empires in what are referred to as "colonial wars." Many of these wars had characteristics of civil wars, such as high casualties over long periods of guerrilla confrontation, but they also had a flavor of international war, since the colonial powers were ruling from afar and trying to hold on to distant territories, and the "freedom fighters" often obtained assistance or safe havens in neighboring states.

Following the disintegration of the colonial system, identity-based groups have waged self-determination wars often hoping to secede from what they view as artificially manufactured post-colonial states with repressive regimes. Such was the case when the Kurds, whose population spreads across parts of Central Asia, sought repeatedly to secede from Iraq from the 1960s through the 1990s. In May 1967 the Biafra region of eastern Nigeria, dominated by Ibo ethnic communities, declared independence and pursued a violent campaign—with the goal of secession—that lasted until it was put down in 1970. One of the key questions concerning the success of secessionist wars is whether they gain the support or intervention of outside powers or regional states. In the case of Biafra, outright recognition by major powers remained elusive. Although France offered covert military assistance to the secessionists, Britain and the USSR continued to recognize and support the Nigerian federal government. The covert armaments provided to the rebels were insufficient to offset the federal government's advantages, and as a result, the die was cast for the Biafrans to fail (O'Connell, 1993).

Secessionists might also pursue "irredentist" goals. Irredentist movements are those where rebellious identity-based groups, such as the

Kurds, wish not only to secede from the nation-state to form their own independent state but also to attach themselves to groups that share their ethnic identity and seek the return of formerly held territories, whether in a new state or as part of another existing sovereign nation. Thus, the Kurds dream of establishing "Kurdistan" by uniting ethnic Kurds from Iran, Iraq, Turkey, and parts of the former Soviet Union. Of course, some movements can become divided about whether to unite with others across a border or to seek their separate identity. There were irredentists among the Kosovar Albanians, for example, who hoped to join "greater Albania" next door. Similar opinions have been seen or demonstrated among certain strata of Greek Cypriot society who hoped to be absorbed by Greece (in what was referred to as "enosis"), while others preferred a separate national identity in Cyprus. These views, of course, are affected by the course of Cyprus's still unresolved civil struggle between the Greek and Turkish communities, a struggle that attracted significant, defining Turkish military intervention in the 1970s.

The stated goals of civil violence, as discussed above, help determine the response of the nation-state. We can distinguish these stated goals from the underlying needs of the insurgent groups. Although we will be exploring the factors that contribute to the outbreak of internal state violence in later chapters, it helps to understand here that although groups may seek revolution, autonomy, or secession, these goals are often determined by a set of unmet needs (see Burton, 1990). Most often such underlying motives relate to issues of power, territory, security, access to resources, simple cultural recognition, or a combination of these factors. It has been argued that satisfying or meeting the underlying needs is essential to resolving these disputes. The Kosovo example illustrates many of these concerns, along with the frustration and sense of deprivation that results from having prior rights and privileges suddenly revoked. These are often cited as triggers of violence, and as we shall see, these needs and reactions manifest themselves differently depending on the group and its political environment.

TRENDS AND PATTERNS

Despite the various definitions of intrastate violence and civil war, observers agree that such violence has become the dominant form of political conflict in the international system, particularly in the

16

post-Cold War era. In 2004, despite the headline-grabbing US "war on terror," civil wars and lower levels of intrastate violence continued in Israel and the Palestinian territories, Sudan, Georgia, Chechnya, Turkey, Kashmir, Sri Lanka, Algeria, Rwanda, Uganda, and Colombia, just to name a few. The prevalence of civil and internal war is illustrated in Figure 1.1. Clearly, interstate and extrastate wars have been on the decline, falling well below the levels of intrastate war onset since World War II.

Figure 1.1 Interstate, Extrastate, and Intrastate War Onset, 1816–1997
War Frequency (1,000 battle death threshold) per Decade

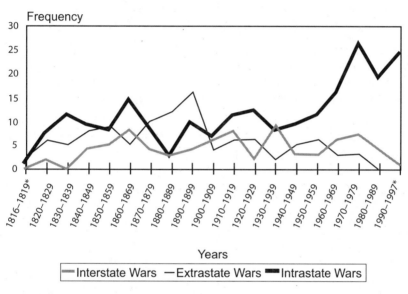

Data Source: Sarkees, Wayman, and Singer (2003).
* Indicates that data for war onsets during that time frame were normalized for a 10-year period.

After the breakup of the Soviet Union and the lessening of hostilities between the United States and Russia, civil war took main stage as the dominant perceived threat to international peace and security. As the proliferation of civil wars emerged, it was argued that the Cold War rivalry from 1945–89, and offshoots such as the firm grip of President Josip Tito on the multi-ethnic Yugoslavia, had kept a lid on the various animosities in several regions throughout the world. Once that lid was removed, groups were able and often willing to engage in violent confrontations with each other, sometimes seeking to settle old scores or to prevent one group from gaining power at the other's expense.

This view continues to be debated, however, especially in light of research on the prevalence of civil war throughout history. By focusing specifically on the onset of civil war over the broad expanse of the 1816–1997 period, and by using the COW definition of civil war (i.e., 1,000 battle-related deaths occurring within a member state among armed combatants), trends in Figure 1.1 show that civil war onset began to increase immediately following the end of World War II rather than at the end of the Cold War. A proliferation of civil wars also was evident in the 1970s. Nevertheless, there definitely was an upsurge during the 1990s, but perhaps a less dramatic one than originally thought, and still less than the number of onsets during the 1970s.

The spawning of civil wars in the post-World War II period, and particularly during the 1970s, is even more dramatically illustrated when a lower threshold level (100 or 200 battle deaths) is used, which is perhaps more appropriate for a discussion of intrastate violence where even relatively small amounts of violence can be quite devastating. Figure 1.2 presents the numbers of such civil war onset. Clearly the trends are in the same direction, but the frequency of lower-level violence adds significantly to the civil war totals.

Figure 1.2 Civil War Onset Threshold Comparison, 1940–1999

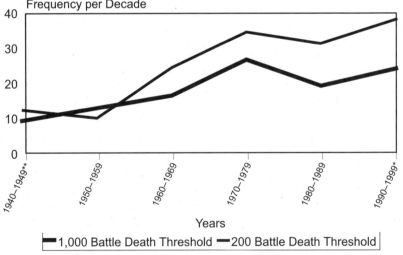

Data Sources: Sarkees, Wayman, and Singer (2003); Regan (2001).
** 200 battle death threshold includes cases initiated during the 1945-1949 period.
* 1,000 battle death threshold includes cases initiated during the 1990-1997 period.

As indicated earlier, civil wars can be distinguished by the identification of the groups involved in opposition to the government. The 1990s seemed to involve an extraordinary number of ethno-political conflicts, whereas during the prior era the international system had been intently focused on ideological and other political conflicts. Figure 1.3 presents the number of civil wars (based on a 200 battle death threshold) by type, using Regan's religious, ethnic, and ideological categories. Wars involving groups defined by their ethnicity seem to have replaced so-called ideological struggles as the most prevalent type during the 1970s (noting that like identity, ideology can also be a cover at times for political power and personal ambition), precisely when civil war onset was at its highest. Conflicts involving groups defined by their religious affiliation do not appear as frequently as other forms of ethnic or ideological conflicts, although religion too experienced higher onset numbers in the latter half of the time period under study.

Figure 1.3 Civil War Onset by Type, 1945–1999

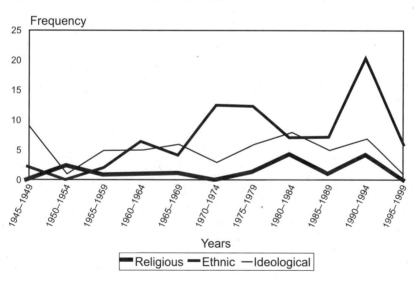

Data Source: Regan (2001).

Although civil wars can and do occur throughout the international system, they tend to occur in higher numbers in particular regions of the world. Figure 1.4 presents the numbers of civil war onsets per region for the period 1945–99. Africa has tended to experience the most civil war since 1975, following its era of decolonization, perhaps because of the artificially drawn nature of African state boundaries. Asia reached its insurgency peak during the volatile years of the 1960s and '70s (e.g., Vietnam, Laos, Cambodia), also in the immediate aftermath of colonial rule. Europe also saw an increase in civil war occurrences following the breakup of the Soviet Union as new states struggled to form independent governments and wrestled with problems of majority-minority rule. On the positive side, though, states such as Canada were able to employ political rather than military means to deal with ethno-political conflict, as in Quebec. The Baltic republics of Lithuania, Latvia, and Estonia, where ethnic Russians had previously been dominant under the Soviet system but were now resented minorities, also averted open warfare. Most regions of the world, then, have experienced civil war in the post-World War II period, with exceptions such as Oceania, which represents a small number of relatively homogeneous nation-states primarily in the South Pacific (relative to other regions of the world) and areas where political compromise and economic advancement have proven more possible.

Figure 1.4 Civil War Onset by Region, 1945–1999
War Frequency (200 battle death threshold) per Decade

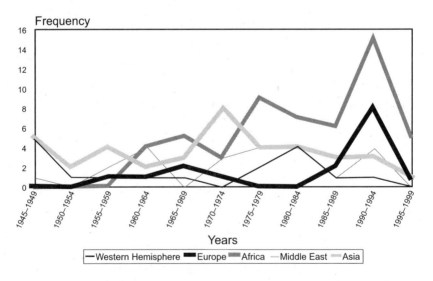

Data Source: Regan (2001).

The trends presented here illustrate the prevalence of intrastate violence relative to other types of war within the international system. Although the figures show a decrease in the last five years of the 1990s, it is unclear to what extent that trend will continue. We know as well that certain regions are particularly challenged to cope with civil war. This is especially the case in less affluent portions of the world such as Africa, where temptations exist to reunite ethnic groups across borders and to gain control of the lucrative, often corrupt, trade in commodities such as diamonds, gold, minerals, and oil, and where governments as well as institutions for peacekeeping or peacebuilding are weak and ill-funded. In subsequent chapters we will review these challenges.

CONCLUSION

Civil wars, in all their various forms, have been the subject of much discussion in the field of international relations, particularly in the post-Cold War era. The next chapter will begin an exploration into the various factors contributing to the outbreak of civil war, beginning with a discussion of the individual and groups and what motivates people to take up arms against their government or their neighbors in society, including disparities in group status and wealth, group identity, and security concerns. The role of personality, charisma, interests, and the role of individuals as leaders of revolutions and other forms of violent social movements within states will be explored. We will note, of course, that today's revolutionary movements are seldom isolated; they have formed connections and networks in this era of global communication that make it difficult to confine them.

Chapter 3 will continue the discussion with an examination of state-level factors leading to war. In the process we will discuss factors, including the adoption of certain types of governmental policies and regulations that privilege some groups over others.

Chapter 4 will explore the challenge that such wars represent for the "international community" as it struggles to curb violence, deal effectively with issues of human rights, and at the same time uphold the principle of state sovereignty as outlined in the United Nations Charter. The discussion will continue with a presentation of ways in which the international, regional, or global system and its structure affects the internal dynamics of civil wars, as in the flow of arms that fuel the fires of violence.

As indicated earlier, civil wars evolve and change over time, involving new actors, spilling across borders, and forcing reconsideration or adoption of new goals. In Chapter 5 we discuss what we know about these conflict dynamics and what challenges those changes represent in terms of conflict management. The resolution of civil war is explored in further detail in Chapter 6 as we examine various patterns of war outcomes. In Chapter 7 we summarize our discussion and conclude with a detailed presentation of the potential for rebuilding wartorn societies. The effectiveness of local, regional, and global responses will be considered.

NOTES

1   Early versions of the Armed Conflict data contained a third intensity category considered "intermediate" level conflicts. These conflicts involved at least 25 battle-related deaths in a year and more than 1,000 deaths over the course of the conflict. However, since these conflicts did not reach the 1,000-battle-death-in-a-year requirement, they were not considered "wars." Researchers at UCDP/PRIO have since eliminated such a designation.

2   Elements of such warfare may not be entirely "new" on the world stage. Insurgency, cross-border smuggling and crime, terrorism, and unsavory multiparty alliances of convenience have been seen throughout the ages. World War I began with an act of international terror with the assassination of the Austrian archduke by Serb nationalists in the Bosnian city of Sarajevo. What may be new about the current manifestation of "new war" is the speed of international communication and interaction and the increased number of states vulnerable to fragmentation and external penetration in today's expanded international system. According to Henderson and Singer (2002: 174), what others, including Kaldor, have identified as "new wars" are really a "hodgepodge of several types of war (i.e. interstate, extrastate, and intrastate) whose distinctiveness as a category derives from the diverse morphologies of its constituent wars rather than its novelty as a 'new and distinct' form of war."

3   Some in the political arena might disagree, seeing the opposition to Iraq's government or coalition forces as unorganized terrorist-type activity. The timing and nature of the opposition attacks, however, demonstrate that although opposition groups may vary in allegiance, they are indeed organized.

4   According to COW, extrasystemic wars, or those involving a recognized member of the nation-state system versus a nonstate actor, are imperial or colonial in nature. The fundamental difference between a civil war and that which is considered extrastate is whether or not the nonstate actor can be considered "an integrated or incorporated territory" as opposed to a "dependency" (Small and Singer, 1982). These terms were later revised to "extrastate" and "intrastate" by Sarkees, Wayman, and Singer (2003: 59), who stated that extrastate wars were conflicts involving "war between a territorial state and a non-sovereign entity outside the borders of the state," such as a colony rising up against a colonial power.

CHAPTER TWO

The Causes of Civil War: Individual and Group Analysis

"The problem of the twentieth century is the problem of the color-line—the relation of the darker to the lighter races of men in Asia and Africa, in America and the islands of the sea. It was a phase of this problem that caused the Civil War."

—W.E.B. DuBois

n his treatment of the origins of the American Civil War, University of Virginia historian Edward Ayers makes the case that causation is complicated and that each war must be seen in its own context.

In one field of human understanding after another … causality has come to be understood in terms of "increasing specificity, multiplicity, complexity, probability, and uncertainty." Historical understanding needs the same perspective … called deep contingency. The perspective argues for the intricate interplay of the structural and the ephemeral, the enduring and the emergent. Simple stories of intrinsic qualities and unfolding inevitability are not worthy of history. We should simply refuse to settle for simple explanations for complex problems ... To understand deep contingency we must try to comprehend a society as a whole, its soft structures of ideology, culture, and faith as well as its hard structures of economics and politics. (Ayers, 2005: 143, quoting Kern, 2004: 6)

Of course, political scientists have tended to differ somewhat from historians on the degree to which each separate case is unique and must be studied exhaustively unto itself. Political scientists have tended to compare and generalize over many cases, looking for consistencies in patterns and factors leading to phenomena such as wars. They have been somewhat more willing to posit general theories of causation. Nevertheless, the historian's caution about complexity is extremely pertinent. Whatever theories we pose must account for multicausality and complexity. "Deep contingency" is built on the realization that a broad social environment, as well as certain event sequences, condition the actual outbreak of war, and that turning points exist where war may or may not have occurred. For such contingent outcomes to occur, the cards can be stacked by background conditions, trends, or forces to make the events and their outcome more probable.

In analyzing international wars, one must speak of a gradation of causation, ranging from what might be termed "background conditions" to "proximate causes." This range of factors can be thought of as the situations that make war possible, even likely on the one hand, and the triggering events that actually launch the war, on the other. As background for World War I, for example, one might note: (1) the polarized alliances—the Entente Cordiale consisting mainly of France, Russia, and Britain versus the Triple Alliance of power including Germany, Austria, and Ottoman Turkey, which heightened tensions and froze relationships and commitments; (2) Germany's failure to renew its nineteenth century "Reassurance Treaty" with Russia that pledged to keep them out of mutual warfare; (3) the rise of challenging powers—Germany and Japan—threatening Britain's global dominance; (4) the rise of ethnic nationalism threatening to divide the major empires of the day in upheavals and struggles for new states; and (5) inflexible military plans that required rapid mutual mobilization of forces in order to implement strategies such as defending Germany from a potential two-front war. Specific triggering events leading up to the war included the notorious assassination of Austria's Archduke Franz Ferdinand by Serbian/ Bosnian nationalists (ironic in light of the persistence of these issues at the end of the twentieth century), and bungled diplomacy, such as Germany's failure to restrain Austria's ultimatum against Serbia, hence implicating Russia, and Britain's delayed indication of commitment to France (see for example, Pearson and Rochester, 1998).

Similar background and proximate perspectives must be employed to understand the origins of civil wars as well. Almost any monumental historical episodes depend on a concurrence of sometimes predictable and sometimes unlikely events as precipitants. Again referring to the US civil war, Ayers has proposed the following panoply of causation:

> Slavery [the single "cause" often posed for the war] was a profound economic, political, religious, and moral problem, the most profound the nation has ever faced. But that problem did not lead to war in a rational, predictable way. The war came through misunderstanding, confusion, miscalculation. Both sides underestimated the location of fundamental loyalty in the other. Both received incorrect images of the other in the partisan press. Political belief distorted each side's view of the other's economy and class relations. Both sides believed the other was bluffing, both believed that the other's internal differences and conflicts would lead it to buckle, and both believed they had latent but powerful allies in the other region that would prevent war. By the time people made up their minds to fight, slavery itself had become obscured. Southern white men did not fight for slavery; they fought for a new nation built on slavery. White Northerners did not fight to end slavery; they fought to defend the integrity of their nation. Yet, slavery, as Abraham Lincoln later put it, "somehow" drove everything. (Ayers, 2005: 134)

Therefore, the background conditions that Ayers (2003) identifies for the American Civil War include the unresolved constitutional provisions for "state sovereignty" and the role of slavery in the nation's future, along with the breakdown of the party system with the fall of the Whigs, and the inability of the Democratic and emergent Republican parties to foster a plan for the treatment of slavery in the newly expanding territories in the midst of new immigrant populations, social and economic rivalries, and jealousies. The Democrats particularly were cross-pressured in trying to remain a "national" party, thus accommodating both Northern and Southern social opinion and interests in a way that increasingly alienated the North. Some historians dwell on the differences in sectional economies, with a supposedly industrial North confronting a supposedly rural South, though Ayers points out that these were somewhat exaggerated characterizations, since the less populated South was partaking of modernity and the early industrial system along with the larger North. The South utilized slavery for both farm and town and, unfortunately, saw this anachronistic and destructive institution as compatible with both advancement and union.

Another background condition to the Civil War had to do with the development of communications (telegraph, print, transportation), whose increased speed made it difficult to moderate rhetoric in one part of the country when viewed by other parts.

> The Civil War was brought on by people imaginatively constructing chains of action and reaction beyond the boundaries of their own time and space. In distinctly modern ways, people North and South in 1860 and 1861 anticipated events, made warnings and threats, imagined their responses, imagined the responses of others. This is one reason the Civil War seems to have, as Lincoln put it, "come," why the war seemed both inevitable and surprising, easily explainable yet somehow incomprehensible. People on both sides were playing out future scenarios even as they responded to immediate threats. They recognized how deeply contingency could run and how quickly things could shift; a Supreme Court decision or a presidential election could change the evolution of vast structures of slavery and economic development. (Ayers, 2005: 141)

For example, sociobiologists might note that whites on both sides of the border, imagining unpalatable futures, feared forceful integration and the prospect of racial intermarriage. The condition of "racism" as we would term it now also prevailed in the war's approach, as Northerners opposed slavery in large part to keep the new territories "free" for white labor, and as some abolitionists and Lincoln himself evidently felt that blacks should be sent abroad to their own country. All such factors contributed to the stacking of a "house of cards" ready to implode with a spark of violence, just as pre-World War I Europe was poised for the ill winds of war in 1914, despite confidence on both sides that the crises could be contained with cooler heads prevailing.

Looking at the nearer term action-reaction events as causes or triggers of the "War Between the States," we note Lincoln's election in 1860, striking fear of radical reform in the hearts of Southern leaders and citizens generally, along with the uprisings by abolitionists such as John Brown. Generally we may note that wars tend to start when one side or the other anticipates an imminent loss of power or control. A certain fatalism can set in, leading to a slide toward the "inevitable" war. We also note the precipitant of the firing on Fort Sumpter in South Carolina, which telescoped the perceived time available for war preparations and response, including the safeguarding of Federal stores at Harper's Ferry, Virginia. Telescoping of time has been cited as a contingency factor for "the guns of August" in World War I as well (see Holsti, 1972; and Tuchman, 1962). Mounting pressure and threat perception in 1860 lent urgency to the congressional compromise discussions in Washington. However, one Southern state after another elected delegates to secession conventions and this fostered intransigence in President Lincoln, who assumed that cooler pro-Union heads would prevail in the South, just as Southerners assumed that cooler pro-peace heads would prevail in the North. All of this meant that it became possible practically overnight to reverse predominantly pro-Union sentiment throughout the South, particularly in the border areas, and to galvanize a new Southern "nationalism" as the North took "aggressive" measures to respond to the threats and provocations it perceived (Ayers, 2005).

It is likely that event sequences and evolutionary buildups such as these are also evident in each civil war situation. It may take time for the momentum toward violence to build, with periods of debate and moderate deliberation or negotiation being punctuated by excesses on one or both sides to drive the situation further and ultimately beyond its limits (on chaos theory and the breakdown of peaceful equilibrium as a lead-in to war, see Saperstein, 1996). Underlying attitudes and prejudices, along with changes in objective conditions such as relative power balances and economic fears or setbacks, pave the way for such warlike turns in the road.

Thus, there is no "one thing" that causes something as complex as the outbreak of civil war. To suggest, for example, that we can blame Slobodan Milosevic, former president of Serbia and of Yugoslavia, for the 1998 war in Kosovo is to be simplistic. Of course, politicians and policy-makers play a key role in driving a situation either toward or away from violence, and they frequently attempt to sway public opinion and make a case for their policies, sometimes cynically rousing age-old hatreds in the process. Milosevic, with his opportunistic bombast against non-Serbian communities in the former Yugoslavia, certainly did not help promote peace, but the process of Yugoslavia's unraveling was long developing, and it helped to inspire his tirades and a sympathetic audience for them. Students and scholars of civil war must move beyond simple and convenient answers to the question of war causation if we are to have any hope of preventing such situations from arising in the future. What follows is a presentation of the significant factors that can, when combined with other factors, create conditions in which civil war is possible.

LEVELS OF ANALYSIS

The notion of deep contingency causation leads us to consider the "levels of analysis" at which to study the onset of civil war. Levels of analysis have long been known as relevant to war studies in general. The outbreak of international war, for example, can depend on changes or elements at three fairly distinct levels: the individual or personal level of leadership and participation; the state level of nationalism, including what might be termed national characteristics; and the international or "system" level of interaction among states in the immediate region or more broadly in the world at large (Waltz, 1979).

At the individual level, the assumption is that specific leaders and individuals who follow those leaders make a key difference in the path toward war (or peace), based on their predilections, perceptions, and performance. Thus, Lincoln's election was seen as a key turning point in hastening the US civil war. Certainly Lincoln is seen as a pivotal figure in prosecuting the war and envisioning the peace, particularly in his struggles to force more decisive action and engagements on his generals and in his counsel of moderation regarding the post-war South. Analysts debate the importance of individuals in crisis and war decisions, with some arguing that the roles individuals occupy in government often dictate how they behave. When individuals gain certain offices or power, the responsibilities of their roles tend to mold them and their decision-making. They come to represent the interests of the agencies they work for, or they take on the responsibilities they think come with their jobs, suggesting that perhaps individual personalities matter less than the individual's role (see Rosenau, 1971).

Thus, the debate rages on about the way other potential presidents, say Stephen A. Douglas, might have reacted if Fort Sumpter were attacked during their administration. Of course, the attack itself might not have happened if Douglas were president, leading into the tricky and ultimately fruitless consideration of "counterfactual" history. It is indeed possible that both explanations, the role and the individual, have merit. Certain individuals may indeed play pivotal roles in civil war scenarios, while at the same time individuals are partly defined by their roles. Regardless, exploring the individual level of analysis seems imperative in order to effectively explore the multiplicity of factors contributing to the outbreak of civil war.

Individual-level factors are also closely linked with the group. Ultimately, for civil war to occur, mass involvement is necessary. Otherwise, individual frustrations with government might take the form of isolated episodes of violence (perhaps in the form of individual assaults or even individual or small group terrorist events such as John Brown's raids). Indeed, civil war is only possible if enough individuals share group goals and are willing to engage in sustained combat or resistance. Lichbach (1998) has referred to this as the rebel's dilemma. Individuals must become organized collectively and be willing to participate actively in the cause, thereby overcoming the "free riding" problem that occurs when rational individuals would prefer to have others do the work and take the risks of fighting for them. It has also been noted that insurgencies, or large-scale uprisings, need not necessarily have the backing of the majority, but only their toleration (see Leites and Wolfe, 1970).

Group dynamics, therefore, are well worth exploring. Psychologist Irving Janis suggests that individuals appear to behave peculiarly in groups, with the classic example being Janis's (1972) famous "groupthink" analysis of crisis decision-making whereby group norms and expectations prevail over individual preferences or dissent. The group can have a dominating effect on its members, taking on a decisional momentum and orthodoxy of its own. Whereas Janis explored group-level decision-making, a factor that may indeed bring about civil war, understanding the group-level factors that lead to mass-based mobilization also seems key. Group-level analysis is important to civil war analysis because group uprisings often trigger the outbreak of sustained violence. Some of the Iraqi insurgent groups resisting American "occupation" after the war to oust Saddam Hussein also resorted to attacks on other Iraqi ethno-political groups, apparently in order to escalate the level of fighting and make Iraq less "governable" for Americans or predominant ethnic communities—thus ushering in a condition labeled, even by some US officials, as civil war.

The second level of international war analysis also entails "national characteristics" and factors that describe the nation-state itself. It appears that certain states in certain circumstances might be more volatile and war-prone than others, though this is certainly a debatable notion. Thus, the proposition has developed that state wealth, resources, boundaries, culture, and regime characteristics matter in war probabilities (the first to examine such notions systematically might have been Quincy Wright in his monumental *A Study of War*, 1942). For example, the famous and controversial "democratic peace" thesis that became influential following the Cold War posits that democracies, while often warlike and involved in wars, almost never fight each other (Rummel, 1979; see Cashman, 1993; and Brown et al., 1998 for a discussion of the debate). The equivalent argument in explaining civil war might be that the type of state matters. It can be hypothesized that democracies or wealthy states might be less prone to civil violence because they are in a better position to satisfy their populations and factional groups. Then again, authoritarian regimes might be better placed to repress ethno-political uprisings that might lead to civil war. Evaluating such rival hypotheses takes careful study of evidence and counterevidence across time.

The third level of international war analysis concerns the interactive system whereby actors become engaged in mutual conflict and competitive relationships that take on a life of their own, much like group dynamics take on their own momentum. Hence, the United States and Soviet Union shadowed each other around the world, with each state mainly preoccupied with "defense" planning and spending against the other for a period of nearly 50 years. Priorities in each state were heavily affected, some would say for the worse, by this preoccupying competition. Thus, analysts speak of "balance of power" or "hegemonic" systems at the international level, either regionally or globally, conditioning the options available to state actors (see Dougherty and Pfaltzgraff's 1990 discussion of Kissinger; Gilpin, 1981).

The system level of analysis seems relevant when seeking to explain civil war as well. We might note the balances of power between insurgents and governments, or among varied insurgent groups. We might look as well at the involvement of international actors from the surrounding region or further abroad when explaining a state's civil war. Civil wars can depend on the fuel, in the form of armament, supplies, personnel, and money, supplied by outside parties to support the domestic war participants. The failure of the Confederate States of America to gain British recognition and backing after seemingly decisive battle losses in Pennsylvania in 1863 appeared to deal a substantial blow to their overall chance of sustaining their rebellion over the long term. Likewise, Kurdish uprisings against Iraq were temporarily squelched in 1975 when Baghdad agreed to a territorial settlement with Iran, which had been supplying and aiding the Kurds to weaken its Iraqi opponent. In 1979, however, after the fall of Iran's Shah Pahlavi government, when Saddam Hussein sought to take advantage of American-Iranian hostilities to redress that dictated border agreement by attacking Iran, the Kurds once again sprang into action in a renewed civil struggle that ultimately entailed Baghdad's use of poison gas to repress it.

Thus, one must approach the question of civil war causation from a number of different, though possibly interrelated, directions and levels. In this way, individual/group, state, and interactive system categories might help to sort out the background and proximate conditions and the events leading to war. We will explore these factors and category levels in the discussion and chapters to follow.

The Individual Level and the Elite

Why are individual men and women motivated to put their lives in danger to join a fight against their government or to take up arms against their countrymen? What motivates leaders to set the course of war and the individual citizens to follow it? Many writers have speculated about humans' so-called violent nature or, put differently, their genetic, "instinctual," or psychological predisposition to resort to violence (see Bandura, 1973; Lorenz, 1967). Building on the work of Sigmund Freud (1900–39) and his assessment that individuals have a destructive instinct in need of an outlet, others have argued that violence and aggression are a natural outlet for one's frustrations (Dollard et al., 1939). Therefore, if one is attempting to explain the outbreak of civil war, we might view group organization and mobilization against a government as a unified expression of frustration experienced by all or most of the participants involved. Clearly, although humans may be "wired" for potential violence, not all humans are violent all of the time—most political and social grievances or everyday conflicts are settled without a resort to force (see for example, the Carnegie Commission report on Preventing Deadly Conflict, 1997). Further, most states do not experience civil war on a continual basis (Fearon and Laitin, 1996). Therefore, based on the occurrence of civil war, explanations of human nature tend to fall short.

Conversely, others have argued that violence is a learned behavior (hence, the "nurture" as opposed to "nature" school of thought; see American Psychological Association, 2003). The reason why some individuals exhibit more violent acts has more to do with their environment than with their genetic makeup. In others words, children who witness violent reactions to frustrating situations will be more likely to repeat these actions later in life rather than interact in a nonviolent manner. Indeed, societies that have experienced war must often go through a process of re-educating individuals in order to effectively transition from a warring society to a peaceful one, and in the process minimize the chance of future war. When such a process is retarded, or purposely negated by ambitious and unscrupulous politicians such as Germany's Adolf Hitler or Bosnia's Slobodan Milosevic, new rounds of fighting can ensue.

The generational impact of a wartorn society can easily be witnessed in the perceptions of children raised in such situations. For example, children of Israel and Palestine learn early not only whom they should fear, resent, and consider an enemy but also, more importantly, often come to believe that their enemy does not accept their existence, is only capable of violence, and understands only violent and aggressive actions. While such education may serve an immediate societal purpose (i.e., getting children to recognize the dangers present in their environment), it does little in the way of fostering the trust-building or reconciliation necessary for peace. Though such "nurture" explanations may help us understand the conditioning that allows violence to erupt and the reasons conflicts can appear to become intractable and resistant to resolution, they do not necessarily help us understand why violence breaks out in the way, and at the time, that it does.

In order to effectively understand how the individual contributes to civil war, two further distinctions need to be made. First, there are significant differences between the motivations of those who lead rebellion versus those who follow leaders into rebellion. What motivates an individual to take up arms against his/her government or neighbors can be quite different from what motivates leaders, such as the Hutu Interhamwe militia chiefs in Rwanda during the 1990s, to encourage their constituents or those they could intimidate to take up arms and even engage in wanton killing (see Weede and Mueller, 1998; and Kaufman, 1996, 2001; Banton, 2000). Leaders, for the most part, are not in harm's way in the midst of a civil war. They do, however, play a huge role in ensuring that such an outbreak occurs in the first place.

Second, although all civil wars do indeed share similar characteristics by definition, individual motivations can vary in relation to varied categories of war. The reasons to engage in ideological war, for example, can differ significantly from the motivations regarding so-called identity war. While both forms ultimately relate to struggles for power, ideological wars tend to be wars of revolution, where rebellious participants aim to overthrow or radically restructure their form of government, thereby changing the nature of the regime in the process. These are essentially struggles to define political and economic structures and futures. Identity groups, on the other hand, will more likely find themselves engaged in struggles for political rights, autonomy, security, territory, or secession. Such groups are interested in achieving varying amounts of political/economic power, security, and representation, typically involving some separate recognition without necessarily changing the form of government.

It is not surprising, then, that the large majority of wars of secession or political autonomy are fought along ethnic, religious, or cultural lines. That is not to say that ideological conflicts are void of other forms of identity, or of goals such as territorial control or ethnic representation in the revolutionary state, or that identity groups do not on occasion have revolutionary goals (indeed, the US war for independence had aspects of both). However, we can distinguish civil wars by the primary affiliation of the groups, in addition to the goals of the movement. As a result, what follows is a discussion of the complex and interdependent elite and mass motivations for engaging in ideological and identity civil wars.

Leaders are often seen as acting out of interests, if not needs (such as the need or "drive" for power). Interests frequently relate to political gains through warfare, i.e., the acquisition of more territory, more control and extended tenure, more authority. In this, leaders may or may not represent the interests of their constituency, though in theory leaders are responsible in what we term a "fiduciary" relationship on behalf of their constituents' welfare and security. We have noted that leaders, such as Serbia's Milosevic and Hutu activists in Rwanda, may utilize outside threats and fears to motivate the masses to take up arms even when they lack a direct grievance. The drumbeat of hatred and blame channeled through the national media can be a powerful driving force in nurturing violence and overcoming qualms about murder or attacks on neighbors.

The personality of leaders thus plays a role in the movement toward war. Some people are more "risk acceptant" than others (Bueno de Mesquita, 2000: 255–56). They might be quicker to push for violent decisive action, despite risks and uncertainties, than their more "risk-averse" counterparts. Risk acceptance can be a key factor in violence calculus for both governmental and insurgent leaders. The latter particularly risk death for their perceived treasonous behavior. Rebellious leaders, as well as governmental officials, have been known to play on their constituents' fears by utilizing the outgroup as scapegoats and motivating the masses to take up arms. This "instrumentalist" process benefits the leader politically by solidifying their hold on power and ensuring their continued support (Gagnon, 1994–95; Saideman, 2001; Saideman and Zahar, 2008; and Saideman and Ayres, 2008). Indeed, some rebel leaders, for example in Africa, have been known to profit handsomely from their war involvement in the form of illegal smuggling and trade in commodities such as diamonds and oil, as well as in the various "perks" that come with power and office.

The economic incentive for elite rebellion has led some World Bank scholars to argue that greed is a more powerful predictor of civil war than grievance (Collier et al., 1998; and Collier and Hoeffler, 2004). Findings do indeed suggest that states dependent upon primary commodities (commodities that are ripe for exploitation) are more prone to civil war (at least to major civil war involving at least 1,000 battle deaths per year). However, other scholars (Regan and Norton, 2005) have modified the greed-versus-grievance argument by finding evidence to suggest that in order for greed to become a significant factor, grievance must first create a situation where a segment of the population is in opposition to the state, allowing elites to mobilize this opposition, and in so doing, offer protection from the state or from other feared groups. Regan and Norton's findings confirm this revised argument, albeit using a lower battle death threshold of 200 per year. Both studies, however, suggest that greed can indeed motivate individuals to lead belligerent masses to war.

Such explanations for elite involvement in civil war tend to portray these individuals as exploiters preying upon somewhat unsuspecting, yet disgruntled, masses. Although that image may be true in many cases, not all elites who find themselves engaged in civil war or large-scale rebellion do so for selfish or opportunistic reasons. Leaders may also emerge out of desperate situations involving oppressed constituents and may be motivated by an altruistic sense of obligation to do what is right and just. Nelson Mandela is a notable example of an individual who led an ultimately armed resistance movement in an effort to overturn South African apartheid and establish majority rule.

Regardless of the type of elite motivation, scholars tend to agree that leaders will not emerge in situations that appear futile. As (for the most part) rational beings, individuals first ask whether the fight is worth the candle (i.e., can they win?) and whether or not the fight will serve its purpose before deciding to engage the masses and take up arms (Weede and Mueller, 1998). Given that humans are subject to misperception, as we have noted, the answers to these questions may be skewed or misinformed, as when rebel groups miscalculate the state's willingness or capability to repress opposition, but these calculations are significant nonetheless.

Most and Starr (1989) have proposed that international war will occur when the opportunity presents itself and the actors are willing to engage. This logic can easily be extended to civil wars. Elites, or political entrepreneurs, may be motivated to lead rebellion when the opportunity, or odds of a successful revolt, are detected and it is reasonably clear that the masses are frustrated enough to follow. Gurr (2000b), in his study of minorities at risk, found that opportunity (what he termed

37

"opportunity in the political environment") and willingness ("collective incentives") are indeed predictors of group rebellion.

There are several scenarios in which such opportunity may occur, including one that Blainey (1988) has referred to as "the death watch." When a nation's leader dies or is otherwise removed from power in a state with questionable succession processes, instability may occur as a "power vacuum" becomes evident. President Josip Broz Tito's death in Yugoslavia ushered in such a period of dissolution. Elite struggles to fill the void are likely to follow. This explains the Cuban exile community's interest in Fidel Castro's health after August 2006. Expectations that control of the communist country might return to capitalist hands sparked demonstrations/celebrations in the streets of Miami. It was unlikely that those currently in power under Castro and his brother Raul would be willing to relinquish control without a fight. However, power vacuums occurring after the death or during the grave illness of a leader (dictators, in particular) can easily create at least the illusion of opportunity for counterelites to take control.

Opposition can also occur in situations when leaders have a precarious hold on power. The 2006 military coup in Thailand occurred under such conditions. A nullified election and proposed shifts in the power structure of the military led to the bloodless overthrow of Prime Minister Shinawatra Thaksin while he was at the United Nations in New York (BBC News, 19 September 2006). The conflict could have progressed to the point of war had sections of the military, or the Thai populous, felt sufficient allegiance to the deposed prime minister or to the principle of civilian rule. This apparently was not the case, thus explaining the essentially peaceful transition.

Elites most certainly play a significant role in facilitating or preventing the occurrence of civil war, but as the Thai coup case illustrates, mass participation or nonparticipation is critical. One can imagine a different outcome, for example, if the population had taken to the streets and the military had resorted to force, or if the armed forces ousted a leader of one ethnic derivation in a country delicately balanced in terms of identity groups, such as in Iraq, or if election results favoring one party in such a delicately balanced state (such as Kenya) had been nullified. If efforts to entice the masses or rally the troops fail, civil war does not occur. Determining what factors will motivate a significant number of individuals to join the cause is a line of inquiry we explore in the following section.

The Masses and Group-Level Analysis

The formation of groups (i.e., aggregates of individuals with a collective incentive) is a significant topic of concern when discussing intrastate conflict. By definition, groups are a primary party to any civil war. As a result, we must first understand how these groups are formed and how they are mobilized into action.

Ethnic conflict theorists have noted the importance of parenting in determining people's reactions to social differences; how children are socialized affects how they deal with "the stranger" (see Sandole, 1999; Volkan, 1998). This in-group identification can lead to functional benefits, such as cooperation and pride, or to dysfunctional and destructive displays of prejudice and xenophobia, even extreme racism. Ultimately, children and adults come to identify with groups for which they would struggle and even for whose defense they would die. The group identity dimension runs from the family on out to the ethnic (clan) and religious group or nation.

It is almost mystical to think that the concept of the "nation" can be imbued with the same fervor of identity as one's family, clan, or religion. Yet, classically this is the case, leading to the phenomenon of nationalism. Nationalism is the struggle to defend and advance the nation, or place it in an autonomous or independent position vis-à-vis other nations, ideologies, or groups. We certainly saw the lengths to which men and women would go in order to win their "civil war" in Vietnam against foreign occupiers (sequentially over centuries China, France, and the United States) and the political opponents allied with those powers (see Box 2.1). The military might of the United States could not win the "hearts and minds" of the Vietnamese majority. We have seen this same nationalistic spirit and commitment from Eastern European nations and Afghanis resisting Soviet occupiers during the Cold War, and subsequently from fighters in Chechnya, the Basque country, and Iraq struggling for group empowerment. In fact, these cases have led some to argue that the threat of an external enemy is exactly what is needed to instill a significant sense of nationalism, strong enough for the nation-states to overcome internal ethnic, religious, or cultural divisions within their population (see Blainey's 1988 discussion of scapegoat theory). This is a topic that will be explored in more detail in the following chapter.

BOX 2.1: A CASE STUDY: THE VIETNAMESE CIVIL WAR (1954–1975)

The division of the country into a communist North, led by Ho Chi Minh, and the non-communist South, led by Ngo Dinh Diem, created a new dynamic. Diem, a Catholic, disliked the communists and rejected Ho Chi Minh's vision of one socialist republic of Vietnam. Thus, the conflict turned into a civil war with Vietnamese fighting Vietnamese. Ho Chi Minh had the support of the USSR, and initially the Chinese. Ngo Dinh Diem received U.S. support because the U.S. wanted to control the spread of Communism in Southeast Asia.

As the civil war began the government in the South became more repressive, canceling a promised election and forcing a large portion of the rural population of the South to relocate in its "strategic hamlet" program. This program entailed moving people from their home villages into heavily fortified pre-fabricated villages in an attempt to isolate the populace from infiltration by the Viet Minh. This program backfired, greatly increasing anti-government sentiment amongst peasants. Meanwhile, a loosely organized force of communist insurgents managed to infiltrate the urban population of South Vietnam. Communist insurgency, coupled with an extremely corrupt and unpopular government, led to a coup in 1963, which resulted in the assassination of Ngo Dinh Diem.

Meanwhile, U.S. President John F. Kennedy sent American military advisors to work with the South Vietnamese army. The Americans too found those in power in the South to be generally ineffective and corrupt, but turned a blind eye as coup after coup was staged. The American participation in the war escalated and by 1964 there were 200,000 American military personnel in South Vietnam and they had changed from being "advisors" to being full participants in the struggle. In 1964, the Destroyer USS Maddox was fired upon off the coast of North Vietnam. While it was maintained for years that this was an unprovoked attack, later information revealed that the American ship was indeed in North Vietnamese waters at the time. With the attack on the Maddox, President Lyndon B. Johnson began to wage an undeclared war against the North Vietnamese, further escalating the number of US military personnel in South Vietnam to a wartime high of over 500,000 in 1968. The major turning point in the war was the Tet Offensive of 1968.

Shattering the serenity of a holiday morning, this attack on U.S. and the Army of the Republic of Vietnam (ARVN) military installations, as well as on nearly every South Vietnamese city, came as a complete surprise and shocked the Americans. Even the American Embassy in the heart of Saigon was attacked by snipers. This Communist offensive was, for the most part, beaten back within a few days, but from that point, it was clear that the Americans could not win in South Vietnam. In America, anti-war sentiment reached an all time high as Americans and the U.S. Government began to scramble for ways to reach an agreeable solution to its embroilment in the Vietnam conflict. Within months of the Tet Offensive, President Johnson halted the bombing of North Vietnam and began to negotiate with the North Vietnamese.

In November of 1968, Richard Nixon was elected President in the U.S., inheriting a nation that was impatient to see American involvement in Vietnam come to a close. Nixon began a policy of "Vietnamization" which entailed the withdrawal of U.S. troops and "handing over the reigns" to the South Vietnamese military. With this program, Nixon reasoned that the South Vietnamese could take over where the U.S. left off, using the superior firepower and technology of the U.S. to win the war. With the Secretary of State, Henry Kissinger, Nixon also opened up clandestine channels of communication with the North Vietnamese. In theory, Nixon's ideas may have seemed to be an answer to the problem; however, in reality, they were not effective. U.S. involvement, though scaled down, was still significant.

To curtail Communist use of eastern Cambodia as part of the Ho Chi Minh Trail, the U.S. staged a coup and invaded the country in early 1970. This plan backfired, dragging neutral Cambodia into the Vietnam conflict. Public sentiment in the U.S. was critical of the U.S. invasion of Cambodia. This sentiment crested with the shooting deaths of four student protesters at Kent State University in May of 1970. In the wake of this event, Nixon announced that all American military personnel would be withdrawn from Vietnam by June 30, 1973. The fighting raged on throughout 1971 and 1972, while Kissinger and the North Vietnamese tried to negotiate a settlement in Paris. Finally, after the Chrismas [sic] bombings of Hanoi and Haiphong in December 1972, an agreement was reached in January of 1973, that called for a ceasefire and withdrawal of American forces within 60 days. Both sides signed, but no one stopped fighting. Both sides felt that ignoring the ceasefire was justified because they were defending their respective territories. Amid this rapidly deteriorating situation, the U.S. finally withdrew in 1975.

With the withdrawal of the Americans, South Vietnam's economy went into a tailspin and inflation ran rampant. In 1974, Saigon was the most expensive city in the world due to the heavy demand and limited supply of almost all goods. Throughout 1974, the situation in South Vietnam deteriorated even further[,] and the North Vietnamese began to assess their strategy for the next year, settling on surprise attacks on provincial capitals. By the end of March 1975, Hue and Da Nang had been lost to the advancing North. As the Communists advanced, populations of entire cities panicked and many fled south. On April 30th, 1975, the North Vietnamese forces marched into Saigon and took over the city, thus ending the civil war.

Source: Nguyen, Windows on Asia Website, Asian Studies Center, Michigan State University. Reprinted with permission.

One additional reason for group identification can be the reality of "safety in numbers." Situations arise where individuals do not feel as though they have a choice—where it is either kill or be killed. Indeed, it seems that the longer a war progresses, the more likely individuals will be asked to choose a side and become a part of the conflict. Neutrality no longer seems a viable option. Thus, a reality of Confederate nationalism developed remarkably rapidly in 1860, with the adoption of national and cultural symbols such as the "Stars and Bars" flag, loyalty to a new government, and the willingness to accept new script money in the American South, binding nonslave holders to slave holders, merchants to farmers, and Whigs to Democrats. More than a few "Yankee" transplants living in the South identified fully with this new "nation" as well (Ayers, 2003).

Group symbols appear to play a significant role in mobilizing individuals to identify with a group, and for that group in turn to mobilize in a progression toward civil war. Stuart Kaufman (2001) has argued that emotional responses to ethnic symbols and myths are particularly likely when group survival appears to be at stake. Ethnic myths work to justify stereotypes of other identity groups, allowing for blaming (i.e., scapegoating) of the other. Fear of group extinction, whether accurate or not, combines with the opportunity to fight to make ethnic war more likely.

National and group inculcation can be either a conscious or gradual unconscious process of attitudinal change, or it can be brought about by force. In several African civil wars and in the former Yugoslavia, individuals, and especially youth and even children, have been forced into armies and taken up arms against the government and their neighbors. Coinciding with safety issues, men and women are given a "choice" either to join the cause or become a casualty. Young people are especially prized recruits because not only are they vigorous and quick but they can also be well motivated by the authorities to believe in causes without question. They tend to lack the range of experience that produces skepticism and attachments to alternate groups and causes. This was the case in Uganda when the Lord's Resistance Army created an army of child soldiers through abduction (Gettleman, 15 September 2006).

Sociologists have noted that it is relatively difficult to instill civil violence among people engaged in "cross-cutting" allegiances and groups (Ross, 1993; this pattern was noted even among Muslims and non-Muslims in Chicago after the events of September 11, 2001, as noted by the Chicago Council on Global Affairs, 2007). If a person shares a number of memberships in civic and professional organizations and clubs with people of another ethnic community, it is less likely, though not impossible, that they would polarize into hated enemies.

Nevertheless, depending on the political and economic circumstances pressuring individuals and groups, neighbors who have lived together and gotten to know each other for their entire lives can still turn to violence and victimization. For example, despite integrating at least to a permissible extent into the life of their cities and towns, Jews were betrayed and killed in many European countries during the Holocaust by local ethnic communities with whom they had lived peacefully and with whom they had at least a modicum of interaction. It was a Dutch policeman who evidently turned in diarist Anne Frank's family, who were hiding in Amsterdam, much to the lasting shame of many in the Netherlands. Although there were notable acts of courage by non-Jews protecting and hiding Jewish neighbors, large numbers of French, Latvian, and Eastern European citizens were all too eager to cooperate with the German authorities in disposing of the "Jewish problem" in their countries when Hitler's forces conquered their territories. Mendelsohn writes of a search for the fate of six of his family members, who perished among six million in the Holocaust, in a small town (schtetl) in what is now Ukraine, a territory fought over and ruled across centuries by Austrians, Poles, Russians, and Germans. He notes the ironies of Jews and Ukrainians forced to compete in situations beyond their control.

> The Jews, nationless, politically vulnerable, dependent on the Polish aristocrats who owned these towns, and for whom so many of the Jews inevitably

worked as stewards and moneylenders, for their security; and the Ukrainians, who for the most part
were workers of the land, who occupied the lowest
rung of the economic totem pole, a people whose
history, ironically, in so many ways was like a mirror image, or perhaps a negative image, of that of
the Jews: a people without a nation-state, vulnerable, oppressed by cruel masters of one description
or another—Polish counts, Soviet commissars. It
was because of this strangely precise mirroring, in
fact, that in the middle of the twentieth century it
evolved, with the precise, terrible logic of a Greek
tragedy, that whatever was good for one of these two
groups, who lived side by side for centuries in these
tiny towns, was bad for the other. When, in 1939,
the Germans ceded the eastern portion of Poland
(which they had just conquered) to the Soviet
Union as part of the Molotov-Ribbentrop Pact, the
Jews of the region rejoiced, knowing they had been
delivered from the Germans; but the Ukrainians,
a fiercely nationalistic and proud people, suffered
under the Soviets, who then as always were determined to stamp out Ukrainian independence—and
Ukrainians. Talk to Ukrainians about the twentieth century ... and they will tell you about their
own holocaust, the deaths, in the 1930s, of those
five to seven million Ukrainian peasants, starved
out by Stalin's forced collectivization [of farms]....
So the miraculous good luck of the Jews of eastern
Poland, in 1939, was a disaster for the Ukrainians
of eastern Poland. Conversely, when Hitler betrayed
the Molotov-Ribbentrop Pact two years later and invaded the very portion of eastern Poland that he'd
given to Stalin, it was, of course a disaster for the
Jews but a blessing for the Ukrainians, who rejoiced
when the Nazis arrived, having been freed from
their Soviet oppressors. It is remarkable to think
that two groups inhabiting such close quarters for
so many years could be so different, suffer and exult

over such different, indeed opposite, reversals of
fortune. (Mendelsohn, 2006: 120)

In a further cruel irony, of course, the Ukrainians, who might not have
much mourned the fate of the Jews at that time, would themselves be
treated and victimized by the Nazis as subhuman members of the Slavic
"race."

In a sense, then, civilian violence can depend on relative polarization in which groups come to see each other as alien, untrustworthy,
privileged, or different, and not as having much in common even
if they have remained in close proximity. This happens despite often
demonstrable similarities, as with the Serbs and Croats sharing what
amounts to a common language, Arabs and Israelis sharing a Semitic
sociolinguistic heritage, and Northern Irish Unionists and Republicans
sharing much the same culture.

One convenient divisive element among otherwise similar groups
can be religion. We say "convenient" because such factors can be seized
upon by unscrupulous and ambitious leaders and drilled into major
hatred and dread. Religious leaders might themselves have conditioned
their flocks to hate, distrust, or resent "nonbelieving" neighbors, and
these patterns can lead to scapegoating of the "other" when times get
difficult, as they did during the global Great Depression of the 1930s.
Religion can be used as a convenient marker, when actually it is other
deeper interests that cause the outbreak of warfare, interests such as
nationalism and group insecurity. Religion can be attuned to some of
the basic human needs (identity, security) that Burton (1990) highlights
(see Box 2.2). Nationalist religious zealotry is compounded by a doctri-
nal view that rewards heroic fighters defending a religious identity. This
is apparent for some of the so-called suicide bombers of our day, though
secular nonreligious forces can also employ such extreme measures in
defense of a nation.

Individual and group identity is a particularly complex concept. The
construction of group identity is itself a topic of debate among scholars.
"Primordialist" notions suggest that a person's identity is a fixed entity
once imprinted by parental training. This argument has been dismissed
by "constructivist" scholars, who argue that identity is more fluid and
that individual/group identity can be constructed, deconstructed, and
reconstructed over time. Fixed primordialist arguments are indeed
problematic as individuals can in many instances redefine themselves

(for example, religious conversion). Yet, it is often noted that even religious converts retain many aspects of their old culture or beliefs.

In the midst of economic and political crisis or violent conflict, identity tends to become hardened (Van Evera, 2001) (the blaming of scapegoats, for example) and even potentially externally imposed. Clearly, each individual has many identities, either self-ascribed or ascribed by others, including racial, ethnic, religious, gender, political, or occupational categorizations, to name a few. Which identity becomes more salient to the individual tends to depend on the circumstances.

People are motivated to join a rebellion because they are passionate about the cause or because they see it being in their interest to do so. Commitment to causes begins to move us from the individual to the group level of analysis of war motivation, entailing the fascinating process by which people come to identify with each other in groups, and identify against "outgroups." Here, the distinction between ideological or utilitarian ("what can I get out of it?") motivations and those involving identity groups becomes pertinent. When people feel a certain "comfort zone" of shared group norms and expectations, frequently found in cultural identity, their adherence to each other, especially in a time of strife, can be boosted. A sense of shared fate can be enhanced.

Group and societal polarization is inevitable if civil war is to occur, but shared identity and collective incentives in a conflict can vary depending on whether a sense of primordial unity or pragmatic calculation prevails. As the march toward war progresses and societies become polarized, an individual's ability to relate to others with similar identities will be tested. In such situations, the nation-state and/or belligerent groups seeking to define parties to the conflict (i.e., us versus them) may attempt to impose identity on groups or individuals.

Indeed, identity formation was purposefully manipulated by the Soviet regime in Moscow in order to ameliorate the potential of civil war and insurgent uprisings. The construction of the "new Soviet man" was posed as an antidote for old pernicious ethnic nationalism and hatreds among constituent groups in the Soviet Union, groups such as the Azeris, Armenians, Tatars, Uzbeks, Ukrainians, and Russians. If social identity could be re-engineered and remolded, it was reasoned in Moscow's modernizing socialist ideology, then the vast state could be unified and both class and ethnic warfare would cease. While Joseph Stalin's iron fist, along with external threats (German, American, etc.), kept such national violence to a relative minimum, once the Soviet regime was removed, old grievances—such as previously forced population movements and insecurities—soon re-emerged, as they also did in Tito's Yugoslavia.

The underlying "causes" of ethnic conflict are often not exclusively to be found in differences of identity. Despite terminology such as "ethnic conflict," ethnicity itself does not cause war. It serves as a group marker, but understanding various group identities and the significance of identity is only part of the puzzle when exploring group-level motivation for civil war. As a result, issues that underlie the appearance of identity-based war seem key to understanding group motivation. As indicated earlier, civil war simply cannot occur without masses who are willing to follow the lead of a political entrepreneur, whether to defend the integrity of a nation or to rebel against it, or whether to respond to perceived injustices against one's group by a current or former government. History reveals certain key themes that characterize the mass resort to arms used to settle domestic political disputes.

One theme relates to the psychology—perhaps even the biology—of security and honor, particularly, though not exclusively, as it affects males. The importance of honor and the notion of "serving one's nation" has certainly played a significant role in motivating individuals to defend their country during times of international war (see for example, Ellis, 1976). This motivation extends to those willing to engage in civil war as well. Those already enlisted in the nation's military may feel compelled to defend that nation even if the threat comes from within. The implications of domestic warfare, however, are quite unique. Defending one's nation from an internal enemy, and in the process potentially killing a neighbor or even a relative, poses challenges—some psychologically or biologically based—that enlisted men and women might not otherwise face. Long-term occupation of adjacent territories and hostile populations may also become necessary and especially onerous. Such duty might be too difficult a request for some, though clearly not for all (particularly when a country is divided in such a way that a certain group's identity is pitted against the identity of the state). Despite these challenges, military men and women might still feel motivated by honor and a sense of responsibility to engage in civil war on behalf of the state.

Honor and service can also, of course, motivate rebels. The American South has long been noted for a tradition of military service as a way of attaining status and honor. One of Ayers's (2003) findings from an extended review of ordinary people's perspectives on the approach of the War Between the States was that both sides, amid whipped-up rumors and media reports, feared the loss of their "way of life." For various individuals this meant the fear that, among other things, slaves would be freed and unleashed on their masters; Africans would flood into Northern towns and cities; enemy troops would violate women and children; and the republic or state's prerogatives as they had been known would be torn asunder. Ironically, the unimaginably destructive and deadly war that ensued, which was intended to forestall these feared outcomes and to restore each side's honor, instead resulted to some extent in all of these feared outcomes.

It seems clear that individual interests, and particularly economic interests, can condition war support and participation. Thus, civil war and rebellion can be seen as a process of "rational choice," though the irrationality of the outcomes is all too apparent (see Blainey, 1988). Kaufman (1996: 113) has indicated that it is difficult to motivate an economically satisfied population to take up arms against their government. If one explores the underlying factors associated with cases such as the Cuban Revolution, the American Civil War, and the Vietnam War, economic issues appear significant. History is replete with cases of ideological conflict involving peasant uprisings aimed at righting unjust economic systems.

Often these wars, in one sense involving the identity of class interests, coincide with struggles to depose corrupt governments or leaders. This was certainly the case in Nicaragua in 1979, when the Sandinista National Liberation Front overthrew the government of Anastasio Somoza Debayle, a dictator whose family had long oppressed the country while enriching itself, thus beginning a long and drawn-out civil war. The Somoza regime had benefited from significant US support, but the corruption surrounding it only became more evident after it managed to embezzle much of the international aid flowing to Nicaragua following the devastating earthquake of 1972 (see Goodwin, 1988). Sandinista rebels and their followers sought not only to rid the country of this corruption but also to establish a more equitable economic system, including significant agrarian reform. Eventually, the US backed the Sandinistas' opponents, the so-called Contras, with arms, training, supplies, and funds, which perpetuated the war.

Economic motivations to engage in civil war can, therefore, readily intertwine with issues relating to identity, justice, and honor. For example, quite a number of the so-called suicide bombers resisting the Israeli occupation of Arab lands have been well educated and come from reasonably well-to-do families. They appear to be motivated by a sense of honor arising from collective humiliation and bitterness at what they see as unjust treatment by their occupiers. Of course, many individuals might also feel such humiliation and not resort to violence; the trigger mechanism might be in the individual's acceptance of martyrdom as a means of restoring honor. Osama bin Laden himself has participated in and led uprisings against Soviet forces in Afghanistan, American forces in the Arabian Peninsula, and Arab governments that have cooperated with outside occupations. We all know that Bin Laden came from one of Saudi Arabia's wealthiest families, and clearly he became a political entrepreneur with outstanding organizational and motivational skills that were very appealing to those prone to seeking honor through both individual and collective action.

Likewise we can also expect that men and women without any viable economic pursuit or prospects can become desperate or disillusioned enough to join a rebellious cause, particularly when those perceiving disadvantages tend to identify with a particular identity group, highlighting perceived injustice ("structural inequality"). They may see little to lose in resorting to violence, combining somewhat rational calculation with emotional bitterness, pain, hopelessness, and anger. Further qualifying the pattern, however, Gurr (1970) and others who investigate "why men rebel" note that very often it is not the poorest of the poor who become aggressive. Rather a process of what is known as "relative deprivation" sets in (as opposed to "absolute deprivation" described by Davies, 1962). Those who have seen some improvement in their living conditions but are denied their ultimate "fair share" (i.e., those who compare their own economic levels to those of others nearby) become embittered at their relative disadvantages. Thus, political rebellion is seen as transitional. This is not so prevalent among the poorest and hopeless or among the richest and most satisfied, but rather it can become concentrated among those for whom change, whether political change such as democratization or economic change such as new industries, has raised hopes only to have hope dashed by various aspects of reality (Victor, 2003).

As a result, noted conflict theorists such as Burton (1990) have proposed a "human needs theory" to explain the extent to which people dispute with each other. Basic human needs such as affection, sustenance, self-worth, or autonomy might be threatened by opponents. In order to offset the violence potential of such unmet needs, governments and authorities are advised to address needs as an underlying factor in order to avert uprisings. Economic motivations for mass participation, as they relate to the causes of so-called identity wars, are more likely to coincide with other forms of grievance or various unmet needs felt by the group.

BOX 2.2: CONSEQUENCES OF UNMET HUMAN NEEDS

Writing for the conflict resolution website "Beyond Intractability," Sandra Marker (2003) has encapsulated human needs theory as handed down by Burton (1990) and others: "According to the renowned psychologist Abraham Maslow and the conflict scholar John Burton, these essentials go beyond just food, water, and shelter. They include both physical and non-physical elements needed for human growth and development, as well as all those things humans are innately driven to attain."

Maslow (1954), posing a hierarchy of needs, begins with the basics of food, water, and shelter, and adds consideration of love and self-esteem, safety and security, and personal fulfillment. Burton (1990) lists needs without hierarchy, needs that might be pursued simultaneously or in varied order. He adds such factors as identity, cultural security, freedom, distributive justice, and participation—factors that might be debated as to their applicability across all human societies. When unmet, either wholly or partially, these needs represent the underlying seeds of human and political conflict as parties struggle over their fulfillment.

Unlike interests, such as money, political power, or land, such underlying needs cannot in themselves be compromised, traded, suppressed, or bargained over. Thus, negotiation becomes complicated when combining "nonnegotiable" needs or demands. Human needs theorists pose problem-solving workshops as one approach to needs reconciliation and fulfillment, as parties work toward mutual identification and understanding of needs, and then toward creative solutions for joint needs achievement (i.e., so each side is, to a tolerable extent, satisfied). It is argued that if bargains are struck only over surface issues or interests, unfulfilled underlying needs will drive parties back toward war.

As Marker notes, though, critics of human needs theory are quick to point out supposed shortcomings:

Many questions and uncertainties surround the human needs approach to solving conflicts. For instance, how can one define human needs? How can one know what needs are involved in conflict situations? How can one know what human needs are being met and unmet? Are human needs cultural or universal in nature? If they are cultural, is the analysis of human needs beneficial beyond a specific conflict? Are some needs inherently more important than others? If some needs are more important, should these be pursued first?

Clearly, though, solutions to complex political conflicts leading to civil war require attention to both needs and interests. One approach that circumvents the definitional problem might be to let disputants themselves define or explore their own and each other's needs and weigh them against stated interests. This could mean, for example, that if a need for religious or cultural recognition is cited, various means for achieving that need might be devised, such as sharing space, having separate schools or languages, or writing guarantees into a constitution. The means may still be controversial and subject to debate, but the least objectionable means might be adopted to satisfy each side's unmet needs.

Issues of relative deprivation and unmet basic needs become particularly powerful motivators when individuals who find themselves comparatively deprived link that deprivation to issues of identity. When the "haves" and "have-nots" are thought to be as easily identifiable by their ethnic, religious, or cultural origins or characteristics, mobilization is more likely. Groups feeling a systematic sense of discrimination, whether economic, political, or social, have the tendency to protect and assert their group identity, finding convenient scapegoats in pursuit of a more just and equitable system (Gurr, 2003). How the state responds to this mobilization may well determine whether or not war is likely.

Clearly, discrimination is not limited to the economic realm. In fact, economic discrimination often begins in the political realm. Feelings of deprivation and grievance can occur among the masses when political rights and access are denied or limited. Some have even argued that political discrimination is more likely to invoke feelings of unjust group status strong enough to lead to rebellion when hierarchical status has been reversed (Olson Lounsbery, 2003). This situation occurred in several post-colonial states as previously disadvantaged majorities under colonial rule found themselves in power as newly independent states adopted majoritarian democratic regime types.

For example, the creation of Rwanda and its next-door neighbor Burundi as states with varied Hutu and Tutsi ethnocultural balances and identities involved elements of status-reversal culminating in civil war, intergroup violence, and vengeance cycles in both states. When what is now Rwanda was a Belgian colony, the Tutsi minority, itself a somewhat artificial ethnic construct, enjoyed a privileged status. That changed, however, toward the end of colonial rule in the 1950s as the Belgians began to implement democratic reforms. By August 1962, Rwanda was granted independence under the Hutu leadership of Gregoire Kayibanda, but not before over 160,000 Tutsis fled the country. Tutsis in exile, recalling past violent attacks, mobilized and reorganized as the Rwandan Patriotic Front, attacking the Rwandan government in 1990. This strategy ultimately backfired after a plane carrying the moderate presidents of Rwanda and Burundi was shot down, resulting in the blaming and slaughter of more than 800,000 Tutsis and moderate Hutus in a period of less than three months. The status-reversal that provided the majority population (Hutus) with political power at the expense of the previously powerful Tutsi minority ignited a chain of events that brought the country to both civil war and genocide.

What also seems clear in this discussion is that group actors are frequently motivated by a need for security, whether to protect themselves from various forms of discrimination or to counter status-reversal and the perceived possibility of group eradication. Groups mobilize in an effort to gain such security. The government, seeing growing "instability" on the borders or in various provinces or sections of the country, might respond with military force, even excessive force. The irony, therefore, is that the very process of mobilization is itself dangerous in many situations. As discussed by Chaim Kaufmann (1996) and Stuart Kaufman (1996), the security dilemma arises in which the very acts and policies meant to fend off enemies provoke them to greater preparations and countermeasures of their own, leaving neither side more secure. How the state responds to such dilemmas and to perceived illegal rebellion will often determine whether war will ensue. The pivotal role of state policy will be explored in detail in the following chapter.

CONCLUSION

Individual and group motivations are an integral part of the civil war puzzle. Without the participation of both the elites and the masses, conflict within states will not reach the intensity of war. As we have demonstrated, what motivates the elites and what motivates the masses are a myriad of issues ranging from greed and political opportunism, to identity, inequality, and unmet human needs (such as the need for justice or security). Fully understanding how such issues interact with government policy and the formulation and salience of group identity, regardless of type (religion, ethnicity, ideology), is central to understanding war mobilization. While passions may run high in the heat of war and during the preparation for war, individuals and groups do not enter into something as dangerous and destructive as civil war without feeling, at least initially, that the fight is worth it. That said, understanding the individual and the group is one dimension of the multidimensional and multilevel explanation of war. In the next chapter we explore the dimension of state characteristics.

CHAPTER THREE

State-Level Factors Leading to Civil War

"God requireth not a uniformity of religion to be enacted in any civil state; which enforced uniformity (sooner or later) is the greatest occasion of civil war, ravishing of conscience, persecution of Christ Jesus in his servants, and of the hypocrisy and destruction of millions of souls."

—Roger Williams

Certain nation-states seem more susceptible to violent intrastate conflict than others. Some nations have experienced very little war in their history, while others seem to be engaged in some form of war or another repeatedly, and often seemingly endlessly. What accounts for these differences? Civil wars, by definition, occur within the geographic boundaries of the state, though certainly outside intervention and the internationalization of civil war does happen. Further, the nation-state is generally both a party to the conflict as well as the setting of the conflict. Groups (nonstate actors) and individuals engaged in large-scale violence against the state often are doing so in reaction to the state's political, economic, or social policies, as well as its structure and institutions.

As a result, in order to fully understand civil war propensities, we must explore the structure of the state itself and the various state-level factors that interact with individual and group motivations in setting the stage for civil war. We see, for example, that countries with mountainous terrain seem to have higher rates of civil war (Fearon and Laitin, 2003; Gurr, 2003). Certainly, the mountains do not "cause" the warfare, but they do create an environment more conducive to guerrilla activities by providing cover for base operations and escape from government pursuit. Opposition groups in states without mountainous terrain may also pursue armed strategies, but they may find it more difficult to sustain themselves with fewer hiding places. Instead, they may revert to urban or "bush" ("jungle") warfare as appropriate.

State characteristics can be categorized along political, economic, and social dimensions. These are not mutually exclusive categories, in that political institutions have a significant impact on the economic factors of the state, as well as its various social factors. In fact, political, economic, and social factors typically reinforce one another, as in the supposed necessity for a well-developed middle class as a prerequisite of democracy (see Moore, 1966). Nonetheless, the three categories are separately useful if one is attempting to provide a structural road map to civil war. What follows, as a result, is a discussion of the various state-level factors that have been identified as particularly salient for state volatility.

THE POLITICAL STATE

First and foremost, nation-states tend to be identified by their political regime (i.e., type of government). In essence, regime type determines both the openness of a state to various political actors within and also the extent of rights enjoyed by its citizens. The spectrum of political openness can range from the fully democratic regime to that which is fully autocratic. Prototypical democratic regimes experience active and open political competition within a constitutional structure with an unfettered rule of law and a concept of human rights protected by an independent judiciary, as well as an active citizenry participating in the election process. Meanwhile, autocratic regimes experience quite the opposite, including limited executive competition, impeded judicial processes, and minimal citizen involvement in the selection of leaders. In between can be either flawed, partial, or transitional regimes that incorporate elements of democratic form with elements of autocratic style.

Thus, pure democracies and pure autocracies are exceedingly rare. Even the United States, which boasts of democratic governance, is not a democratic state in its purest sense. For example, US presidential outcomes, themselves typical of republican rather than mass democratic structures, are determined by an electoral college and not by the popular vote. This was witnessed in the 2000 presidential election when Al Gore, despite national electoral victory, lacked the necessary electoral college votes to defeat George W. Bush, a decision that was ratified by the Supreme Court.

Understanding the various dimensions of a state's political regime, and how those dimensions influence the mobilization of opposition, requires that one resist the temptation to separate the world's state governments into those that are either democratic or autocratic. It is the various shades of gray that provide the "stuff" that makes war possible. The more regimes fall short of full participation and protection of minorities, or the more they depart from pure repression, the more prone they may be to suffer rebellion and uprising. For example, the shah's social reforms in Iran, in the context of his continued autocratic rule and use of secret police, may have driven the society toward the rebellion that ultimately became the Islamic revolution in 1979.

We begin our discussion about regime type with an exploration of the democratic peace thesis, introduced briefly in Chapter 2, and its potential applicability to intrastate warfare (for a fundamental study of the subject, see Hegre et al., 2001). International relations scholars tend to agree that no mature democracies have ever fought against each other (Mansfield and Snyder, 2005; Doyle, 1986). In an even more controversial assertion, it has further been argued that democratic states experience less international war in general (Rummel, 1979), because if citizens are required to consent to war (as they are in a democracy), they are unlikely to do so given the costs they will bear. Related to the democracy and peace theses is Immanuel Kant's (1795) thinking about peaceful republican communities, both domestic and international.

As a result, scholars and policy-makers alike have been tempted to propose the spread of democracy and liberal ideals as a way to lessen the occurrence of war (Doyle, 1986). Former US President Bill Clinton's push to spread democracy was evident in his 1994 State of the Union Address: "Ultimately, the best strategy to ensure our security and to build a durable peace is to support the advance of democracy elsewhere. Democracies don't attack each other; they make better trading partners and partners in diplomacy" (*The New York Times*, 26 January 1994). It can be argued that the Bush administration's subsequent involvement in Iraq, spurring an Iraqi civil war, came because of the belief—however unfounded it might have been—by influential officials that they could remake the Middle East into some sort of Western democratic image, thus ending regional warfare and instability.

Applying the democratic peace thesis to peace within borders, however, has proven even more problematic. The United States, despite its semidemocratic institutions (during the nineteenth century, nonwhites, nonproperty holders, and females were excluded from democratic participation), experienced a particularly bloody civil war from 1860–65 resulting in over 650,000 dead. Indeed, democratic peace theorists regarding international war have argued that Britain refrained from intervening against the North (in light of its substantial economic ties to the South) in the civil war because of its underlying perception of the USA as democratic (Owen, 1996).

Democracies of various sorts do experience civil war or significant rebellions and uprisings, as seen for example in campaigns against ethnic autonomy movements in territories such as the northeast tribal hill country in India. Perhaps, however, mature democracies (those that are institutionally consistent and developed) experience fewer or lower levels of such wars. Perhaps citizens within nations with a democratic history or tradition are more likely to address their grievances, as in Canada, through the political process and without feeling the need to risk their lives by engaging in armed conflict with or within the state.

Interestingly, however, and perhaps for different reasons, autocracies appear to share the potential for a diminished occurrence of civil war also seen in democratic regimes (Hegre et al., 2001). Citizens living in autocratic regimes might have grievances, but mobilizing to address them can be dangerous. The same may also be true in democracies as the majority of citizens come to political consensus and strongly reject aberrant or critical views, even to the point of arrests, prosecution (e.g., the US alien and sedition laws at the time of the French Revolution), or forceful repression (as in antiterrorism arrests seen in many countries in our own time). In addition, in democracies as well as in autocracies, there might be significant unwillingness to countenance autonomy or secessionist struggles to control parts of the country, even though these may go on, as mentioned in the Indian example above.

As a result, scholars have found that nation-states that are neither democratic nor autocratic are the most prone to civil wars (Hegre et al., 2001; Fearon and Laitin, 2003; Henderson and Singer, 2000). We refer to these states as "semidemocracies," "transitional democracies," or "anocracies." This type of state political structure does not yet provide the openness that allows citizens to address and redress grievances consistently, but it is also not as repressive as an autocracy so as to thwart mobilization, thus making a political situation potentially ripe for conflict should grievances arise.

Since democracies and autocracies are more internally peaceful, and democratic dyads (i.e., two democratic states) are statistically perhaps less likely to fight one another, foreign policy initiatives that promote democratization would seem warranted. Not only would the spread of democracy provide political rights and freedoms to more people, but we would also be able to predict fewer international and civil wars. The actual democratizing process, however, can be rather volatile (Snyder, 2000). States rarely transition quickly and effectively from an autocratic or anocratic regime to one that is solidly democratic. Where leaders and institutions may require the time necessary to adjust to a more liberal system, the population may be motivated to seek a quicker transition. Once again, the interests of the elites and the masses tend to diverge.

Transitions to democracy inevitably mean a loosening of the control leaders once held. Accountability becomes an issue, and repression a less acceptable tool for dealing with dissent. Not only must institutions adjust to provide citizens a voice and a free flow of information (e.g., freedom of the press) but elites must also adjust to the idea that their power is now limited and subject to the sanction of an independent judiciary. Masses, on the other hand, often embrace the democratization process, though they can be suspicious that their ethnic or cultural or regional voting strength may be overwhelmed in the new political order. The political freedom extended to citizens of newly democratic states is a typically welcome change, though in some cultures and states, such as contemporary Russia, citizens also retain a preference for order and a certain tolerance for semi-authoritarian rules, such as suspension of liberties, restrictions on the press, or removal of regional governors or administrators. When citizens do campaign for democracy, though, they often have little patience and seem to expect that such a transition should occur rapidly if it is to occur at all.

Further, transitional states' progress can be complicated by social and economic issues. Not only are these states seeking to adjust to or create newly democratic political institutions but they are also often seeking to provide economic or social relief to the population as well. Dealing with these types of issues simultaneously is difficult and takes time. This reality is part of what makes the democratization process volatile.

The Soviet regime in Moscow during the late 1980s under President Mikhail Gorbachev sought to foster increased freedom of discussion and inquiry (glasnost and perestroika), leading to economic progress while retaining a single party structure. This proved impossible as the regime ultimately fell, first to a rather chaotic political free-for-all and then to a form of "guided" or strongman democracy under President Vladimir Putin. By contrast, during much the same period, China sought to fully repress political liberalization (as seen most starkly in Beijing's Tiananmen Square incidents of 1989) and concentrate exclusively on economic liberalization and modernization. This proved effective, at least throughout the early twenty-first century, offering a great deal of economic opportunity to new generations of Chinese citizens. However, some analysts still note a high potential for eventual political uprising, regional autonomy struggles, and economic corruption in the country. As political freedom becomes available, masses may begin to mobilize for political action. Where institutions are not yet able to absorb issues of grievance, especially if the economy should turn sour, and political elites are not yet accustomed to accommodating protest, the stage may be set for a resort to repression. Mason and Quinn (2003: 27) have identified this type of situation as one ripe for a "subsequent reversion to authoritarian rule," making revolution more likely.

Political stability in and of itself appears to impact a state's propensity for civil war. Fearon and Laitin (2003: 85) found that instability (measured to indicate whether or not a country "had a three-or-greater change in Polity IV regime index in any of the three years prior to the country-year in question") within a country increases the odds of civil war onset by 67 per cent. Interestingly, their findings do not support the link between democratization and civil war discussed above, but rather support the opposite position. According to Fearon and Laitin, dramatic shifts away from democracy are more likely to produce the conditions ripe for civil war. Not surprisingly, populations that are used to a certain amount of political freedoms (i.e., those associated with democratic governments) would look unfavorably upon the curtailing of those freedoms.

Type of government may also play a role in the facilitation of civil war as groups internal to the state struggle to align politically. War, both domestic and international, tends to be a struggle over political power, though other factors can come to the fore, such as the ideological (philosophical) struggle over the direction of the state or society, or religious or ethnic hatred and distrust. The world witnessed many power struggles within these different guises during the Cold War and during the years of anticolonial struggle following World Wars I and II, such as the internal war in Northern Ireland, fought within and by a recognized mature democracy (see below).

BOX 3.1: A CASE IN POINT: NORTHERN IRELAND

The conflict in Northern Ireland has never reached the level of full-scale civil war; however, the persistence of the conflict, as well as the fact that it occurs within a mature democracy, has made it one of the most publicized and researched during its time. What follows is a brief description of the modern history of the country leading up to the outbreak of violence, or the "Troubles."

The six counties of Northern Ireland were left in disputed autonomous status in 1921 after the four-year Irish rebellion led to the independence of southern Ireland. The Irish nationalist parties in Dublin reluctantly accepted this arrangement, while pro-British (mainly Protestant) elements in the Ulster Unionist Party (UUP) and its militant extremists, known as "Loyalists," inside Northern Ireland welcomed the terms as allowing for continued association with the UK. Opposition nationalist (mainly Catholic) elements in the north chafed at the pro-British dominance, and maintained a sometimes armed resistance. The struggle was about political dominance and subservience, along with the question of Ireland's ultimate national boundaries.

Thus, a Catholic-based civil rights campaign along with street demonstrations emerged in 1968, leading to Protestant counterdemonstrations and growing sectarian clashes. The Northern Irish government, under Terrence O'Neill, proposed reforms that satisfied neither side, leading to new elections, and a stronger UUP majority, as well as more riots. British troops were invited in to keep order and control all security forces in the province; a prolonged period of direct British involvement resulted.

The presence of British forces at first reassured Catholics about their protection and rights (voting, housing, etc.), but as time passed without a political solution, the Irish Republican Army (IRA and later its militant wing the Provisional IRA) initiated armed resistance to the British "occupation." The British cracked down on the unrest with a policy of arrest or detainment without trial, further enraging the nationalist side. Polarization worsened with the formation of the ultraloyalist Democratic Unionist Party in 1971 led by Reverend Ian Paisley, along with the militant Ulster Defence Association.

Violence worsened once again in 1972 after the "Bloody Sunday" civil rights march degenerated into clashes with British forces, resulting in the deaths of 14 unarmed civilians. British Prime Minister Edward Heath was unable to come to an agreement with Northern Irish governmental authorities on the issue of responsibility for law and order, and Britain removed the government and reinstituted direct military and political rule. Death totals for 1972 reached a peak of 478, and by 1999 the "Troubles," including many acts of terrorism, had claimed some 3,300 lives.

The situation began to stabilize with an emerging Anglo-Irish dialogue in the 1990s, provisions for reintroduction of a Northern Irish parliamentary assembly, and accords for ceasefire and disarmament of militants that also cleared the way for closer association and growing prosperity within the European Union framework for southern Ireland. Yet, tensions and grassroots distrust and resentment had not been totally eliminated.

See: Banks and Muller (1999).

Clearly, the Northern Irish situation was strongly conditioned by British and Irish interests. With major power interests in countries that were divided ethnically or by class, the structure of the international system itself had much to do with the so-called ideological conflicts and civil wars that arose between 1945 and 1989 (these factors will be discussed in the next chapter). However, wars fought over the political nature of the state and which social or political classes might dominate it fall solidly under state-level discussions. Battles such as those in Cuba (1955–59), Nicaragua (1978–89), Vietnam (1955–75), and, more recently, Nepal (see Box 3.2) serve as examples of civil wars with such socio-political overtones. Nepal also illustrates the interplay of social class conflict and environmental factors such as the potential for rural sanctuaries and anti-urban warfare, patterns seen in other areas where

Maoist guerrilla tactics were applied, including China during its long civil war.

BOX 3.2: A CASE IN POINT: "WHO ARE NEPAL'S MAOIST REBELS?"

Just when it seems that revolutionary communism has all but disappeared in the world, Nepal's Maoist rebels seem to grow stronger and stronger.

It is estimated that they now have between 10,000 to 15,000 fighters, and are active across the country, with many parts completely under their control.

So how did the rebels transform themselves from a small group of shotgun-wielding insurgents in 1996 to the formidable fighting force they are today?

The disillusionment of the Maoists with the Nepalese political system began after democracy was re-introduced in 1990. (Lawson, 6 June 2005)

Patterning themselves after the Peruvian Shining Path guerrillas, but with notable Nepalese variations, Nepal's Maoist rebels participated in overthrowing Nepal's absolute monarchy even as they participated in new parliamentary elections representing the poverty-stricken rural masses. They, like the government troops they fought, utilized ruthless violent tactics including torture and summary executions.

Calling for a single party Marxist republic, the rebels launched armed resistance to the government in 1996 with attacks on police outposts and the confiscation of arms. They continued such raids but modified their tactics as necessary for political advantage over the next several years, retaining only the commitment to the removal of the constitutional monarchy. In the process, they took advantage of the severe resentment of lower social castes against dominant elite castes. Thus, they came to be seen as the only currently viable alternative to the repressive traditional social order; yet still lightly armed, they remained relatively obscure on the world scene. However, with audacious actions such as notorious abductions and kidnappings, and with the acquisition of greater firepower and funding, probably smuggled across the Indian border, they emerged as one of South Asia's best-organized and most potent insurgent forces, next to the famous Tamil Tigers of Sri Lanka.

Maoist guerrilla strength has been demonstrated in widespread and effective general strikes in the capital city of Katmandu, as well as through headline-grabbing "re-education" abductions of school children near the capital. Their forces cannot fully win a "people's war," but they take refuge and advantage of grievances in the poorer rural areas of the country where government development programs have been stymied and where government troops cannot effectively reach without heavy-handed attacks that further alienate the population.

Source: Lawson (2005).

Transitions for newly independent states are equally problematic, if not more so, than democratic transitions for older, more established states. Civil wars in the post-World War II era have taken place primarily in Third World countries (Mason, 2004), particularly in former colonies (Henderson and Singer, 2000, 2002). In fact, statistically, the first two years following independence appear to be the most volatile time, increasing the odds of civil war onset by a factor of 5.25 (Fearon and Laitin, 2003: 85). During this period, new states struggle to establish control over state territory, as well as legitimacy with the citizenry. That control and legitimacy may not come easy, and the ability to gain it is often closely connected to the colonial experience.

Colonial administrations clearly left their mark in many ways, beginning with the arbitrary nature by which colonial boundaries were established (Henderson and Singer, 2002). Where one colonial territory ended and another began was typically a political decision made by colonial powers over resource distribution with little or no regard for the demographic layout of the existing area. The formation of Iraq and Lebanon, for example, were two such materialistic designs by colonial powers (Britain and France) and resulted in states with significant and politically challenging ethnic divisions.

Further, as decolonization gained momentum following World War II, the creation of newly independent states mirrored more closely the arbitrary boundaries of colonial territories rather than any pre-existing tribal or cultural borders. The issue of boundaries and cross-border kindred groups has been identified as a problem more for Africa than perhaps other regions. Arbitrary boundaries clearly divided groups and created diverse polities. As newly forming states transitioned from independence, the new central or federal governments sought to expand their control and assert their power throughout the territory in order to demonstrate legitimacy as a nation and to control the wealth and resources (e.g., gold, diamonds, copper) so necessary to pay for the state and its development. The arbitrary nature of state boundaries made this assertion of control difficult as national identity had perhaps yet to emerge, while group-level identity and mutual suspicions persisted. Some of these tensions were exacerbated by outside powers intervening in the affairs of these fledgling states for their own gains, and by the emergence of increased corruption after the first generation of national leaders following independence. Transitions to independence and possibly democracy were thus complicated in many respects by colonial history itself.

Territories subjected to colonial administration often experienced policies identified as "divide and rule" or "divide and conquer." British colonies are most noted for this experience, but other colonial powers such as Belgium utilized the technique as well. Essentially, the policies entailed providing advantage to one segment of society, usually a demographic minority, at the expense of other groups in society, most notably the demographic majority. The minority, as a result, would gain some of the spoils of colonization, including educational advantages, at the expense of the majority and presumably assist the colonizer in maintaining and prolonging its rule. The benefit of such a policy for the colonial power was that any frustrations felt by the majority of people within the territory would be redirected from the external power to the internal one, i.e., the influential and advantaged minority.

The significant impact of "divide and conquer" policies is that group identity became solidified. In addition, years of colonization meant years of group frustration with an internal target. During this time, fairly high levels of European migration to colonial territories also occurred. These migrants often held privileged positions in society. By the time decolonization occurred, animosity and frustration on the part of the masses aimed at privileged groups was already in place and the potential was there for social polarization.

Decolonization also often meant democratization or, more specifically, majoritarian democracy. We have discussed the challenges of democratization, but this becomes particularly perilous as previously disadvantaged groups obtain power over previously advantaged groups. Combine that with high levels of animosity and frustration, and once again, civil war becomes possible.

Cases in point are Zimbabwe (formerly Rhodesia), as well as its neighbor South Africa. Politically dominant white minority groups led both countries during the period of British rule, and even during the post-independence period. Efforts on the part of these minority-led governments to maintain power as surrounding countries transitioned to majority rule resulted in internal strife, repression, and violence. In fact, it has been argued that minority-ruled governments are particularly prone to civil war as such governments violate the "nationalist principle" (Gellner, 1983). Majority groups may resent their politically inferior position and further recognize that their numeric majority should lead to political power over the minority. Though systematic evidence of the warlike effect of minority-rule discrimination has been found to be weak (Fearon, Kasara, and Laitin, 2007), in Zimbabwe, South Africa, and elsewhere, ultimately significant and sometimes violent internal and external pressure for majority rule developed successfully.

South Africa experienced years of apartheid policies that were met with both armed and nonviolent resistance by the black majority and their sympathetic allies among other ethnic communities. The eventual transition to majority rule finally occurred, mainly peacefully, in 1994 when Nelson Mandela became president (with some ironic inter-African conflict between the African National Congress and Zulu tribal groups) after years of struggle and brutal repression. Zimbabwe, which transitioned to majority rule in 1979 when its independence was finally recognized,[1] experienced subsequent internal unrest and discrimination as the government sought to right past wrongs by expropriating property from the white minority. After a two-year civil war between President Robert Mugabe's government and the opposition led by his former anticolonial colleague Joshua Nkomo—a division that was created during the previous war of independence—conflict also emerged between white landowners and black settlers seeking to retake land obtained during colonial times under white privilege. Thus, majority rule in South Africa proved far more harmonious than in Zimbabwe.

In 2003 the American intervention in Iraq, also a former British mandate territory, unleashed similar and destructive majoritarianism on the part of previously subjugated Shi'a Islamic population groups against the previously dominant Sunnis. Both Sunni and Shi'a militias also sporadically attacked outside coalition forces and newly emergent Iraqi governmental troops and police. While minority rule can lead to civil war when the "lid" of colonial rule, authoritarian rule, or outside occupation comes off, majoritarian rule has also been identified as a potential predictor of civil war in divided societies (Sisk, 1996). Although democratic systems of government are designed to provide a voice to the citizens, and while constitutions might protect minority rights, majoritarian democracy means that the majority often wins. This works well when minority groups do not feel significantly threatened by the majority. In many societies, however, this is not the case, particularly in what are referred to as "divided societies," or societies where group identity has become politicized and/or polarized, making identification across groups difficult. When safeguards of minority rights are lacking or violated, and minority insecurities regarding their security or their economic livelihood are great, civil war is possible as groups struggle for what they see as survival.

We might expect that countries having previously been subjected to divide-and-conquer colonial administration and/or minority rule would be more likely to face these types of majoritarian democracy problems. Politically dominant majorities or aspiring opponents may attempt to use their newly obtained power to assert their dominance by correcting past injustices or by pursuing policies of retribution.

Certainly, both minority- and majority-led governments have been guilty of utilizing the government apparatus to benefit their own identity group. When a single politically dominant identity group within a country controls much of the significant state apparatus, such as the executive, legislative, and military branches of government, and begins to use that dominance to the advantage of the group, the government has in essence been captured by that group. What can follow are policies that systematically provide advantage to the dominant group or disadvantage subordinate groups. In a democracy, the national government is conceived as something of a neutral arbiter of disputes within society. When that government becomes a tool of the politically dominant group (whether a demographic minority or majority) and begins to enact policies beneficial strictly to that group, other identity groups within society can feel threatened. The previously mentioned apartheid policies of South Africa's minority-led white government are an example. Black South Africans were systematically disadvantaged by such policies to the point of taking up arms, after more nonviolent approaches failed to correct and reverse such policies.

Other examples of politicized ethnic dominance patterns would include the Sinhala-only policies and anti-Tamil language laws of the late 1950s in Sri Lanka. Previously advantaged Sri Lankan Tamils found themselves in a politically inferior position when the majority Sinhalese group declared Sinhala the national language, Buddhism the national religion (as opposed to Hinduism), and then guaranteed a certain amount of civil service employment to the Sinhalese. The enactment of these policies was immediately followed by rioting in the streets of Colombo, Sri Lanka's capital. Whether such discriminatory policies are designed to correct past grievances (as in the case of Sri Lanka) or to sustain a situation of privilege (e.g., South African apartheid), legislating identity, as seen in the authors' analysis in Box 3.3, is associated with the outbreak of ethno-political conflict (Olson Lounsbery, 2003; Olson Lounsbery and Pearson, 2003).

BOX 3.3: TESTING A MODEL OF DISCRIMINATORY POLICY CHANGE AND ETHNO-POLITICAL VIOLENCE

Query: Does the occurrence of discriminatory policy change predict the occurrence of ethno-political violence?

Hypotheses:

(1) Country years with discriminatory policy changes are more likely to experience ethno-political violence than country years without such policy changes.

(2) Country years with "negative" discriminatory policy changes are more likely to experience ethno-political violence than country years with "positive" discriminatory policy changes.

Spatial-Temporal Domain: 1,193 country years from a random sample of 30 countries for the period 1960–2000.

Variables:
Outcomes: ethno-political violence occurrence (any level)
Predictors: Policy Characteristics
   (1) discriminatory policy change occurrence (DPC)
   (2) policy orientation
      State Characteristics
   (3) economic fluctuation
   (4) regime type
   (5) colonial history

68

(6) cultural polarization

(7) persistent protest

(8) regime instability

(9) territorial concentration

(10) level of state terror

Data Sources: Data on ethno-political violence were compiled using Regan (2002), the Correlates of War (COW) data (Small and Singer, 1982), and Keesing's *Contemporary Archives*. Policy data, colonial history, and information on persistent protest were gathered using Keesing's, *Political Handbook of the World*, and US State Department country reports. Economic data were found in the International Financial Statistics (IFS) and Penn World Tables. Regime type and instability were identified by Polity IV (Gurr, 1997). Cultural polarization was coded by Henderson and Singer (2000). State terror data were that of the Political Terror Scale (Gibney, Cornett, and Wood, 2008). Minorities at Risk (MAR) data (Gurr, 1993) were used to identify territorial concentration.

Data Operations: The dependent variable in the study was any mass-based ethno-political violence, either intergroup or violence against the state involving at least one conflict-related death using news reports to supplement COW and Regan (2002) data.

Policies were coded as discriminatory (DPC) (predictor 1) if they provided linguistic, religious, or economic or political advantage, or disadvantage, to a particular identity group within the country. A code of one indicates such policy change occurred and zero indicates otherwise.

In addition to identifying the occurrence of discriminatory policies, we were also concerned with what types of discriminatory policies were more likely to lead to ethno-political violence. As a result, each discriminatory policy was identified as either "positive" or "negative" (policy orientation, predictor 2) in nature, based on the supposed view of the subordinate group affected. For heuristic purposes, then, a national policy that declared Hindi the state language of India would be coded negatively (i.e., from the viewpoint of non-Hindi speaking groups). On the other hand, a policy that provided autonomy for a certain minority group, or which allowed for multiple language use, would in most circumstances be coded positively, being seen as supposedly protective of or sensitive to minority concerns, even if technically discriminatory from a majority viewpoint.

Economic fluctuations (predictor 3) were represented by the percentage change in gross domestic product from the prior year available in IFS (2001, 1985).[2] Regime type (predictor 4) was derived by subtracting a state's Polity IV autocracy score from its democracy score. Given the apparent volatility of semidemocratic regimes, a dichotomous regime type score was also used comparatively. Regime type scores ranging from between -5 and 5 were coded as *semidemocratic*. State colonial history (predictor 5) was coded dichotomously using US State Department country reports. A culturally polarized state (predictor 6) is one in which "the distribution of a state's cultural groups approximates a 50:50 split" (Henderson and Singer, 2000: 285).

Persistent protest (predictor 7) was measured using Gurr's (1993, 2000) approach (MAR data), where a country year was considered to have experienced persistent protest if ethno-political protest occurred during at least five years in the previous decade.[3] Regime instability (predictor 8) was identified using Polity IV, with each country year being coded as unstable if an abrupt regime change, or a transition to independence, occurred at all during the previous four years. If a state's first or second largest "minority at risk" groups received a group concentration score of one ("'majority in one region, others dispersed' or 'concentrated in one region'" [Gurr, 2000: 297]), then the country was considered to have territorially concentrated (predictor 9) minorities. State terror (predictor 10) scores were limited to the years 1977–94, with terror scores at time period one$_1$ predicting ethno-political violence at time period two$_2$ with a range from zero to five, with five being the highest level of terror.

Data Analysis: Analyses used to predict the occurrence of ethnopolitical violence are frequently challenged by the fact that the war or ethno-political violence in one year has a way of repeating itself in the next. This problem of autocorrelation in the dependent variable makes it difficult to isolate the impact of independent variables in the model. In addition, data gathered on multiple countries over several years means that country characteristics not accounted for in the model could influence the performance of the independent variables (i.e., referred to as panel effects) as well. As a result, binomial cross-sectional time series analysis was employed, which controls for both autocorrelation and panel effects.

Findings: Table 3.1 below provides both bivariate and multivariate regression results, which indicate that discriminatory policies are significantly correlated with increased levels of ethno-political violence, thereby confirming hypothesis #1. Both positive and negative discriminatory policies are associated with the occurrence of ethno-political violence as regimes become more democratic; the relationship is positive and statistically significant. Positive discriminatory policy changes appear to be less volatile than negative discriminatory policy changes, however. Negative discriminatory policy changes, those that tend to reinforce the interests of the dominant communal groups, are indeed associated with higher odds of ethno-political violence than positive policies.

TABLE 3.1: MULTIVARIATE ANALYSES RELATING TO ETHNO-POLITICAL VIOLENCE

	Bivariate	Equation One	Equation Two	Equation Three
DPC (All types)	.755*** (.151)	.778*** (.158)		
Positive DPC	.417** (.186)		.456** (.19)	
Negative DPC	.855*** (.201)			.823*** (.219)
Per Cent Change in GDP	-.005 (.007)			
Regime Score	.037** (.018)	.088 (.019)	.012 (.019)	.021 (.019)
Semidemocracies	-.101 (.214)			
Colonial History	-.894*** (.361)	-1.1*** (.363)	-1.07*** (.363)	-1.07*** (.37)
Cultural Polarization	-.230 (.336)			
Persistent Protest	1.39*** (.37)	1.19*** (.397)	1.42*** (.397)	.983** (.406)
Regime Instability	.353 (.241)	.48** (.264)	.451* (.266)	.458* (.261)
Territorial Concentration	-.611 (.426)	-.811* (.428)	-.783* (.426)	-.811* (.436)
State Terror (1977–1994 only)	.088 (.098)			
Constant		-.064 (.456)	-.083 (.454)	-.03 (.465)
Model		N = 1,193 X2 = 48.49***	N = 1,193 X2 = 31.50***	N = 1,193 X2 = 35.90***

*p<.10; **p<.05; ***p<.01, two-tailed significance

Three control variables appear statistically associated with the occurrence of ethno-political violence in the bivariate analyses: regime score, colonial history, and persistent protest. It appears that as a regime becomes more democratic, the occurrence of ethno-political violence becomes more likely. Interestingly, states with colonial histories appear to be less likely on the whole than those without colonial history to experience ethno-political violence. This finding is surprising given that most civil wars in the post-World War II era have occurred in post-colonial states (Henderson and Singer, 2000). As in Gurr's (2000) study, persistent protest does predict violence in the following decade, although state terror, territorial concentration, and regime instability do not consistently do so (at least in the bivariate analyses).

Multivariate findings presented in Table 3.1 (Equations One, Two, and Three) again support the linkage of discriminatory policy changes to violence, regardless of policy type (positive, negative, or both). Years in which such policy changes occur are more likely to experience ethno-political violence, particularly under conditions of persistent protest, recent regime instability, and in states without colonial histories or territorially concentrated minorities. Regime score was included in these models, but was not a statistically significant variable. Thus, we find some evidence that ethno-territorial dispersal, and perhaps ethnic mixing in the midst of policy change, might condition more violent outcomes.

In an effort to provide a voice to many competing identity groups within society, including those that might object to discriminatory policy, policy-makers have suggested the use of certain institutional remedies, such as "devolution" or decentralization in democratic societies. By allowing regions within the state to influence policies that will affect those regions directly, groups that are a minority within the state, but a majority within their region, will have a larger amount of control over regional legislation. This control, in theory, should raise satisfaction and help counter potential threats to minorities in a majoritarian democracy.[4] India has attempted to alleviate concerns over political privilege among its diverse population through the creation of regional (or state) governments with their own legislatures in a federal structure, although the central government maintains greater power than the individual states and, in emergency legislation, can suspend state governments. Federal systems vary on these power balances, as between the US and Canada for example (the latter affording more provincial discretion in general).

Decentralization, however, can have some fairly significant negative effects as well, and recent research has also cast doubts on the

likelihood that such forms of institutional tinkering will fully alleviate ethno-political and sectional conflicts and divisions (see Christin
and Hug, 2004, 2003). Brancati (2006) has found that decentralization
does indeed lower the intensity of ethnic conflict, but indirectly; decentralization encourages the formation and solidification of identity-
based political parties. Such parties, while perhaps increasing the sense
of security for the groups represented, make it difficult for various
identity groups to find common ground and form the cross-cutting ties
thought to be important for national unity (Ross, 1993). As an example,
India has had its share of civil violence in the Kashmir region and elsewhere, and lower levels of conflict on a yearly basis in other parts of
the country (see Olson Lounsbery and Pearson, 2003). Identity-based
political parties, such as the Hindu Nationalist Bharatiya Janata Party,
have become more prevalent over time, pushing what sometimes are
seen as divisive agendas (as in anti-Muslim campaigns) and tending to
displace the larger, more unified and secular Congress Party that was
the bulwark of the independence struggle against Britain.

Governmental composition also seems to impact the propensity of
states to experience civil war. The role of women in government has
been explored in this regard. Feminist scholars have argued that war
would be less likely to occur if there were more female leaders because
women are naturally less violent or competitive than men. It has also
been argued that women would be less likely to want to risk the lives of
their children and would choose to explore resolution through diplomatic channels, opting for violence only as a last resort. Proponents of
the feminist peace theory, much of which has been applied to international rather than civil war, have had a difficult time, however, reconcil-
ing theory with reality, particularly as it relates to war. Women leaders,
such as Indira Gandhi, Golda Meir, and Margaret Thatcher, have led
their nations in international wars, but it has been argued that this is
not a fair test of female propensities since these women had to rise and
rule within a male-dominated hierarchy. Prime Minister Gandhi was
also seen by some Indian regional communities, such as the Sikhs (one
of whom eventually assassinated her), as stepping on their domestic
rights by assuming strong central powers in times of "emergency," and
Prime Minister Thatcher, who survived an Irish assassination attempt,
certainly mounted a quite forceful response to Irish Republican Army
attacks and terror. Female Sri Lankan presidents have carried on the
anti-Tamil civil war as well.

When one explores other levels of political power, however, the feminist peace argument gains support. Caprioli (2000) found that the percentage of women in a nation's parliament, women's suffrage, the fertility rate, and the percentage of women in the labor force are all associated with fewer militarized interstate disputes, as feminist theory would predict. The feminist peace argument has had some empirical success as well when used to explain the occurrence of civil war. Although female leadership at the executive level does not appear to influence the propensity for civil war, Melander (2005) found that the more women in parliament and the lower the educational attainment ratio between men and women, the lower the level of intrastate conflict, though once again strength of democracy itself might be an intervening variable explaining these findings. It also appears that fertility rates and the percentage of women in the labor force are associated with civil war just as they are with interstate war (with higher fertility rates and lower percentages of women in the labor force predicting more war). It could be that these factors are reflective of other trends occurring in a society, such as a lack of equal opportunity, general economic vitality, or income inequality across households, but the importance of the life conditions of females in society is marked.

It has also been theorized that militarization of society (i.e., the dominance of the military, military values, and the military economy) appears to relate to state volatility. In their study of post-colonial states, Henderson and Singer (2000) found that the more militarized a society is, in terms of spending or budgetary factors, the more likely it is to experience civil war. We might expect that states that embrace something of a military culture will be more likely to rely on the military to resolve disputes, even if those disputes occur within state boundaries. Gurr (2000) found indirect support for this argument when he concluded that the use of state repression techniques leads to a higher incidence of ethno-political rebellion. In addition, of course, ongoing or long-running civil wars can markedly increase the state's military spending and militarization.

The general association between militarization and civil war is not surprising. If groups mobilize in order to address grievances, and the government does not respond aggressively but rather works to come to terms with the group, then civil war is unlikely. Actors will find it unnecessary to take up arms if the alleviating of grievances can be done without risking lives (at least within a reasonable time period). However, once a state moves to repress grievance-based mobilization, groups are either forced to settle for what they perceive to be an unjust outcome or they further mobilize and respond more likely in kind, meaning through the use of force. Once such mobilization and fighting takes place, a set of rebel leaders may gain an interest in persevering in the struggle, sometimes gaining power and prestige and also accruing economic benefits by controlling resources and trade. They come to have a persistent interest in rebellion (see O'Brien, 1986). This action-reaction process will be explored in more detail in Chapter 5, but it is important to note here that the availability of weaponry, due to previous bouts with the government or in neighboring wars, increases the opposition's ability to respond to government violence in kind. One of the most significant predictors of civil war is a history of civil war. Conversely, the longer a state experiences peace, the more likely that peace will continue. States with recent periods of civil war are more prone to revert to violence to resolve their internal differences than to pursue nonviolent options.

Thus, a nation's socio-political structure has definite implications for its propensity for civil war. As we have demonstrated, however, the state's political structure and policy choices are often influenced by its social composition. We explore this state-level aspect in the next section.

THE SOCIAL STATE

Our discussion of social aspects of state structure as related to the propensity for civil war begins with the size of a state's population. It appears that larger states are more prone to civil war onset (Fearon and Laitin, 2003). The ability of a national government to assert its control and gain legitimacy, especially across a wide territory, is often challenged by large populations. This appears to be the case regardless of the demographic composition of the population. Governing diverse populations is clearly a challenging reality for many states. In fact, it has been argued that a state's demographic structure in and of itself can create an environment that is ripe for conflict. Countries with varied ethnic, religious, linguistic, or cultural groups are likely to find that a certain amount of ethnocentrism exists, though certainly social diversity can also reduce ethnic tensions when cultural groups get to know and interact with each other positively.

Vanhanen (1999) has argued that diversity and ethnocentrism lead to ethnic nepotism, where a person's ethnic affiliation (Vanhanen includes other forms of identity in this definition) becomes politically relevant. Identity-based parties are likely to emerge as groups vie for political power and, therefore, societal privilege. Indeed, Vanhanen finds that diverse states have higher levels of institutionalized ethnic conflict in the form of significant "ethnic parties and organizations, significant ethnic inequalities in governmental institutions and customary ethnic discrimination" (1999: 60). Ellingsen (2000) further finds evidence that multi-ethnic states are more likely to experience civil war.

Others have explored the relationship between a nation's demographic structure and its propensity for conflict. As noted, Fearon and Laitin (2003) found that the size of a country's population in and of itself seems correlated with civil war. Henderson and Singer (2000) tested the theory that nations with two significantly large cultural groups (i.e., those that approximate a 50:50 split in population) see more interethnic competition, and therefore potentially more civil war, than states with wider ethnic group size gaps. Their findings did not support this hypothesis, however. Other scholars have argued and found that states with a large ethno-political group comprising between 45 and 90 per cent of the total population will create a competitive environment significant enough to produce violence (Collier and Hoeffler, 2001, 2002). Fearon and Laitin (2003), on the other hand, did not find support for demographic diversity and polarization as predictors of civil war when they controlled for the wealth of a nation.

We can certainly see how a diverse population can create an unstable socio-political environment, yet the reality, of course, is that nearly every state in the international system is multi-ethnic or diverse to some degree. Although civil war is prevalent relative to other types of war, intrastate cooperation generally far exceeds intrastate violence (Fearon and Laitin, 1996: 715). In other words, most people get along with, or at least tolerate, each other most of the time.

Blimes (2006) proposes that contradictory findings regarding ethnic fractionalization and civil war onset can be explained by recognizing that the effect is indirect as opposed to direct. In other words, the demographics of a state do not in and of themselves create war, but fractionalization can make war more likely if other explanatory factors are present. As instrumentalist theory suggests (see Chapter 2), ethnic, religious, and social divisions within a state can be manipulated to serve as fault lines for conflict among power rivals. Therefore, while disregarding the complications surrounding diverse populations is problematic, to suggest that there would be less civil war if all countries were more culturally homogeneous (if that were even possible) neglects the significance of confounding potential causes of war. The next section will explore economic indicators of civil war, allowing us to delve further into possible explanations using factors, such as class and ideology, that can also be related to identity conflict.

THE ECONOMIC STATE

Not surprisingly, civil war researchers have spent much of their time exploring the link between a state's economy or economic factors and the outbreak of violence. In fact, ideological conflicts, by their very nature, tend to revolve around a state's economic issues and structures. The civil wars in Vietnam, Guatemala, Nepal, and Nicaragua, to name a few, fit this description. In all of these cases, opposition groups sought to restructure the state along more egalitarian, socialist, or communist lines involving land and income redistribution. Disruptions in Zimbabwe and Lebanon have shared this dimension as well, for example, in the gaps generally present between whites and blacks or between Christians and various Muslim communities (e.g., Shi'a and Sunni). Such propensities toward economic or class-based civil violence are particularly the case in agrarian-type societies. In fact, the link between economic inequality, the percentage of a state's population engaged in agriculture, and intrastate violence was first established statistically by Russett (1964).

Nearly every nation in the international system is constructed of unequal parts. It is a mark of some states' (e.g., in Scandinavia) success that they can promote greater economic equality, though even states that have done so sometimes have gravitated toward civil war, as attended Saddam Hussein's fall from power in Iraq. Iraq in the 1970s, before a disastrous series of international and internationalized internal wars, had one of the best distributed economies in the Middle East by measures such as the Political Quality of Life Index (PQLI). Yet, when the US-led invasion in 2003 removed the authoritarian lid, previous prosperity did not prevent segments of the society from rising up to redress perceived unfairness in the distribution of power and wealth.

Once again, however, not every state in the system experiences violent opposition to economic inequality. What accounts for states where violence emerges as compared to those where it does not? Over time, empirical findings have both provided support for and against the association between economic inequality and violence. The relationship between economic disparity and civil war is indeed complex. Nagel (1974) suggested that the relationship is actually curvilinear; that is to say that low, as well as high, levels of inequality are unlikely to produce violence. Satisfied people appear less prone to rebellion, while hopeless and destitute people appear ill-suited for rebellion. Just as we saw earlier that transitional states somewhere between authoritarianism and democracy experience the upheavals and dislocations that can lead to civil violence, it appears that moderate levels of economic inequality create the potentially volatile environment ripe for conflict. People's expectations and demands begin to rise as they experience improvements in circumstances and prospects. If the society is either unable or unwilling to fully satisfy these demands, frustration and disillusionment can result. It is then that citizens are most likely to compare their lot to others inside or outside the country and feel that the ability to do something about the perceived injustice or inequality is within their reach through the use of force, either in protest or even rebellion.

Economic inequality can take several forms. Some scholars (Russett, 1964) have focused specifically on land distribution. For example, the inequitable distribution of land in Guatemala was a significant factor leading to coup, regime change, and ultimately civil war in the 1950s. What proved most volatile in that case was the redistribution of land to the peasants, particularly during the regime of social reformer Jacobo Arbenz Guzman, which included land re-appropriation involving the US-based United Fruit Company. Of course, land reform policies in Guatemala did not alone account for the years of violence that ensued. The US (the Central Intelligence Agency in particular) became an active party in the socialist-leaning country, supporting Arbenz Guzman's ouster as part of its Cold War strategy aimed at combating what it viewed as expansionist Soviet ploys in the Western hemisphere. In fact, it has been argued that economic inequality and land reform are not necessarily direct factors leading to civil war (Moore, Lindstrom, and O'Reagan, 1996) but rather, as the Guatemalan case illustrates, important contextual conditions that are seized upon by ambitious leaders either inside or outside the country.

Interestingly, conflicts involving issues of economic inequality often tend also to involve ethnic, religious, or cultural groups. In fact, Gurr's study of "minorities at risk" (2003) identifies economic grievance as one of several factors that can move identity groups toward mobilization. The state's reaction to such mobilization, whether forceful or conciliatory, whether redressing or reinforcing the inequality, is a factor that will be explored in Chapter 6, and is of significance in driving a situation toward or away from war. In states such as Sudan, a consistent correlation has been noted between ethnicity and access to resources, often enforced by state policies that are ethnically discriminating across regions in a pattern of "fiscal federalism" (Yongo-Bure, 2007).

We might expect that a shared identity might make it easier to recognize inequality and, therefore, to mobilize to correct perceived injustice. Besancon (2005), however, argues that economic inequality is a better predictor of revolution than of ethno-political conflict (the former being the primary topic of concern for Gurr's studies). She argues and finds evidence to suggest that among diverse societies, economic equality actually leads to higher levels of conflict as identity groups compete with one another for economic spoils. Her findings would appear to support the curvilinear theory of violence proposed by Nagel.

A nation's wealth (or lack thereof) has also been identified as a predictor of civil war. Wealth here means the funds available to the population and is related to but distinct from the state's natural resources per se. While some oil-rich Middle Eastern states have seen wealth accrue to at least some segments of their population, some of the poorest African states sit on vast deposits of valuable resources (diamonds, gold, oil, minerals) whose value is appropriated by corrupt leaders or foreign powers and never reaches large segments of the society. We might expect that the poorer the nation in terms of resources or available funds, the less likely its population will benefit from whatever economic activity exists. As indicated above, most states have some level of inequality, but those states with lower levels of economic resources or with totally misappropriated resources are also more likely to experience the negative effects of inequality and to experience the breakdown of governmental and civil order. Conversely, in wealthier states, although inequality is likely to exist, as long as much of the population is economically viable, the odds of civil war occurring are low. According to Fearon and Laitin (2003) wealthier nations are better able to thwart initial intrastate opposition should it occur. Poorer nations do not have that ability. However, the American Civil War began, we must recall, when one part of a nation experiencing growing prosperity came to fear that its supposed economic lynchpin, namely slavery, might be threatened and restricted as the economy of other parts of the country expanded perhaps even faster.

Thus, the pattern and controversies surrounding a nation's economic development may influence its propensity for civil war. As states develop economically, not only do they become wealthier but they also see differential rates of growth regionally within the state and establish more beneficial trade relations abroad. The liberal model of peace suggests that higher levels of economic development will lead to more democratic regimes (as states interact with other democratic or "open" regimes and emulate them), thereby supposedly making for more peaceful states (both externally and internally—see Gissinger and Gleditsch, 1999). Although Krause and Suzuki (2005) found evidence to suggest that economic development does dampen the possibility of civil war (at least in Asia and sub-Saharan Africa), Melander (2005) found that the positive effects of economic development and wealth were overshadowed by gender inequality. One might suspect that other forms of social inequality, such as slavery, might also increase the chance of resentment and conflict.

CONCLUSION

Liberal internationalist theorists tend to support foreign direct investment into less developed states so that they may become better developed, therefore more democratic, and therefore more stable and peaceful (note the studies cited above by democratic peace theorists). The findings we cite do indeed point to the need for economic and social development, but they also present cautions about the dangers inherent in transitions and change. Empirically, for example, in a study of globalization, foreign trade, and direct investment for the period 1965–93, Gissinger and Gleditsch (1999) found that foreign direct investment actually predicts higher rates of political instability and civil war. This negative effect, related to the debate about the positive and negative effects of "globalization" in economic and cultural activity, is not uniform, however.

Countries able to manufacture and trade goods do indeed benefit from active trade, but countries reliant upon agricultural exports do not benefit as much. We have noted research findings that associate rural economies with war. These economies seem especially subject to dislocation in the global marketplace as prices for crops fluctuate wildly and as incentives lead to substitution of cash crops, such as cotton, for food crops, such as corn, or conversion of corn from a food to a fuel crop (E-ethanol), thus creating social hardships. Additional findings by Collier et al. (1998) also show that states dependent on primary commodities (e.g., natural resources), as opposed to manufacture goods trade, are more prone to war than those without such dependence.

It seems clear, then, that a healthy functioning diverse economy, able to provide food and sustenance for its population and to export manufactured products, has the best chance of discouraging civil disruption and war mobilization. The population itself, whether large and diverse or small and homogeneous, stands a better chance of remaining at peace if the country's resources, political power, and economic benefits are distributed in a way that is perceived as being fair, and if policies do not discriminate harshly on the basis of region or ethnic identity. The chances for such peaceful patterns are significantly influenced both by conditions within the state and by actions and events occurring outside the state itself, in the international system. We turn to those external factors in the next chapter as a way of further completing the war-causation story.

NOTES

1   Prime Minister Ian Smith had declared independence in 1965. The United Nations refused to recognize this declaration primarily due to minority rule.

2   Gross Domestic Product (GDP) figures or percentages for Somalia were not included in IFS. As a result, per cent change in GDP from the previous year for Somalia was calculated manually using raw GDP figures identified through the University of Pennsylvania's World Tables.

3   MAR data use the ethno-political group as the unit of analysis, while this project used country year. Therefore, persistent protest was considered to have occurred in the previous decade if any group or combination of groups engaged in ethno-political mass-based protest.

4   A variant of the local empowerment approach to peace resides in sociologist Amitai Etzioni's concepts of "communitarianism." He notes

the virtues, in an ideal sense, of local communities taking responsibility for their members, keeping order and cohesion among themselves, dealing positively with each other but exercising the right "to be left alone," and balancing the individual's autonomy and collective responsibility (Etzioni, 1996).

CHAPTER FOUR

International Effects on Civil Wars

"Verbal promises of the British Government and their American allies are utter rubbish because we are in this plight through deliberate colonial policies of the British."

—Joshua Nkomo

The international system experienced significant changes during the latter half of the twentieth century. In addition to the increase in the occurrence of civil wars illustrated in Chapter 1, imperialism and colonialism were no longer the accepted norms of international relations. Indeed, increasingly the idea of "aggressive" or offensive warfare became discredited, with "self-defense"—an admittedly vague claim—the only valid excuse for using international violence, at least as enunciated in the United Nations Charter. Yet, the UN was also structured to feature a Security Council dominated by major powers, which was authorized, if its members mutually agreed, to enforce decisions even against the will of misbehaving (e.g., aggressive) member state governments.

The international system, as reflected in the UN and various regional intergovernmental organizations, therefore came to have something of a split agenda regarding intervention across borders. On the one hand, emphasis continued to be placed on state sovereignty, even as actual sovereignty (i.e., the ability of states to fully control their own territories and affairs) ironically weakened during the century. What began with the Treaty of Westphalia in 1648, premised on the notion that peace is dependent on sovereign states leaving each other alone, persisted as a normative underpinning of international relations. Oddly enough, even new states with borders drawn by former colonial powers, such as those in Africa, zealously guarded both their territory and their newly won sovereign status.

However, while sovereignty and its attendant legal rights remained a watchword for newly emerging post-colonial states during the 1950s and 1960s, in some regions "pan" ethnic movements, as in "pan-Arabism" and "pan-Africanism," emerged at the same time expressing affinities and interests that promised to bring formal and informal interventions into each state's affairs. The main underlying principle of international law, though, remained state sovereignty. This principle was also enshrined in new regional security organizations, such as the Organization of African Unity formed in 1963, later to be designated the African Union (AU).

States within the international system had also learned another major lesson during World War II. The horrors of the Holocaust and the international aggression demonstrated by the Axis powers could not be ignored. It was evident that states could not always be trusted with their own populations and could not always be trusted to refrain from premeditated attacks on citizens of other states. As a result, the UN further developed treaties and conventions, such as the Genocide Convention of 1948, which endorsed human rights and outlawed mass killing. UN peacekeeping evolved in response to such global changes to what Bellamy, Williams, and Griffin (2004) have suggested is now "post-Westphalian" in nature, involving the promotion of liberal regimes based on the democratic peace thesis.

Interestingly, what emerged out of the dual quest for sovereignty and human rights were two parallel international rules of conduct whose actions and enforcement could run contrary to one another. By enforcing one principle, the other might be violated. Nevertheless, international law, like its domestic counterpart, is fluid. In recent decades it has become increasingly evident, through actions and rhetoric, that states in the international "community" are attempting to find a place in law where sovereignty and humanitarian intervention can be reconciled. No state is interested in dissolving the state sovereignty principles espoused in the UN Charter, yet most states can agree that crimes against humanity should be prevented and that some enforceable action is required to back up the rhetoric. Indeed, it was the UN that first broached the subject of intervention for justice, as had its predecessor the League of Nations in taking up the issue of "non-self-governing territories" and in moving toward the dismantling of colonial empires.

The tension and interplay between the noninterventionist and interventionist norms, therefore, have become ever more apparent given the prevalence of the terribly violent civil conflicts as introduced in Chapter 1. This chapter will explore the challenge that civil wars represent for the international community in terms of legal and ethical principles. The growing and interesting interplay between the Westphalian nation-state system and the principle of sovereignty, on the one hand, and the evolving international legal pressure for the protection of human rights and remediation of conflict on the other —as evidenced by the creation of the International Criminal Court and War Crimes Tribunals at the Hague at the turn of the twenty-first century—present a dynamic tension for the future.

INTERNATIONAL LEGAL DILEMMAS AND INTERVENTION

The contradiction between the right to state sovereignty and human rights centers on the enforcement of those rights. The UN Charter, with the exception of Chapter VII on threats to the peace and Chapters XI and XII on non-self-governing territories, does not provide for intervention into countries' domestic affairs. It is quite explicit in that regard. Yet, the Charter also authorizes the Security Council to make decisions regarding situations that threaten international peace and security, including decisions concerning the action that should be taken (Chapter VII, Article 39). In some cases, civil wars themselves can be deemed to threaten international order, especially when they spill over across borders or generate multitudes of refugees.

Without obtaining this UN mandate, technically states or organizations that take it upon themselves to intervene in the internal matters of another state, even in the event of apparent human rights violations, can be acting illegally. This is a rather strict interpretation of the UN Charter and is more supportive of state sovereignty than human rights. As we will discuss later in the chapter, the relative legalities and moral imperatives surrounding such interventions create quite an international dilemma. Furthermore, there have been more interventions than Chapter VII mandates, indicating that states or organizations have operated at times without formal UN approval. The general framework for when military interventions in civil conflicts are considered legal is presented in Box 4.1.

BOX 4.1: LEGALITIES OF INTERVENTION IN CIVIL WARS

The basic international legal presumption is that sovereign governments have the right to hold the monopoly of force in their domains. Thus, international interventions in situations of civil violence can legitimately only respond to invitations to back the government side in civil disputes; supporting rebels or insurgents is illegal (see Dinstein, 1977). At some point the government's control and authority may erode so badly that there is a complete breakdown of civil order and certainty over who is the established authority. With such a breakdown, which of course can be difficult to identify conclusively, the presumption is that foreign governments can recognize whichever contending group or side they feel should be the legitimate successor, but there is also a presumption that they should refrain from invading the country or becoming engaged in the conflict. Presumably they should instead do whatever they can to promote a peaceful settlement (see Institute de Droit International, 1975).

Since international law is adaptable over time to new circumstances and interpretations, these classical noninterventionist legal doctrines have become debatable in more recent years, especially since the end of the Cold War in the 1990s, as intergovernmental organizations and nation-states have legitimized interventions to uphold humanitarian goals and offset potential abuses and genocides, including those that might be perpetrated by a government (see Talentino, 2006). Still, the principle of sovereignty presumptively prevails even in light of such human rights concerns, though with far less clarity than in previous legal theory (see Roth, 2005).

A growing number of scholars, particularly in light of the post-Cold War era conflicts, argue that state sovereignty is based on something other than a government's effective level of control. They assert that in order for a state to claim sovereignty, and therefore immunity from international intervention, the people of that nation must support such a claim (Waltzer, 1995). This constitutes a relatively fluid and open-ended interpretation of state sovereignty that would theoretically allow for humanitarian intervention, without violating sovereignty principles, in situations where a large portion of a state's population are victims of human rights abuses and have therefore not provided their consent to the government. Waltzer's provocative argument rests on the concept of "fit," where the noninterventionist principle must be maintained when the people of a state consider their own government to be legitimate.

The problem with such arguments, however, is evident in many intrastate conflicts discussed in this book. Often, the government of a state may have the presumed or expressed approval (and hence legitimacy) of a majority of citizens (thus meeting Waltzer's definition of "fit"), but at the same time, it might deny rights or commit acts of violence against a minority group within the state (Slater and Nardin, 1986), and those minorities might engage in rebellion of various sorts. According to Waltzer, the sovereignty of a state such as Serbia in 1998 would not have been in question because the majority of the total population supported the Milosevic regime in Belgrade. Nevertheless, approximately 90 per cent of the largely Albanian population in Serbia's Kosovo province did not support the repressive Belgrade regime, which was implicated in many human rights abuses. If Serbian sovereignty were no longer valid in Kosovo, as argued by Slater and Nardin, then theoretically the international principle of human rights would take precedence, thereby allowing for international intervention in support of the Kosovar Albanians. Indeed, North Atlantic Treaty Organization (NATO) forces undertook such an intervention in 1999, though they were careful to indicate that they did not wish to see Kosovo immediately declare independence. The contentious question of long-term rule in the province would have to be determined by peaceful political processes (as documented by *Frontline: War in Europe*, 1999), which led it to become a contentious international issue, pitting pro-Serbian Russia against NATO members in the UN Security Council.

Other scholars share Waltzer's interpretations, but the overall picture is not clear-cut. As Waltzer himself recognizes, outside intervention in civil violence has traditionally been deemed illegal unless invited by the government, thus biasing most international interventions toward supporting the status quo, unless the government itself ceases to function effectively or loses sovereign control in a civil war. Indeed, part of Serbia's highly repressive and violent tactics throughout the

Bosnian and Kosovo conflicts might have stemmed from its resentment of an early recognition by outside European powers of the breakaway former Yugoslav republics of Slovenia and Croatia. The fact that this supposed interference came from states such as Germany, which had invaded Yugoslavia in World War II, and received varying degrees of welcome from various ethnic communities, added to this resentment and bitterness.

According to some international legal scholars, a state's sovereignty refers more accurately to the sovereignty of the people, or popular sovereignty (Reisman, 1995, 1990). This analysis allows for humanitarian intervention whenever the "sovereignty of a people" is violated. To carry this logic a step further, sovereignty is maintained through the use of international intervention on behalf of the people being violated (Kresock, 1994). In this regard, sovereignty is a manifestation, not a contradiction, of self-determination. However, the international legal community is far from united on this view.

The implications of popular sovereignty logic are problematic. Although this view of international law as it relates to humanitarian intervention would allow the international community to skirt the issue of state sovereignty, we could envision how many unpopular governments in the world would suddenly feel threatened if the international community formally adopted this interpretation. What degree of uprising would be necessary to conclude that the government is no longer legitimate? Who would decide and by what rules? Would violent rebellion be the only route an oppressed population could use to legally generate international assistance? The question of whether or not to recognize regimes that have seized or claimed power has proven contentious and provocative enough in history (see for example, the Taiwan-China dispute); adding a legitimacy standard to decisions about humanitarian intervention could further complicate and delay remedial action in support of human rights (see Roth, 1999).

Essentially, we can view the debate and dilemmas outlined above as presenting two extremes, one representing sovereignty as a condition whereby the government enjoys a monopoly of legitimate force inside its borders as expressed through effective control of its territory, and the other viewing sovereignty as an issue of popular rights entitlement that is threatened or violated by governmental abuses. Indeed, governmental abuses, including genocidal acts, have often historically stemmed from efforts to put down popular uprisings, protests, secessions, or rebellions (e.g., Turkey's treatment of ethnic Armenians prior to and during World War I; Saddam Hussein's brutal poison-gas attacks on ethnic Kurds in northern Iraq during the Iran-Iraq War).

Many scholars of international law tend to fall somewhere in the middle of the sovereignty-human rights debate. They recognize the need for both state sovereignty and human rights protection, and as such promote small modifications to the current system, utilizing the dynamic nature of international law and jurisprudence to argue for adaptations to the evolving complexities. Most recognize the important roles the UN and the International Court have to play in human rights crises. The UN system is considered best situated to deal with such situations of global importance and to develop norms of both recognition and intervention (see Murphy, 1996).

The matter of human rights versus state sovereignty, however, rarely escapes political interpretation. Often states that have experienced humanitarian intervention, or those that find they are being threatened with the prospect, claim that the matter is internal and therefore protected by sovereignty. On the other hand, many international interventions in the midst of civil wars have been undertaken by individual states or groups of states with or without a legitimating mandate, as from the UN. Stated reasons for such interventions might stress concerns about humanitarian or human rights (ethnic rights), or, as in the case of the American-led NATO invasion of Afghanistan after the events of September 11, 2001, states wishing to intervene might stress the notion of self-defense against attacks launched from the offending state's territory (the acts of al-Qaeda for example). However, such interventions can also harbor power-related and self-interested motives, such as trying to gain more influence, resources (e.g., oil), territory, or weaken opponents in a region. Therefore, to better understand the interaction between state sovereignty, politics, and human rights, we delve into a historical analysis.

HISTORY OF INTERVENTION AND CIVIL WARS

In 1648 the modern international system began with the noninterventionist live-and-let-live solution to the Thirty Years War between Catholic and Protestant princes in Europe. While the resulting European "nation-states" (actually, princely states) hardly had the mass-based nationalist character they would later develop, the nation-state emerged as the primary actor of the international system; international relations would be conducted through arrangements and treaties between "sovereign" states. For some time, sovereignty remained something of a myth, as some states had clear power advantages over others. All states were not in reality equal, but they were equally entitled to sovereign immunity under the treaties and interpretations that constituted international law. As a result, a nation's borders became a defended and legal barrier to intervention.

The dynamic concept of state sovereignty changed both with the tendency of princes to "cheat" and occasionally intervene against each other and also with the emerging international commerce and communication that generated interests inside each other's territories. Following Westphalia, the concept of sovereignty was meant to refer to more than a home state's borders. Once again, in reality the concept did not apply to all members of the system. Sovereignty was primarily designed to protect certain existing older states in Europe or other regions (e.g., Siam, now known as Thailand, in Southeast Asia), as well as the colonial powers. These powers, including France, Britain, Spain, Portugal, the Netherlands, and Russia, along with the later-formed Germany, Italy, and emerging Japan and the United States, continued to expand their imperial domains with little concern for smaller states' borders or sovereignty claims. When the United States and the breakaway province of Texas provoked a war with Mexico in 1846 (LaFeber, 1994) and claimed as a prize the current American Southwest, the international community hardly raised an eyebrow in defense of Mexican sovereignty. Today, such a conquest would technically be deemed illegal under international laws barring expansion through warfare, though even now the sovereign status of territories "occupied" in wars is in political dispute, as in the Middle East. Expansionist foreign policies were not new to colonial powers, nor to those that were the targets of colonialism.

Views on sovereignty in various parts of the world changed subtly over the course of the nineteenth century, both with the rise of the nation-state and downfall of monarchies after the French Revolution and also with the formation of mass-based industrial states in Europe. Gradually, nationalist independence movements began among colonized peoples in Europe (Greece) and the Middle East (Arab regions), and human rights concerns began entering into the field of international law even with the first laws of war and humane treatment of prisoners following the American Civil War. Further steps along these lines were taken at the Hague

Conference of 1907 and in the wake of World War I and its profoundly disillusioning attrition, with the formation of the League of Nations in 1919 and the Kellogg-Briand Pact of 1928, the latter of which attempted a renunciation of aggressive war. Later came the antigenocide and human rights declarations made following World War II. In addition, expansionist policies were not only curbed but in some cases reversed.

In place of a world of dominant colonial powers, a hierarchical system of many nations at different levels of power and development gradually emerged. Former colonies gained independence through a variety of means, including agonizing anticolonial wars (often guerrilla-based), independence in exchange for support during global wars, or by shifts in colonial power policy looking to quickly extricate from costly and unpopular colonial entanglements. This process was accelerated through the formation of the United Nations. Rhetorically, the US and USSR generally backed these anticolonial principles (America has been referred to as the "first new nation" in view of its early split from Britain), even while acting to promote colonial (Puerto Rico, Philippines) and "neocolonial" (Cuba, Haiti, Poland, Czechoslovakia, Hungary) spheres of their own. Moscow championed the cause of many newly emerging post-colonial states in order to weaken the hold of the Western powers on developing regions. The UN, initially a coalition of victors in the war, would come to be viewed as the foundation of post-war global governance.

The right of states to self-determination became the rule as espoused in Article 1 of the UN Charter. This right was later reaffirmed in Article 1 of the International Covenant on Civil and Political Rights of 1966 (ICCPR) and in Article 1 of the International Covenant on Economic, Social and Cultural Rights of 1967 (ICESCR). Many of the world's remaining colonized states began, in succession, to declare independence throughout the 1950s and '60s. In turn, the Westphalian concept of sovereignty was transformed as it began to be applied to these newly independent states. The threat of expansionist policies was no longer tolerated, at least in principle. More importantly, the UN hesitantly and gradually provided mechanisms for human rights enforcement through the Security Council when disagreements and a major power veto could be avoided. Still, the actual definition of what constituted a just struggle for national liberation by oppressed or victimized people remained murky and open to political manipulation.

We have noted the irony of an international order that seeks to balance sovereignty and the need for human rights declarations. After 1945 the inequalities of colonialism were no longer acceptable, though the reality of military, economic, and social inequalities remained stark. As the evidence of genocide and mass extermination unfolded in the aftermath of World War II, the international community made a commitment to collective human rights. The Universal Declaration of Human Rights that developed at that time, along with the Genocide Convention (both adopted in 1948), and followed by the Torture Convention of 1984, enunciated humanity's revulsion at the bloody history of the twentieth century and supported, at least in theory, measures that would protect populations and prisoners of various types. The UN presumably would serve as an organization of peace-loving states that valued self-determination, human rights, and sovereignty, while frowning upon expansionism, colonialism, and aggression.

Problems inevitably developed in this dual sovereignty and human rights system. Volatile civil conflicts began to emerge in post-colonial states as they struggled to create viable political, economic, and social institutions. The polarized Cold War environment played a significant role in maintaining both the international system and its tensions. As newly formed states struggled with their own populations, often within artificially drawn borders that separated ethnic kinship groups, they also frequently found themselves deeply involved in the greater hostilities of the Cold War (see Box 4.2).

BOX 4.2: A CASE IN POINT: THE BELGIAN CONGO AND A LEGACY OF CIVIL WAR

Some states were especially ill-prepared for independence by their former colonial rulers, as in the famous circumstances of the Congo in 1960, where only a handful of university graduates existed in the entire country, and where the army remained under Belgian command. A brutal Congolese civil war resulted that taxed the UN's consensus and pacificatory abilities, as Belgian-backed factions sought to gain control of the most resource-rich provinces, and as the army mutinied and rampaged through the countryside threatening foreigners. The UN attempted to pacify this situation with a peacekeeping force, and for the first time found it necessary to fight solely within a state and back one political faction against another—a fact that brought bitter protest from the Soviet Union when the "legitimate" government of left-leaning Premier Patrice Lumumba was allowed to fall in 1962 (leading to Lumumba's assassination and Soviet Chairman Nikita Krushchev's famous shoe-banging speech at the UN).

In a "zero-sum environment," as viewed from the two superpowers' perspective ("you're with us or you're against us"), loyalty presumably could be purchased through economic and military assistance. In many cases, brutal dictators who were friendly to one Cold War power or the other, as with the later corrupt Congolese (and Zairian) ruler Joseph Mobutu, were able to repress discontent and opposition by utilizing military assistance gained from their friends (Pearson, Sislin, and Olson, 1998). Although the United States and the Soviet Union were unwilling to engage with one another in the potential disaster of direct confrontation, they were perfectly willing to use post-colonial states as pawns.

In such civil war examples as the post-independence fighting in Angola from 1975 to 1999, one might argue about whether the small state or the rebel groups manipulated the Cold War powers to engage in their regional disputes, or whether the powers manipulated their small clients to gain regional control, or whether both were true. Either way, human rights issues and questions of minority rights became entangled in political power struggles, often taking a back seat to other superpower goals such as economic or political control and "stability." In the midst of ideological struggles, violations of human rights continued, particularly ones related to violations of minority rights within state borders.

The value of state sovereignty came to be questioned in other ways during the Cold War. Small states' dictators were often propped up and popular leaders deposed, as in Iran in 1953 with the forced replacement of the economically nationalistic Mohammed Mossadeq's government by the Shah Reza Pahlavi regime in 1953, or in the 1954 Guatemalan military coup that toppled the democratically elected left-wing leader Jacobo Arbenz Guzman from power and resulted in a civil war and the ultimate loss of some 150,000 lives, mostly among the Mayan Native population. In both these cases, external support through the US Central Intelligence Agency helped bring about the overthrows, leading to years of repressive policies and ultimately further uprisings (see Immerman, 1982; Copeland, 1970).

Smaller states often feared for their independence on the chance that major powers would return to expansionist policies similar to those of the colonial past. Time and again the internal policies of smaller countries were dictated by outside forces in an effort to prevent states in a Cold War camp from defecting. For example, Washington's overt and covert military and diplomatic policies in states such as the Dominican Republic, Nicaragua, Grenada, Honduras, Guatemala, and Chile and throughout the Western hemisphere following the rise of Cuba's Fidel Castro were designed to prevent the rise of assertive leftists or nationalists. Similarly, Soviet military interventions in East Germany, Hungary, Poland, and Czechoslovakia during the 1950s and 1960s, culminating in the ill-fated Afghanistan intervention in the 1980s, were designed to maintain friendly client socialist regimes in nearby countries.

Although the UN had reiterated its commitment to state sovereignty, and seemed to extend that commitment to states that had exercised their right of self-determination, the commitment was often ignored when smaller states' sovereignty ran counter to larger states' security interests. This was not surprising given the Security Council's veto powers. It was apparent that state borders continued to be permeable and subject to aggressive diplomatic, economic, military, and intelligence intrusion at the whim of major powers, struggling to win their own "war." Human rights likewise often played second string in a much larger game.

Thus, despite a noninterventionist norm in international relations and international law, it is extremely difficult to completely isolate civil wars and keep out international actors and influences. Many of the internal causal factors of civil wars are also exposed to international influences. These range from economic inequalities and environmental degradation, to interest and identity groups' unresolved security and territorial concerns and their relations with friendly or kinship groups abroad and to the plentiful availability of international arms sources. The effects of a globalized international economy certainly pressure individual states, sometimes leading to the breakdown of internal order or the rise of competition and violence between disadvantaged factions.

EXTERNAL FACTORS AS CAUSE AND EFFECT

Civil wars can be "caused" by such outside influences or can trigger outside parties' intervention in the state, either on the side of the government or on the side of rebels and contending groups. In other words, war can be both a "dependent" and "independent" variable related to outside influence and interference. The increased globalization of the international economy has opened the door to external forces that determine the economic opportunities for groups in both developed and less developed countries, and give rise to "internationalized civil wars."

One can point to the obvious start of what became known in US political circles as an Iraqi civil war in the wake of the American intervention to topple Saddam Hussein in 2003 (on the definitional debate, see Box 1.1 in Chapter 1), and the subsequent dependency of the Iraqi economy and political system on American auspices. Concerns among Sunni Muslims grew as their traditional dominant minority status gave way in the new government to a Shi'ite majority and Kurdish control of additional oil-rich provinces. Shi'a militia also resented both Sunni rebellion and American dominance (for a similar scenario in Afghanistan, see Box 4.3). Attacks escalated by insurgents who directly resisted the US coalition's occupation, or by groups seeking to make such occupation untenable by fomenting bitter fighting among the various ethnic communities.

BOX 4.3: A CASE IN POINT: COMPLEXITIES OF THE AFGHAN CIVIL WAR

Afghanistan saw renewed civil war in the wake of America's and, subsequently, NATO's intervention to topple the militantly Islamist and puritanical Taliban regime that had harbored al-Qaeda terrorist trainees leading up the World Trade Center attacks in New York in 2001. In this war, beginning in December 2001, the Taliban was opposed by ethnic tribal and mujahadeen fighters whom it had previously defeated militarily before coming to power during the 1990s.

The Taliban found its ethnic base mainly with the Pushtun tribal population, which is strong in the southeastern part of the country and near the border with Pakistan. Indeed, Pakistan had backed the Taliban with the tacit consent of the US until the World Trade Center attacks and then executed a 180-degree turn to oppose them at Washington's behest. However, Taliban fighters continued to find refuge inside Pakistan, a highly cross-pressured and ethnically diverse state itself.

The Taliban's "northern alliance" opponents were composed mainly of ethnic Uzbeks, Hazara, and Tajiks who were backed by Iran and some former Soviet republics to the north. Control of resources and trade in commodities such as oil and opium was a subtext to the fighting among groups that had been at each others' throats over many centuries.

Washington allied itself with these anti-Taliban Islamic and tribal factions, interestingly, finding itself on basically the same side as the Iranians in this war. The US had also backed these same groups during the 1980s, as they had resisted the Soviet intervention on behalf of the secular socialist Afghan government of that time. To complete the perplexing picture, these mujahadeen fighters had been assisted in their anti-Soviet campaigns by Osama bin Laden and other outside Islamist revolutionaries, who were aided by both the US and Saudi Arabia and who later attacked American interests in the region and throughout the world.

Thus, the interplay of outside and splintered internal parties in a civil war situation can be confusing, contradictory, and convoluted because parties play to their short-term interests and form shifting alliances of at least temporary convenience.

Existing or ongoing civil wars, ranging from the Russian Civil War, right after World War I, to the Korean and Vietnam wars, have also *attracted* foreign interveners. In the case of Russia we saw both the effects of outside factors causing the civil war and the civil war leading to outside intervention. World War I and struggles against Germany and its allies so destabilized and weakened the tsarist regime in Moscow that internal revolution occurred, partly spawned when Germany sent an exiled revolutionary, Vladimir I. Lenin, back to Russia to spearhead a Bolshevik uprising against the state. The revolution led to a brief "White" and "Red" army civil war of pro- and anti-revolutionary factions, which in turn attracted military intervention by Western powers seeking to overthrow the new Soviet republic: France, Czechoslovakia, Japan, and the United States. This unlikely and ultimately unsuccessful group of interveners each reacted from their own interests: the French to retrieve their massive financial investment in the tsarist regime; the Czechs to rescue some of their troops; the Japanese to redress boundaries with Russia; and the Americans, under President Woodrow Wilson, to retrieve lost equipment and defeat a competitive new regime in Moscow (Strakhovsky, 1944; Fogelsong, 1995). Thus, the Soviet regime could always say that its fears of US "aggression" were justified by the history of Washington attempting to "strangle the baby in the crib" —landing and eventually evacuating Marines from the frozen shores of

Archangel in 1918. (In considering the legalities of such international interventions, review Box 4.1.)

Outside penetration of civil wars can, therefore, range from direct military involvement, to financial or military assistance, to commercial ties with one side or another, to diplomatic recognition. One of the keys to the outcome of the American Civil War, after the North was finally able to win an important battle, was Britain's ultimate decision not to back the South militarily and the North's imposition of a reasonably effective naval blockade of southern ports. Until that time, however, Britain's trade and strategic interests had led to London's diplomatic involvement and material assistance to the South, and there was quite a bit of uncertainty as to whether the support would go further and become decisive, with the Lincoln administration making key concessions to the British in the Trent Affair, a naval and diplomatic confrontation, to avoid this possibility.

Once intervention of any sort takes place in a civil war, counter-intervention by the intervener's international competitors can follow. The decades-long post-colonial Angolan civil war was perpetuated and complicated in this way by competitive interventions first by major powers—the US, USSR, and China—mostly in the form of military assistance to favored factions, and then by military interventions by Cuba (assisted by Soviet transport) and South Africa (under the apartheid regime to oppose the Popular Movement for the Liberation of Angola [MPLA] faction that ultimately came to power). Indeed, even as the Nixon administration delivered military hardware to antigovernment forces through Zaire (today's Democratic Republic of the Congo) in the 1970s, US oil corporations continued to trade with the Angolan government for their own economic interests. Finally, the Cuban-South African confrontation proved decisive, both in the form of a Cuban victory to establish the MPLA as Angola's government and also in the ultimate discrediting of South Africa's military prior to the downfall of the white minority South African regime.

As noted, one of the problems leading to uncertainty regarding international intervention is the fact that international boundaries were drawn so arbitrarily in certain regions—particularly, for example, in Africa, where colonialists drew lines mostly for ease of economic extraction and with little or no relevance to the ethnic composition of the states themselves. These borders have been recognized and legitimized in the ensuing years, for example in the doctrines of the Organization of African Unity, now the African Union (AU). However, the temptations to intervene to back ethnic and clan groups remains, along with the spillover effects of one civil war on another, as refugees flee and seek safe havens. The Rwandan civil violence and genocide in the 1990s led Hutu groups to seek refuge in Congo, which added to the political pressures in that state as Hutu forces helped unseat the Zairian government (finally deposing the corrupt American client Mobutu regime). These developments, in turn, led to subsequent Rwandan (Tutsi-led) intervention in Congo to oppose the Hutus, along with counterintervention in Congo by other neighboring states, as well as internal Congolese military revolts backing one ethnic community or another.

Thus, the pressures on societies in conflict can come from close by, from just across borders (indeed states such as Congo have numerous porous borders), or from a considerable distance as major powers become fatally interested in the outcomes of internal struggles. As we noted in the Angolan case, the two sectors (proximate and distant) can interact, as major powers use other states (e.g., Cuba) as proxies to intervene or send their aid and supplies to various fighting factions through local third party states (e.g., Zaire). The lessening of superpower competition after the Cold War eased some of this interplay, but the rise of antiterrorist concerns since 2001 heightened outside interference once again, as was seen in Afghanistan.

Another factor has risen to further complicate the isolation and containment of civil wars in relation to the regional or international systems that surround them. That is the growing tendency of governments to support "private" militia groups to quell actual or supposed rebellions by insurgents. This is done in part to shield the national or local authorities from charges of human rights abuses, and has been seen in the Mexican struggle against Zapatista guerrillas in Chiapas province, in Indonesian campaigns against rebellions in East Timor and in Ache province, and in the Sudanese government's efforts to quell rebellion of "African" (mostly agricultural) against "Arab" (mostly herding) clans in Darfur. Muddying the political and battlefield situations in this way tends to intensify pressures for outside intervention.

The United States, for example, took a rhetorical stance against "genocide" in the Darfur struggle within Sudan in 2005 and 2006 (see Box 4.5), even as the UN was somewhat more reticent about using that term for the complex fighting of militia forces, either sympathetic to the government or to the rebels. Yet, because Washington also relied on the Khartoum government for information and support against militant Islamic terror groups such as al-Qaeda, the US was reluctant to bring full pressure to bear on the Sudanese authorities. China, another UN Security Council permanent member, was similarly seen as lenient with Khartoum because of its growing oil interests in the region. This may have emboldened Khartoum to resist the imposition of large-scale UN peacekeeping troops to try to quell the violence. Conscious of its "sovereign" rights, the Sudanese government initially accepted only a relatively small contingent of AU troops, which proved inadequate to safeguard the civilians in peril. No government likes to admit it cannot handle its domestic security situation, nor admit that it might have committed or enabled human rights abuses.

In other parts of the world, civil violence has emerged or has been perpetuated with less direct foreign military intervention, in the wake of disruptive outside economic forces and in light of corrupt and even larcenous local leadership. In West African societies such as Liberia and Sierra Leone—societies with many natural resources but desperately poor populations—lucrative diamond and oil trade became a crucial interest of militia leaders, who carried on civil wars in part to corner the market on illicit cross-border trade. The very fact that legitimate international economic actors, such as multinational corporations, have tended to bypass regions such as Africa for their investments and manufacturing has left the region open to corrupt systems of black markets and smuggling, as well as the violence attendant on the establishment of local fiefdoms.

NEW OR OLD CIVIL WARS?

We saw in Chapter 1 that the complicated warfare situations now emerging in world politics have led some analysts to coin the term "new wars" to describe internationalized civil or "extrastate" wars involving cross-border intergroup support and supply networks; complex motives including crime and resource plunder; mainly civilian as opposed to military casualties; and multiple state and nonstate actors. Such wars are supposedly less structured as a series of pitched battles over territory and less easily defined as civil or international than traditional wars. They also tend to be more focused on the validation of group identity through means such as ethnic cleansing, as well as through the use of more unorthodox combinations of tactics including guerrilla or terrorist activities. These wars are connected to globalized international distribution and communications systems (see Kaldor, 2006). The Bosnian wars of the early 1990s were perhaps the first examples of such unstructured "new wars," where civilian victimization became the rule rather than the exception.

Other episodes of fighting between nongovernmental groups, such as between Hezbollah and Israel, also illustrate the supposedly new forms of war. While Hezbollah was, and continues to be, an actor in intricate Lebanese politics (e.g., represented as a political party in the Lebanese Parliament), it was also forcefully opposing and acting independent of the government. It had an armed force of its own supplied from abroad (Syria/Iran), capable of preoccupying and even bloodying Israeli forces (for a summary of Lebanon's dilemmas as a "penetrated society," see Box 4.4).

BOX 4.4: A CASE IN POINT: LEBANON: THE ULTIMATELY PENETRATED SOCIETY

Historically, Lebanon has been known as a "penetrated" society highly subject to and delicately balanced against civil war. It suffered formal civil warfare in 1958 and then again throughout the 1970s and into the 1980s, based on the intermixture of clan rivalries and political ambitions, compounded by outside interventions and refugee flows. Syria and Israel have occupied or held parts of the country, and Palestinians have flowed in (and out) of it as a result of wars in neighboring states. Pressure thus increased for renewed violence after Israel's ill-fated intervention against Hezbollah in the summer of 2006.

Lebanon originated as a country severely split between various Christian and Muslim clans and families. The former tended to be European-oriented and traced their lineage all the way back to medieval Christian crusaders dispatched by European monarchs to control the "holy lands" beginning in the eleventh century. Some Christian factions eventually joined anticolonial factions in the nineteenth and twentieth century rise of Arab nationalism, but generally this community has maintained stronger ties to the West than have their Muslim Lebanese counterparts. The cleavages in Lebanese society were, and continue to be, exacerbated by wealth and income differences among these Christian and Muslim groups. (For example, the large Shi'a Muslim population tends to exist at the lower economic levels.)

When Lebanon achieved its independence from Syria in the 1940s, most of the country's political parties did not even support the state's existence. Politics centered on families and clans; even the larger religious groupings were divided—Christians between Maronite Catholics, Greek Orthodox, and other sects; Muslims between Sunnis, Shi'a, and Druse factions. The constitution recognized these confessional divisions and pioneered what came to be called "codetermination," which meant formally dividing the key offices of the state, such as the positions of president, prime minister, parliamentary speaker, etc., between the different ethnic groups. The parties even conveniently agreed not to take census counts in order to maintain the fiction that the country was populated by a Christian majority, even in light of subsequent changes in birth rates.

In a sense, this system functions democratically, but the country's frequent plunges into civil wars, spurred by outside forces, demonstrate a basic failure of confessional democracy or codetermination to insure the peace. Among the outside pressures were regional "Arabism" during the days of Egyptian President Gammal Abdul Nasser's prominence in the 1950s; a Palestinian presence and reaction against them as refugees; prolonged and repeated Syrian and Israeli occupation of parts of the country in order to establish control and weaken hostile parties (Syria, authorized in its role by the Arab League, sometimes changed its support from Muslims to Christian factions in order to do so); Israel's unilateral withdrawal from southern Lebanon as pro-Shia Hezbollah guerrillas became more effective; and more recently, the role of Iran in fomenting support for militant Islamic and anti-Western/anti-Israeli parties, with the United States, France, Jordan, Egypt and Saudi Arabia (the latter three Sunni-dominated states) still interested in countering these trends.

The result is a society very subject to economic booms and busts, to informal and illicit markets for trade, to wartime destruction and crushing demoralizing violence in the midst of a nominally democratic and modern society. Yet, Lebanon also periodically recovers its equilibrium, rebuilds its infrastructure, and functions rather effectively as a Middle Eastern financial and tourism center.

Technically, there is nothing entirely new about "new wars" that involved guerrilla or terrorist struggles, nor about civilian victims, international supply, and smuggling and crime networks. Indeed, such criminal networks tend to thrive in all civil wars because normal economies are disrupted. However, the instantaneous communications linking groups and actors across the world make such factors far more difficult to control and more frequent and interconnected today than in the past. Fueling such emerging and changing forms of war, the "revolution of rising expectations" that we noted as a causal factor of civil war in Chapter 3, and as described by analysts such as Gurr, is spurred on by today's instantaneous international communications. Through media such as radio, TV, mobile phones, and the Internet, people have come to realize how life is lived in other countries; they realize the wealth and opportunities available to others, or the prevailing global standards of human rights.

People's grievances and bitterness can also grow through reports of local corruption and foreign states' political manipulation, exploitation, and hypocrisy. For example, a lack of economic opportunity and the American one-sided partisanship for Israel have been noted as factors contributing to Hamas's and Hezbollah's popularity as militant Islamic reformist parties, and to the growth of insurgent political forces. Such actors are seen as less corrupt alternatives to mainline Palestinian or Lebanese politicians and more devoted to delivering services to the people. Of course, they have also been abetted by external Iranian and Syrian material assistance. Iran's own Islamic revolution in 1979 against the shah's regime, one of the best-armed governments in the world, was termed the first "Sony revolution," in light of the cassette-taped recordings of the fiery cleric Ayatollah Ruhollah Khomenei that were smuggled into the country from nearby Iraq. In those sermons, Ayatollah Khomenei outlined the perverse partnership between the shah's regime and Western powers such as the United States. Since then, militants have drawn similar connections between Western powers, oil interests, corruption, and "nondemocratic" states such as Saudi Arabia and Egypt.

Local media networks, such as Al-Jazeera in the Islamic world, have broken the monopoly on news broadcasting once enjoyed by British, French, and American press agencies, presenting views much more critical of global powers and those who collaborate with them. Thus, the Pakistani government has been increasingly cross-pressured by militant domestic Islamic parties on the one hand, and the United States as a military ally on the other. Islamist parties expect the Pakistani state to follow a militant foreign policy by backing liberation movements in places such as Kashmir against India. At the same time, Washington and New Delhi expect Islamabad to crack down on international

Islamic terrorists and on the supply of nuclear materials abroad. The result is that Pakistani leaders such as former President Pervez Musharaf have tended to play "both sides of the street," fearing loss of power in elections or coups d'état or even assassination attempts, with a possible ultimate result of civil war. This is particularly the case since the Pakistani military, upon which the regime depends, might itself become subject to division along partisan or ethnic/tribal political lines.

INTERNATIONAL REMEDIES AND RESPONSES TO CIVIL WARS

The end of the Cold War has had a significant and further dynamic impact on the potential sovereignty/human rights contradiction we have noted in this chapter. Following the Soviet Union's disintegration, a "new world order" was predicted in Washington. It was thought that nations would be able to reach across state lines under the aegis of international and regional organizations and work together in a cooperative manner toward the development of stable democracies, globally and regionally integrated economies, environmental protection, and human rights. Indeed, as noted by analysts such as Talentino (2006), a new "multilateralism" in international responses and interventions has been pronounced when we count the relative increase of joint as opposed to unilateral interventions, peacekeeping missions, and humanitarian relief efforts undertaken through intergovernmental organizations (IGOs) since 1990.

Alongside this new multilateralism, however, is something quite different from what George H.W. Bush and other optimistic onlookers might have imagined at the time of the Gulf War. In a number of countries, pent-up resentment at years of political subordination brought uprisings by ethno-nationalist identity groups. The degree of bitterness and brutality entailed in these uprisings, especially at a time of economic distress, would shock the world in places such as the supposedly cosmopolitan Bosnia. Furthermore, stung by embarrassing reversals in some of these trouble spots, powers such as the United States have also undertaken unilateral interventions in "important" locations such as oil-rich Iraq, not wishing to share power and control of its operations with the broader international community.

As illustrated in Chapter 1, although the rise in civil war outbreaks began in the 1970s, primarily within post-colonial states, and although the international system was no longer preoccupied with the Cold War, regional and global powers, including the UN, only reluctantly and belatedly took notice of the new violence. It became tragically apparent that civil wars were perhaps even more volatile in terms of human rights abuses than international wars (Miall, 1992). In fact, they tend to generate more deaths in a shorter period of time than their international counterparts and are more difficult to resolve (Licklider, 1995). In addition, the dynamics of civil conflicts tend to make them more prone to genocide (Harff, 1995).

Following the Cold War, several factors became apparent regarding the course and internationalization (tendency for outsiders to intervene) of civil wars. The international community now had the opportunity to jointly address international issues as fundamental as human rights and the sanctity of borders (e.g., the US/UN defense of Kuwait against Iraqi "aggression," but one might also note the defense of oil interests) as the restraints of the Cold War were no longer in place. No longer was it inevitable that a policy favored in Washington would be opposed or vetoed by Moscow, and vice versa. This was the message delivered by UN Secretary-General Boutros Boutros-Ghali on January 31, 1992, when he stated, "A conviction has grown, among nations large and small, that an opportunity has been regained to achieve the great objectives of the Charter—a United Nations capable of maintaining international peace and security, of securing justice and human rights" (Boutros-Gali, 1994). At the same time, however, it was also apparent that the international community was facing new challenges with which it was completely unprepared to deal effectively. This became evident in one of the first multilateral interventions of the new era: the case of Somalia, a state that had suffered governmental meltdown, vicious violence, and mass starvation all depicted graphically on international broadcast networks.

For the most part, the international community was in full support of the 1990 Somali intervention by UN peacekeepers, including US forces under UN command for the first time. Though one could argue about the goals of regional stabilization and security of the Red Sea coast, the operation began primarily as a humanitarian mission in the midst of a great humanitarian crisis, which itself was well publicized by the world's media and therefore difficult to ignore. In addition to large numbers of civilian deaths during the political violence following the disintegration of Somalia's socialist-leaning government, the population faced mass starvation and a devastated state infrastructure. Somalia was lacking a dominant, recognized governmental authority and was beset by clan warfare. However, with the subsequent exit of the American contingent from Somalia after they encountered embarrassing casualties at the hands of the clan militia, a valuable, albeit dysfunctional, lesson had been learned. This lesson would delay similar international interventions in other civil wars, most notably Rwanda, though as seen in Table 4.1, the pace of interventions would pick up again.

Before and during the Cold War, encroachments upon the independence of states were defended primarily under the rubric of the right to self-defense, although occasionally, as in Vietnam, interveners invoked rhetorical justifications involving humanitarian or democratic elements (e.g., "nation building"). In the post-Cold War era, an additional element of this contradiction would emerge. The principle of self-determination, which had historically applied to post-colonial states with arbitrarily drawn colonial boundaries, now became the claim within countries of many politically subordinate groups that felt slighted by governments dominated by certain other ethnic, religious, or cultural parties. Ethnic tension gave rise to fierce and intolerant ethnic nationalism and to repression in civil wars in places such as Sri Lanka and Sudan (see Box 4.5). Once again, the international community seemed to be caught off guard, although in this instance the warning signs had been quite evident as these wars gathered steam over a period of many years.

BOX 4.5 A CASE IN POINT: THE SUDANESE CIVIL WAR: INTERNATIONAL RESPONSE

The government of Sudan has been engaged in a large-scale civil war since 1983. The highly centralized regime of Khartoum is predominately Arabic/ Muslim, while the southern populations tend to identify themselves as African, traditional, or Christian. A peace agreement in 1972 had provided for some level of self-rule, but this was revoked in 1983. This led to the initiation of armed rebellion with the Sudan People's Liberation Movement/ Army "fighting for a unified, democratic, socialist Sudan with religious freedom" (Uppsala Conflict Data Program, Sudan Conflict Summary). In addition to revoking self-rule, Muslim Shari'a law was imposed throughout the country, including its application to non-Muslims.

The Sudanese conflict has gained a significant amount of international attention. The government of Sudan has received aid in the form of arms and military training from a number of states, including Libya and Iran. The southern rebels have received assistance from states such as Ethiopia, Eritrea, and Uganda, all of which blamed Sudan for aiding their own rebellious populations. Both the government and the rebels, however, have experienced fluctuations in assistance over time. By the late 1990s, oil revenues were benefiting the Khartoum regime, making outside assistance less important for their cause.

International actors have also sought to bring about resolution to the Sudanese civil war through mediation. The Inter-Governmental Authority on Development (IGAD) was created in 1994, comprised of Eritrea, Ethiopia, Uganda, and Kenya, with the goal to end the violence. A ceasefire was achieved in 2001, followed by the Machakos Protocol, where "the Parties have reached specific agreement on the right to Self-Determination for the people of South Sudan, State and Religion, as well as the Preamble, Principles, and the Transition Process" (IGAD, 20 July 2002: 1).

While the Machakos process continued, in 2003, the conflict expanded to the Darfur region of Sudan when a March 14 Declaration was made by the Sudan Liberation Movement/Army (SLM/A), which tended to feel left out of the Machakos bargain and the distribution of rights and resources. The SLM/A "demanded a united democratic Sudan based on equality, the separation of religion and the state, complete restructuring and devolution of power, even-handed development, and cultural and political pluralism" (Uppsala Conflict Data Program, Sudan Conflict Summary). The Justice and Equality Movement also began its campaign against the government aimed at "a federal system with autonomy for all states, a rotating presidency, and an equal distribution of natural resources" (Uppsala Conflict Data Program, Sudan Conflict Summary). The Darfur rebels are predominately Muslim and ethnically diverse. Their motivations for rebellion appear to revolve around the marginalization of the region and threats to their settled agricultural lifestyle.

The Darfur portion of the conflict has involved significant human rights violations with blame for many of the atrocities being placed on the Janjaweed, a government-aligned nomadic militia. Although the government has denied responsibility for the Janjaweed, attacks by the government and Janjaweed have at times been coordinated, and there is evidence that the Janjaweed has received arms and financial support from Khartoum. The attacks in the large Darfur region have resulted in great human hardships, rape and killing, and the creation of massive refugee populations spilling over into nearby Chad.

By 2004 the United Nations Security Council was forced to act by adopting Resolution 1556. The resolution demanded that Sudan work to disarm the Janjaweed militias and bring about a negotiated settlement, promising to take further action if Sudan did not comply (UN Security Council, 30 July 2004). The Security Council resolution was met with immediate criticism, with headlines such as "Sudan hails 'softer' Darfur draft" (BBC News, 30 July 2004) and "UN: Darfur Resolution a Historic Failure" (Human Rights Watch, 18 September 2004). Nongovernmental organizations working in the region, as well as UN member states familiar with the conflict, had urged the Security Council to impose an oil and arms embargo on Sudan itself, not just on the rebel groups internal to the state. They also urged the council to expand peacekeeping in Sudan from a small and outgunned African Union contingent to a much larger international United Nations effort (a move later authorized). It appeared as though the international community was reluctant to identify the Khartoum government as a major party to the Darfur human rights atrocities and the conflict itself.

Surely, the UN Charter had not intended for the self-determination of all possible groups. Despite the existence of laws of war, genocide, human rights conventions, the Nuremberg laws of crimes against humanity, and most recently a functional International Criminal Court, it also proved a challenge to gain international support for intervention to prevent discrimination and atrocities, such as those seen in Rwanda and Sudan. Post-colonial states began their struggles with internally subordinate or dissatisfied minority groups in the 1970s, and these were followed by the insurgency of subordinate populations within former Eastern bloc states, such as those in the Baltic region, which began to agitate for independence, autonomy, irredentism, or secession during the 1980s and '90s. Government repression of minorities or dissident groups, as in Sudanese attempts to impose Islamic law throughout the country, added to the difficulties of addressing civil wars before they resulted in local disasters.

Thus, a challenge for the international community would emerge as the number of civil wars increased. With so many wars in play at the same time, and so many populations at risk, would the international community rise to the challenge given the so-called lesson learned in Somalia? The choice of where and when to intervene would become yet another international debate involving issues of sovereignty and strategic significance. In growing numbers of these cases, the UN would be called upon to act, sometimes initially, sometimes in the wake of unilateral moves by various powers, and help restore order. Organizations such as NATO, which had never before held duties of intervention, were also called upon to act in places such as Bosnia, Kosovo, and even outside Europe in Afghanistan when agreements could not be reached involving the UN. Table 4.1 presents a timeline showing the pace of UN civil war peacekeeping interventions in the post-World War II era by region.

Table 4.1 United Nations Peacekeeping Missions in Civil Wars, 1958–2008

UN COLD WAR PEACEKEEPING INTERVENTIONS	DURATION	REGION
UNOGIL (United Nations Observation Group in Lebanon)	6/58–12/58	Middle East
ONUC (United Nations Operation in the Congo)	7/60–6/64	Africa
UNSF (United Nations Security Force in West New Guinea)	10/62–4/63	Asia
UNYOM (United Nations Yemen Observation Mission)	7/63–9/64	Middle East
UNFUICYP (United Nations Peacekeeping Force in Cyprus)	3/64–present	Europe
DOMREP (Mission of the Representative of the Secretary-General in the Dominican Republic)	5/65–10/66	Western Hemisphere
UN POST-COLD WAR PEACEKEEPING INTERVENTION	DURATION	REGION
UNTAG (United Nations Transition Assistance Group) in Namibia	4/89–3/90	Africa
UNAVEM II (United Nations Angola Verification Mission II)	5/91–2/95	Africa
UNAVEM III (United Nations Angola Verification Mission III)	5/91–11/94	Africa
ONUSAL (United Nations Observer Mission in El Salvador)	7/91–5/95	Western Hemisphere
MINURSO (United Nations Mission for the Referendum in Western Sahara)	9/91–present	Africa
UNAMIC (United Nations Advance Mission in Cambodia)	10/91–3/92	Asia
UNTAC (United Nations Transitional Authority in Cambodia)	2/92–9/93	Asia
UNPROFOR (United Nations Protection Force) in the Former Yugoslavia	2/92–3/95	Europe
UNOSOM I (United Nations Operation in Somalia I)	4/92–3/93	Africa
ONUMOZ (United Nations Operation in Mozambique)	12/92–12/94	Africa
UNOSOM II (United Nations Operation in Somalia II)	3/93–9/95	Africa
UNOMIG (United Nations Observer Mission in Georgia)	8/93–present	Europe

UN POST-COLD WAR PEACEKEEPING INTERVENTION	DURATION	REGION
UNMIH (United Nations Mission in Haiti)	9/93–6/96	Western Hemisphere
UNOMIL (United Nations Observer Mission in Liberia)	9/93–9/97	Africa
UNAVEM I (United Nations Angola Verification Mission I)	10/93–3/96	Africa
UNAMIR (United Nations Assistance Mission for Rwanda)	10/93–3/96	Africa
UNMOT (United Nations Mission of Observers in Tajikistan)	12/94–5/00	Asia
UNPREDEP (United Nations Preventive Deployment Force) in the Former Yugoslav Republic of Macedonia	3/95–2/99	Europe
UNCRO (United Nations Confidence Restoration Operation) in Croatia	3/95–1/96	Europe
UNMIBH (United Nations Mission in Bosnia and Herzegovina)	12/95–12/02	Europe
UNTAES (United Nations Transitional Authority in Eastern Slavonia, Baranja, and Western Sirmium) in Croatia	1/96–1/98	Europe
UNMOP (United Nations Mission of Observers in Prevlaka) in Croatia	2/96–12/02	Europe
UNTMIH (United Nations Transition Mission in Haiti)	7/96–7/97	Western Hemisphere
MONUA (United Nations Observer Mission in Angola)	6/97–2/99	Africa
MIPONUH (United Nations Civilian Police Mission in Haiti)	8/97–11/97	Western Hemisphere
MINUGUA (United Nations Verification Mission in Guatemala)	1/97–5/97	Western Hemisphere
UNPSG (United Nations Civilian Police Support Group) in Danube Region of Croatia	1/98–10/98	Europe
MINURCA (United Nations Mission in the Central African Republic)	4/98–2/00	Africa
UNOMSIL (United Nations Observer Mission in Sierra Leone)	7/98–10/99	Africa
UNMIK (United Nations Interim Administration Mission in Kosovo)	6/99–present	Europe
UNTAET (United Nations Transitional Administration in East Timor)	8/99–5/02	Asia
UNAMSIL (United Nations Mission in Sierra Leone)	10/99–12/05	Africa
MONUC (United Nations Organization Mission in the Democratic Republic of the Congo)	2/00–present	Africa
UNMISET (United Nations Mission of Support in East Timor)	5/02–5/05	Asia
UNMIL (United Nations Mission in Liberia)	9/03–present	Africa
UNOCI (United Nations Operation in Cote d'Ivoire)	2/04–present	Africa

UN POST-COLD WAR PEACEKEEPING INTERVENTION	DURATION	REGION
MINUSTAH (United Nations Stabilization Mission in Haiti)	4/04–present	Western Hemisphere
ONUB (United Nations Operation in Burundi)	5/04–12/06	Africa
UNMIS (United Nations Mission in the Sudan)	3/05–present	Africa
UNMIT (United Nations Integrated Mission in Timor-Leste)	8/06–present	Asia
UNAMID (Africa Union/United Nations Hybrid Operation in Darfur)	7/07–present	Africa
MINURCAT (United Nations Mission in the Central African Republic and Chad)	9/07–present	Africa

Source: United Nations, United Nations Peacekeeping: List of Operations.

It is clear that Cold War competition, at the very least, limited the amount of UN peacekeeping during that time. However, attempted remedial action has mushroomed, along with demands on UN resources, during the post-Cold War period. Although civil war activity began to increase in the 1970s, the international community did not appear to take much notice until after the end of the Cold War, as the number of UN peacekeeping missions increased from six to 42. In the post-Cold War era, the UN has experienced a dramatic rise in its responsibility for domestic peacekeeping activity; there have been 21 African civil war peacekeeping missions, nine in Europe, six in the Western Hemisphere, and six in Asia.[1]

Any permanent member of the Security Council has the option to veto enforcement activity. Chapter VII mandates are not possible once that veto has been exercised by any of the five permanent members (United States, Great Britain, France, Russia, and China), which can result in gridlock on important issues of international peace and security. However, the lack of a Security Council mandate has not necessarily meant that intervention does not occur. Other forms of multilateral and unilateral intervention have taken place in civil wars, including regional and major power moves, both with and without UN approval. Although humanitarian issues in civil wars are a serious concern, strategic issues also play a prominent role, as when NATO forces are dispatched to contain the fighting in places such as Bosnia, Kosovo, and, after the attacks of September 11, 2001, Afghanistan.

Regional Intervention

The United Nations has found itself overextended and overburdened in the post-Cold War period. In addition to the dramatic increase in the number of peacekeeping missions it has taken on, it has also been involved in the majority of civil wars identified in Chapter 1 in one way or another. UN envoys and special contingents engage in civil war "early warning," monitoring, mediation, diplomacy, peacekeeping, peacebuilding (bolstering the state's capacity for effective government and sound economic practices), and postconflict reconstruction. Often cash-strapped and without ready forces, the UN has also come to rely on the willingness of member states to provide peacekeeping troops, and on various regional organizations to engage in many similar activities within their spheres of influence.

International support for regional action was utilized on occasion during the Cold War to bypass US-Soviet rivalries in the Security Council (Boutros-Ghali, 1992) or to pave the way for unilateral interveners to exit. By shifting the peacekeeping role from that of the international community (dominated by major powers) to regional organizations believed to be more attuned to indigenous conditions and less swayed by power politics, it has been argued that regional peacekeeping can also be more effective. However, as shown in the Darfur example, regional organizations such as the AU can themselves become overstretched and lack the number of peacekeeping forces and the funding necessary to patrol effectively. Other regional organizations, such as the Organization of American States (OAS), are heavily influenced by a superpower in their midst. At minimum, under the UN Charter, regional organizations are expected to report their interventions on behalf of peace to the UN, which maintains a presumed interest in and potential backup for such actions to promote their success.

Some scholars maintain that regional organizations are not only closer to the situation but that, despite individual states' potential involvement on one side or the other in civil wars, regional organizations retain greater interests in constructive resolution of the fighting, especially when continued warfare could potentially destabilize the entire region (Wehr and Lederach, 1996; Pearson and Olson, 2001). This was the case in the Central American civil wars in Nicaragua and El Salvador. Threats of contagion prompted then Costa Rican President Oscar Arias to lead a successful regional conflict resolution effort under the OAS in

1987. Arias benefited from his position as a leader trusted by all of the parties involved, including the United States, particularly due to his prestige and his country's location in the region. Of course, such discussions can be assisted and given greater impact by the support of key major powers.

Regional organizations' ability to "soften the blow" of humanitarian intervention and intervene with less of a threat of strategic and ulterior motives remains limited, however. Sometimes, as with the AU, noninterventionist norms persist. Also, there can be confusion of mandate and overdependence on one dominant regional power, especially given a shortage of resources among various regional states to effectively participate in the peacekeeping or peacemaking missions. The intervention of ECOWAS (Economic Community of West African States) into the Liberian conflict in 2003 was welcomed by long-suffering Liberians, but criticized as well for the questionable motives and sometime destructive performance of the Nigerian forces leading the action (Ofodile, 1994).

Regional organizations can ease the UN's burden, but they are not necessarily neutral interveners. As regional actors, states' biases will inevitably play a role, though not necessarily one fatal to the mission. As a result, the key to resolving such problems, many argue, is a continuing role for the UN Security Council acting as something of a check against expansionist regional powers (Farer, 1993). In fact, the ECOWAS intervention in Liberia did have the support of a UN mandate, albeit after the fact.

Security Organizations

In addition to interventions by the UN and other regional IGOs, international *security organizations*, such as military alliances (NATO) or political groupings of states, have taken a turn at resolving intrastate conflict. These organizations are generally less inhibited by formal bureaucracies and requirements for consensus among politically diverse members, and can make decisions to intervene more freely than the UN. Historically, one can cite cases of joint security force interventions among like-minded powers in civil wars, such as during the Russian Revolution in 1917, or the "Coalition of the Willing" in Iraq in 2003.

Indeed, the precursors of alliance moves to quell messy civil war situations came from the Eastern bloc, with the Warsaw Pact during the height of the Cold War. Under something termed the "Brezhnev Doctrine," Warsaw Pact members intervened in Czechoslovakia in 1968 to support "brotherly Socialist regimes." As internal popular opposition threatened to overthrow communist rule, Warsaw Pact members, including the East Germans and Poles, as well as the Russians, created a force of 200,000 troops that moved into Prague, effectively ending Westernization and political liberalization (the so-called Prague Spring) in that country for the time being. This would prove to be one of the few formal collective uses of either NATO or Warsaw Pact troops during the Cold War.

Other joint security interventions have been undertaken since the end of the Cold War, as NATO has expanded both in membership (to include former Eastern bloc members) and beyond its Cold War defensive Western European mandate to contemplate peacekeeping ventures in a variety of regions. With the Soviet Union's disintegration, the Warsaw Pact came to an end. Despite the loss of its nominal opponents, NATO would continue on, and its purposes would expand. In 1995 NATO troops took direct military action in the Bosnian civil war, and did so again in Kosovo in 1999. Despite a constitutional controversy about using its forces abroad (given its World War II experience), even Germany, now reunited, joined in with these peacekeeping missions designed to separate warring parties and protect local populations. Both these interventions involved deployments outside of the traditional NATO geographic sphere. In fact, in 1999 NATO outlined its new strategic concept as one that might entail far-flung crisis response, as was the case in Afghanistan beginning in 2001.

The 1990s interventions in the Balkan wars proved complicated given Russian backing for Serbia and suspicions of NATO's new assertiveness, as well as a resurgent German role in Europe. This led to both an uncertain UN Security Council mandate and competitive Russian military moves to shadow those of NATO. With Moscow's threats to veto UN intervention, critics noted that using NATO to bypass the Security Council could have the effect of raising tensions in central Europe and decreasing UN legitimacy, perhaps damaging its ability to manage issues of international peace and security in the future. It was apparent at the time, though, that NATO could respond to such crises more readily than the UN, particularly when such actions were not backed by all of the veto-carrying members of the Security Council.

Though NATO's military and diplomatic interventions could not resolve the underlying tensions and suspicions present in the Balkans, they did provide a prolonged respite from the fighting; foster peace negotiations such as those at Dayton, Ohio, presenting the framework of a political settlement; and move the conflicts toward resolution. However, there was a price to be paid. NATO's involvement was not considered neutral by certain contending forces, particularly those of Serbia, which at times engaged NATO in military encounters. Nor would some NATO members permit the dispatch of ground troops.[2] Aerial bombardment had the effect of killing many civilians (actions that themselves, under some conditions, might be considered war crimes), as well as destroying an infrastructure that the international community would then have to rebuild, indeed in collaboration with the UN.

NATO action was justified on the grounds that humanitarian needs superseded state sovereignty in both the Bosnian and Kosovo cases. According to NATO members, Serbian President Slobodan Milosevic was no longer the legitimate ruling authority for these regions, although this view was questionable under international law, especially for Kosovo province. Washington stopped short of formally backing Kosovar independence from Serbia and gave lip service to disarming the Kosovo Liberation Army insurgents. Milosevic could cite Serbia's grievances against Croatia and other breakaway former Yugoslav republics, both historical and at the time of the fighting, but his crimes against humanity became even more evident as the resulting criminal tribunals unfolded at the Hague in 2001. The legality of the international interventions, especially in light of the intrusions on Serbian sovereignty, became something of a moot point after the fact.

Unilateral Intervention

By far, the most legally questionable form of civil war intervention is that which occurs unilaterally. During the Cold War, superpowers violated the sovereignty of states within their sphere of influence on a regular basis, generally much to the detriment of human rights. The United States, sometimes with and sometimes without IGO support, injected itself into civil wars occurring in Greece (1946), Korea (1950), Guatemala (1954), the Dominican Republic (1965), Nicaragua (1981), and Grenada (1985), and did so in Southeast Asia as well. Operating under the policy of anti-Soviet containment, Washington sought to prevent any "loyal" country from shifting camps (i.e., adopting socialist or communist doctrine or leaving the US sphere of influence). The Soviet Union in turn intervened in its share of civil wars and uprisings as well, for much the same power-oriented reasons as the United States, most notably when it unilaterally entered Hungary in 1956, Afghanistan in 1978, and when it ferried Cuban forces to the Angolan battlefields in Africa during the 1970s and '80s.

Not all unilateral interventions were the product of Cold War politics, however. On occasion, civil war interventions have occurred at the request of the governments or rebels facing internal opposition. As far back as the Spanish Civil War of 1936, outside powers, notably Nazi Germany, fascist Italy, Portugal, and Soviet Russia, tried out their weapons and tactics by backing their favorite civil war clients, while informal brigades of militia volunteers, including the American Abraham Lincoln Brigade, were also dispatched for both idealistic and pragmatic purposes. Both France and the United Kingdom have intervened on behalf of governments in their former colonies in the Middle East and Africa in an attempt to put down uprisings or maintain influence. For example, in 1980 France intervened in the Chad civil war (1980–87) on behalf of Hissene Habre, whose forces were battling those of Goukouni Oueddei, as well as the Libyan forces that had come to Oueddei's aid. Without French intervention, Habre's newly formed government would most likely have fallen. Similarly, French forces were regular participants in quelling civil violence in the Central African Republic, which harbored significant supplies of uranium, among other resources.

Other cases of unilateral intervention into warring countries have come in the context, or as the result, of cross-border attacks or raids. As government troops pursue rebels, they often cross borders to ferret out those seeking refuge in neighboring states. Thus, the Vietnam War spread to both Laos and Cambodia, states undergoing their own internal disruptions. In many wars, ethnic clans and tribes have friends and allies across the border, either as refugees from prior fighting (as in the Democratic Republic of the Congo after the Rwandan genocide) or as citizens of neighboring states. These events have on occasion resulted in intervention by the neighboring state(s) into the civil war state, or vice versa as a besieged government chases or raids rebels in cross-border sanctuaries.

The legitimacy of unilateral intervention is often questionable, yet rarely challenged. For the most part, requests from legitimate governments for foreign assistance are accepted as legal (Doswald-Beck, 1986). However, civil war situations where governmental legitimacy has broken down, or is in question, complicate the issue. For example, when the territory of Chad was divided between Oueddei and Habre, both Libya and France claimed legitimate intervention on behalf of the recognized authority. Under international law, if a civil war entails complete government breakdown, outside states should refrain from intervention. Yet, humanitarian need and the need for governmental reconstruction muddies the legal waters considerably.

Unilateral interventions often have been rationalized through the claim of self-defense and national interest. The United States and USSR certainly claimed self-defense from foreign intrigues in the midst of the Cold War, as did South Africa in its cross-border raids into neighboring Mozambique and Angola. These are clearly the most questionable and most challenged motives internationally. We can generally distinguish unilateral interventions in this regard from their multilateral counterparts, as both justification and motives appear rather different. Forms of multilateral intervention tend to require consensus, and tend to grapple with humanitarian concerns, while valuing state sovereignty when feasible. Unilateral interventions tend to lack international consensus, seem to pay relatively little heed to niceties of either sovereignty or human rights, and are often launched in defense of self-proclaimed doctrines (e.g., the Monroe Doctrine of American involvement in Latin America; the Soviet Brezhnev Doctrine regarding Eastern Europe) and claims of "national defense," or more generally "compelling interests." Sadly, such interventions have also often had the effect of generating humanitarian crises rather than resolving them. Yet, when all else fails, people caught up in civil wars, whether hard-pressed governments, insurgents, or innocent bystanders, may welcome the potential relief of foreign troops riding to the rescue, even if they are lone riders.

CONCLUSION

It is apparent that civil wars are particularly subject to global political debate on issues of human rights and large-scale humanitarian crises. The need to remedy such situations will inevitably run the risk of violating principles of state sovereignty and norms of nonintervention. Debates over the legalities of humanitarian intervention continue among scholars and policy-makers as each new episode of civil war unfolds. History has shown that interventions into civil wars have occurred both with the nod of the international community, typically through

IGO mandates, and also in unilateral or even covert fashion. Interventions may or may not be in support of human rights. In fact, it appears that unilateral and security-oriented interventions are particularly susceptible to exacerbating humanitarian and even environmental crises (note the toxic Agent Orange dioxin excesses of the Vietnam War).

As the international community continues to struggle with and contemplate the legality and effectiveness of intervention, it seems apparent to many that the most significant weapon against the destructiveness of civil war may be prevention. Early warning of civil wars, as well as constructive international preventive measures, would appear to require less resource commitment than intervention. If potential civil wars could be better detected prior to their outbreak, and if effective diplomatic pressure and socio-economic incentives could be mounted, then perhaps lives could be saved and devastation averted.

Recalling the causative factors outlined in Chapters 1 to 3, among the warning signs presumably of interest to potential international interveners would be repeatedly expressed grievances regarding the distribution of power, land, or resources within a country, especially in a society transitioning from harsh autocratic to somewhat more open protodemocratic status; mounting interethnic or intersectional tension within a country; an escalation of "fighting words" or resurrection of historical grievances between communities; the imposition of discriminatory policy changes by governments; scapegoating through governmental and media channels; the mobilization and armament of factions within a state; and rudimentary violence (e.g., raids on police or military outposts), or acts of terror and counterterror reprisals. Once a civil war breaks out, it is difficult for constructive intervention for peace, whether diplomatic or protective military, to take place. The processes by which civil wars are played out, in action-reaction, escalation, or de-escalation sequences, are more fully spelled out in the next chapter.

NOTES

1   There have been international peacekeeping missions in the Middle
     East, but only one was civil war-related; even the recorded case of Leba-
     non involved peacekeeping designed to prevent cross-border interven-
     tion by Syria rather than peacekeeping amidst warring factions within

Lebanon itself. Since the 2006 fighting, though, internal Lebanese peacekeeping by UN forces has been reinvigorated with new missions and responsibilities, though not without questions about the ability to disarm warring factions such as Hezbollah.

2   NATO ground forces were dispatched to Afghanistan following 2001: many of the problems encountered and civilian death tolls seen in the Balkans were noted in that country as well.

CHAPTER FIVE

Conflict Processes During Civil Wars

"Victorious warriors win first and then go to war, while defeated warriors go to war first and then seek to win."

—Sun Tzu

To this point, we have identified and discussed the various factors contributing to the outbreak of civil war at several levels of analysis, particularly the individual, group, state, and the international levels. We have also made clear that not one of these factors alone is sufficient to cause a phenomenon as complex as a civil war. More accurately, several factors at each level interact with one another, creating a volatile mix. Therein lies the complexity of any form of conflict, but this is especially true when discussing large-scale violence within a state.

The complexity does not end there, however. If one looks at the war lists provided by the Correlates of War project (COW) and Peace Research Institute Oslo (PRIO), it may appear that wars start and stop at easily identifiable times. In reality, this is not the case, especially for civil wars, which may tend to recede and restart repeatedly. The progression toward and then throughout war is itself a series of actions and reactions that we refer to here as conflict dynamics. Although it is certainly true that the outbreak of intense intrastate violence may appear rather sudden to outside observers, the reality is that scholars, policy-makers, and others who closely follow events in a particular country will more than likely not be surprised by such violence, having witnessed previous and increasingly destructive group-to-state or group-to-group confrontations and interactions over time.

The "start year" of any war may indicate when that conflict met the operational definition of a particular research group, usually once the specified minimum number of fatalities (1,000, 200, etc., depending on the project) has been achieved. However, conflict and various forms of positive and negative interaction between parties occur well before the "start" of a war. Close observers are likely to have witnessed the communication of an opposition group expressing a particular grievance, for example. They would also have witnessed the government's response to those concerns or demands. As we have indicated earlier (Olson Lounsbery, 2003; see also Gurr, 2000), governments that repeatedly repress dissent appear more likely to experience ethno-political violence, and to be slow in undertaking reforms to relieve the tensions, than less repressive states. On the other hand, this is not always the case. For example, despite the US Congress passing a series of reasonably timely governmental "reforms" meant as compromises on the incendiary issue of slavery in the first half of the nineteenth century, the American Civil War, though delayed, was not ultimately averted.

Often, though, even for moderate and responsive governments, the pace of reform efforts is a step behind the next set of demands made by the opposition or insurgents, since it takes time for ruling constituencies to convince themselves that concessions may be necessary. On the whole, however, if a government responds to a move by an opposition group in a conciliatory manner, opposition members are less likely to escalate the conflict. If a group can achieve its goals, or even a portion of its goals by working within the system, then choosing the violent path is not as enticing and may seem unnecessarily costly. This, of course, explains why democratic states appear to experience less intrastate warfare than transitional states (see Chapter 3), since mature democracies offer avenues of resolution already available when grievances arise.[1] Recognizing that the state typically and nominally has a legal and/or actual monopoly on the use of force within its borders, the opposition group has a choice to make about whether to react to repression by escalating the conflict and persisting in the pursuit of group goals, or to acquiesce (even if such acquiescence may be temporary given that the grievance is likely to remain). If the state utilizes the full brunt of force against its internal opposition, a quick military victory is certainly conceivable, at least early on. In fact, the opposition's ability to survive the beginnings of violent conflict can be considered a victory over the power dominance of the state because international attention and sympathy may emerge (particularly if the repression appears drastic). In turn, how the group responds to the government's actions can be considered a signal to the government for its next reactions. This admittedly rather simplistic action-reaction description (see Figure 5.1) of a potential conflict process and the options of the actors within the process provides a glimpse at the dynamics and decisions that play out as actors move to, from, and through the outset and, subsequently, the course of the war.[2]

Figure 5.1 Action-Reaction Descisional Sequences in Launching Civil War

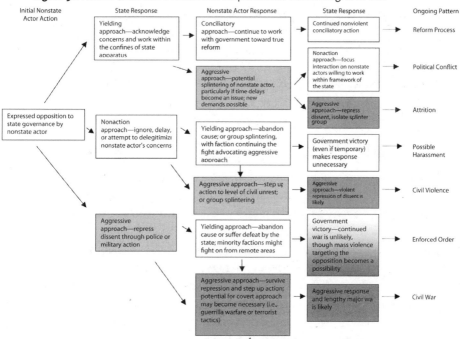

Action-reaction processes help to explain conflict duration, intensity, and even the stability of conflict resolution. Figure 5.1 illustrates the potential interactions between a government and its internal opposition and how choice of reaction sets the stage for future reactions by the other party involved. These dynamics have implications for whether and how war is carried out, whether additional actors become involved, and when outside intervention and conflict resolution is likely to occur. Dynamic activity occurs between parties, but also within parties, as when groups splinter or fracture into factions that disagree about strategy or tactics, or when "rejectionist" extremists stand in the way of agreements, adding yet another layer to the complexity of intra-state war. Structural changes, shifts in leadership, and intragroup divisiveness can have a significant impact, either by bringing about conflict de-escalation or by making matters worse, thus facilitating further escalation. These processes will be explored in detail in this chapter. Conflict dynamics can and do occur at various levels of analysis as well. Through examining each level of analysis we will begin to understand what impact particular changes may have on the course and duration of conflict.

THE INDIVIDUAL AND GROUP DYNAMICS

War has been seen as a drastic though often calculated means by which to resolve conflict. According to Clausewitz, war is "a true political instrument, a continuation of political intercourse, carried on with other means" (Clausewitz, 1984: 87). In this sense war, including civil war, can be seen as akin to political decision-making in general. If, as we indicated earlier, parties can come to terms without resorting to arms, they will likely do so. The reason has to do with the consequences of war itself. Although war may indeed be a calculated "political instrument," it is one that has profoundly damaging costs and consequences—sometimes unpredictable ones, and offers only uncertain prospects for ultimate success (though Blainey, 1988, notes that all contestants have potentially unrealistic positive expectations when they begin fighting). At the individual level, political violence changes human beings and affects their lives in ways that can be unanticipated if not unimaginable. These changes can lead to embitterment and atrocity, as well as to psychological damage (e.g., post-traumatic stress disorder [PTSD]) and overcommitment, and to the corruption of both leaders and the state apparatus, all of which can influence the progress of the war, making peaceful resolution more difficult.

Issues of survival become significant behavior modifiers during war. Although one's experience of war may vary depending on one's proximity to the fighting, a series of changes occur in terms of how individuals and groups view themselves, as well as how they view each other. For reasons of survival and security, it becomes important for individuals to be able to recognize "the enemy." Not doing so could be a deadly mistake, but castigating others as enemies can also lead to unnecessary bloodshed and the erosion of democracy, where it exists.

Many "old" wars between states, or even former civil wars such as in the American South, involved standing and typically uniformed armies fighting pitched battles in a progression toward victory or defeat (e.g., the island-hopping US Pacific strategy in World War II). Parties to a conflict were fairly easy to identify. Conversely, the battle lines of civil war today are quite blurry. Necessity requires, however, that individuals be able to identify those with whom they can feel secure and those by whom their security may be threatened. Thus, a strategy of "walling off" or "cleansing" (displacing or killing) enemies can emerge after tit-for-tat acts of violence or communal attacks; such strategies can reassure the parties that they will be left alone, but they also add to the inhumanity and scars of war.

The "wall" running through the capital city Nicocia, separating the Northern Cypriots (Turkish) from the Southern Cypriots (Greek). Photo courtesy of Benoit Muracciole.

As we have indicated, civil wars can be related to a variety of differences, including ideological, religious, cultural, and economic. To easily identify individuals based on these categories can often be difficult, however. This was particularly true in the Rwandan and Bosnian wars, where physical and even cultural differences between Hutus and

Tutsis, and Serbs and Croats could be difficult to detect. Governments and groups have sought to remedy this potentially confusing matter in a number of ways (e.g., by using identification cards or requiring certain groups to wear symbols, such as the German requirement that Jews wear the Star of David leading up to and during World War II). In Rwanda a relentless Hutu-driven media propaganda storm castigated Tutsis as "cockroaches," making it psychologically easier to tolerate extremist "solutions." Such processes and the need to identify "us" versus "them" begins to polarize any warring society. Interaction between individuals of different group identities—even among those who formerly had reasonably good and harmonious relations—diminishes, while distrust, scapegoating, and hostility increases. These are some of the "enabling conditions" that allow wars to proceed and allow otherwise law-abiding individuals to commit acts that in nonwar situations would be labeled "murder."

As individuals engage in war, the violent experiences and images may prove too difficult for them to manage. Most are familiar with soldiers experiencing PTSD following participation in war, a disorder that is now recognized as a psychological consequence of violence. It is known that PTSD affects both soldiers and civilians, including war refugees (see the work on Iraqi refugees by Kira et al., 2006). Our understanding of what happens to war veterans and victims can help us understand the changes that may occur with various civil war participants, including children recruited as soldiers in many recent wars, particularly in Africa. Situations where it is difficult to identify the opponent and where there is a lack of security regardless of one's position or status in the conflict (i.e., ambiguous "front" lines and combatant versus noncombatant roles) create stresses that may result in war atrocities, or PTSD and domestic violence (Laufer, Gallops, and Frey-Wouters, 1984: 67).[3]

More so than in interstate war, civilians in civil conflicts become entangled as both victims and targets of fire (Miall, 1992). The main casualties of so-called new wars (see Chapter 4) have been civilians killed or wounded either as "collateral" damage surrounding battles or as direct targets of terrorist strategies. Women frequently become victims of rape and other violent acts as part of strategies to demoralize and defeat the enemy. Children are frequently orphaned and are forced to engage in violence themselves.

The impact of such brutal acts committed against civilians in the midst of civil war has significant repercussions for the individual participant, whether shooter or target, as well as on the propensity for future war. Women who have been raped often find themselves outcasts in their own society. Children forced to take up arms and weaponry against others find it a difficult transition once they are in the position to return to a peaceful and normal life. Just as adult soldiers experience PTSD, women and children and refugees both leaving and within the country can also find themselves haunted by the images of their experiences. Children raised in a violent environment not only have fewer options in life and less education but also learn to react to conflict violently. Problems that in other nonwar societies may be resolved through dialogue will be approached differently in a post-war environment because of these experiences. Studies in Northern Ireland, for example, have identified domestic violence and soccer hooliganism as significant problems linked to what one author has termed "hegemonic masculinity," which might relate to or be reinforced by long-term civil violence as a regional pattern (Bairner, 1999; see also Freel and Robinson, 2004, for domestic violence rates in Northern Ireland).

Civil war generates problematic group dynamics as well. When war ensues, group identity becomes solidified and enforced; there is very little room for neutrality. The now famous quote by US President George W. Bush that "you're either with us, or against us" (CNN, 6 November 2001), used to describe a "war on terror," exemplifies what transpires in civil war situations as well. Individuals are forced to choose sides, sometimes quite literally in residential areas. Group identity can be imposed on people based on whatever characteristics are being used within the state to make such determinations, such as first or last names, skin color, or other characteristics. Through this process, group solidification occurs (Kriesberg, 1998).

With little communication occurring between groups, individuals no longer feel safe interacting with those of the outgroup who used to be associates, neighbors, friends, or even family members. As groups become polarized, the image of the enemy can become significantly distorted. Reports of abuse and atrocities can be exaggerated to exacerbate this dynamic, making it easier to justify negative views of and actions toward the enemy. Views of the "other" also become self-fulfilling prophecies (Kriesberg, 1998), meaning that individuals expect the enemy to behave in ways that are aggressive, and so they interpret actions as aggressive regardless of the original intent of the action. Given the significant decrease in intergroup communication, the other's actions are unfortunately left almost entirely up to interpretation and rumors, making miscommunication a significant problem. In such situations, actions by one group may be motivated by a need to take defensive action in response, which in turn can be seen by the other group as entirely threatening and offensive.

This type of interaction, interpretation, and miscommunication has often characterized the Israeli-Palestinian conflict. Ironically, Jews and Palestinians have many cultural and historical similarities, including relatively high educational standards in strong families and the treatment suffered as outcasts by majority populations. Yet, negative characterizations and threat perceptions abound between them, in part due to the perception of "zero-sum" conflict (i.e., competition for the same pieces of land in which if one gains it the other supposedly must lose it). Israeli responses to suicide bombers frequently involve the raiding and bombing of Palestinian territory, and more recently have led to the erection of an extensive "barrier" or wall, complete with separate roads and road lanes, inside Palestinian territory to confine the population and prevent easy access to Israeli cities and settlements. Israeli actions are explained as efforts to identify and arrest terrorists, yet to many Palestinians, the resulting inconvenience, chaos, death, and disruption is interpreted quite differently as discriminatory and repressive. Palestinian anger over their subordination then contributes to another generation of fighters.

Some have observed that it can take bold moves of acknowledgment or reconciliation, such as offers to mourn with victims and for the dead of the other side, to break such cycles of violence and vengeance. Such actions can begin to engender trust and a belief that each side actually values human life and feels remorse. Thus, there might be some formulas whereby both communities could gain satisfactory, if not optimal, levels of security and territory. For example, the late King Hussein of Jordan once went to Israeli homes to offer personal condolences during mourning for Israelis killed by Jordanian border guards, thus creating a major psychological impression of courage and compassion. Of course, Jordan had already established tentative working relations with Israel to weaken the power of the common "enemy" (the Palestinians in each state) and the Jordanian government finally renounced its claims to the West Bank and advocated a separate Palestinian state.[4]

The unfortunate effects of mirror imaging between civil war opponents are likely to occur in many situations of violent interaction.

Groups engaged in civil conflict recognize the danger that the enemy poses to their survival. As a result, group members on both sides become convinced that while they are reasonable, members of the other group are incapable of accepting, collaborating, or compromising with them. Both Israelis and Palestinians believe this about the other. Opponents' actions and even offers of negotiation are interpreted as devious ploys or as signs of weakness. The processes involved here are a function of psychological group solidification, group insecurity, and group survival. Even though group actors are complex and heterogeneous, with good, bad, and various types of intentions and motives, concerns about safety suggest one needs to be cautious with all opponents.

Members of each opposing party have similar thought processes for the same reasons. It is both easier and safer to see the enemy as a singular unit bent upon destruction. All sides become convinced that the sole purpose of the enemy (essentially all members of the opposing party) is to defeat or destroy them. Underlying basic needs or grievances of the opponents tend to get lost in this process, while opponents' actions are interpreted as confirmation of their hostile intent, thus making negotiated outcomes more difficult.

When one is convinced that an opponent lacks legitimate goals and is primarily interested in waging war simply to commit acts of violence and group destruction, emotional responses and overreaction result. If an opponent's actions seem both threatening and irrational, one is left with the feeling that reasoned responses and communication are inappropriate, tending to reward the enemy's aggressive tactics, and may legitimize the enemy's cause. We witness this dynamic when states, whether or not engulfed in civil war, are confronted with "terrorist" activity.

Some would classify terrorism (e.g., bombing attacks on civilian centers) as related to other uses of force, designed in this case to instill fear and pain, convince opponents that resistance or continued occupation of territory is futile, and to publicize the causes of one's own group (see Pearson and Rochester, 1998). Terrorism also tends to be used by actors who lack the means to utilize more conventional and expensive forms of violence, such as through military brigades. However, in reacting to the wanton destruction wrought by terrorists, state leaders frequently refuse to negotiate with them under the belief that to do so would encourage more terrorism, and also due to a sense that negotiations must involve legitimate "rational" actors. In certain circumstances, though, even fanatics are open to long- or short-range negotiated agreements if they find it within their interest. Negotiations may also be inevitable, as when discussions or offers regarding prisoner exchanges are necessary. The question is whether and to what extent one wants to agree with unsavory characters or risk facilitating their causes.

Certainly superpowers have been known to aid and abet the causes of fanatics if they thought these individuals or groups fit in with their own long- or short-term interests in a conflict, as when American arms were dispatched to Afghani mujahadeen "freedom fighters" opposing the Soviet Union in Afghanistan during the 1980s. However, identifying opponents as fanatical or "irrational" does carry with it the political benefit of delegitimizing them in the eyes of in-group members, as well as external actors and the international community. The relatively new and amorphous American war on terror has had such an impact with the labeling of internal opposition in places such as Iraq as "al-Qaeda-linked" terrorists. These groups may or may not have actual or substantive links to the transnational terror network, but the desired effect is to delegitimize them and draw internal and outside support for the cause. Such strategic gamesmanship also plays into the dominant major power's interest in maintaining an internal presence in particular war-ravaged countries and in justifying its own military acts.

During the Cold War, leaders of states experiencing armed internal opposition would on occasion attract the attention of either the United States or the Soviet Union by labeling their domestic opposition as either communists or "lackeys of imperialism," thus hopefully opening the spigot for arms supplies and military support. For example, dictators or factional leaders in countries such as Nicaragua, Guatemala, the Dominican Republic, and the Philippines were able to receive American military aid, weaponry, and sometimes intervention in their fight against left-leaning guerrilla groups as the United States waged its zero-sum proxy game against supposed Soviet influence. Such claims, regardless of their accuracy, brought conflicts to a different level, where compromise and conciliation were no longer options.

Despite the momentum and staying power of hostile mirror imaging, such games of distrust and intransigence, whether or not involving actual terrorists, can be reversed. This may be the case when one's hesitant conciliatory overtures produce positive responses on the part of the opponent. Further incremental concessions back and forth may follow; in this way negative action-reaction cycles begin to "morph" into positive give and take. In game theory, this process of breaking the "prisoner's dilemma" of endemic mistrust through phased-in peace feelers and concessions is termed a "tit-for-tat" strategy. One risks a concession, and if the other side responds in kind, a further concession is offered, and so on. Otherwise, both sides revert to hostile play. This pattern was proposed and verified experimentally by Rapoport and Chammah (1965) and applied in Axelrod's social science laboratory (1997).

STRUCTURAL CHANGES

In addition to the dynamics involving individuals and groups as parties to a conflict, significant structural changes can and do occur, impacting the course of any particular civil war. Structure involves the political, social, and geographic context of the war itself and of the parties. More specifically, it involves the interplay between parties directly involved, those indirectly affected, and those intervening in the struggle. Depending upon the developing circumstances, continued warfare can either seem politically compelling or repugnant to those in leadership positions. Depending on whether actors remain "rational" or not (i.e., whether they are capable of carefully calculating the costs and benefits of violent struggle), the "game" of conflict can appear to be going well or badly, thus affecting the next set of leadership choices and decisions, potentially restructuring the parties' relationships and their goals in the process.

It should be clear at this point that issues of security loom large for all parties involved in organized political violence. In fact, concerns about group survival become paramount and guide many or most of the decisions made within warring societies. Concerns over group survival can easily translate into concerns over territorial "homelands" or political survival for group leaders and elites. As conflict ensues, the ability of any particular leader to provide a sense of security for their group, whether the group in question is the government or that of the challenger(s), will determine their own ability to retain leadership.

Leaders who can provide this supposed security are less likely to be toppled either through election or overthrow. Consequently, the longer one remains in a leadership position during the course of a civil war, the more likely one is identified with that war, in turn increasing one's stake in the ultimate outcome. US President Abraham Lincoln

finally achieved enough momentum in the war reports of Union progress in the American Civil War that he managed to survive the election of 1864, when just a few months earlier it had been assumed that
he would be defeated. On the other hand, even victorious leaders can
be doomed as war-weary constituents seek to replace them once the
war is over or at a stalemate. Psychologically, leaders find themselves
frequently in a situation where they think they need to demonstrate
their strength, while efforts to come to terms with their opponent
appear less useful.

In an aggressive civil war environment, challengers naturally emerge
within parties, particularly when a current course of action appears to
be ineffective at achieving full-scale military victory. Frustration over
a lengthy bloody war can translate into demands for an alternative
course of action. Leadership change in this type of situation becomes more likely as challengers offer new promise to end the fighting.
Zartman and Touval (1996) have suggested that when both parties to
a war have experienced enough futile battles and enough death they
may find themselves in the position of a "mutually hurting stalemate"
(MHS). In an MHS, both parties begin to recognize that military victory
is unlikely, that the status quo has become intolerably costly, and that
negotiating an outcome is perhaps a better choice. As wars progress,
however, such conciliatory efforts, especially if unilaterally initiated,
become viewed as weak, and past sacrifices are viewed as a reason to
persist in the hostilities (on the concept of "entrapment" in conflict,
see Pruitt, Rubin, and Kim, 1994).

When the perception of group survival is at stake, negotiation may
still not be perceived as a viable option for the masses, even as the pinch
of a MHS sets in. Intragroup challengers may emerge offering a different, even more aggressive, course of action aimed at achieving group
victory through continued resistance and military action. Conciliatory
actors might be publicly castigated. By the same token, of course, stalemates can bring conciliators to the fore, calling for immediate cessation
of warfare (see Mukherjee, 2006: 495, who argues that civil wars ending
in military victory afford a better chance for power-sharing agreements
to work than do civil wars ending in military stalemate). For example,
during the American Civil War, Union General George McClellan
styled himself as just such a conciliator who would have sought terms of
settlement with the South, probably including the retention of slavery,
in his challenge to Abraham Lincoln for the presidency in 1864. Thus,

intrawar leadership challengers and changes can lead either toward or away from negotiated settlements. The rules of the game can change as a new set of dynamics emerge.

In some situations where successful challengers have emerged, the group or party as a unit is maintained. In other situations, however, continued loyalty to past leadership may generate group splintering and the emergence of new factions and actors in the war. Splintering might further complicate war dynamics among parties who have already gotten, for better or worse, to "know" each other. In the Philippines, for example, the Moro National Liberation Front (MNLF), a fairly loose coalition of various opposition parties, became engaged in a separatist rebellion on behalf of the Mindanao Muslim communities against the newly formed, predominantly Christian, national government in 1970. By the mid-1970s, however, MNLF had splintered into three parts:

> Differing goals, traditional tribal rivalries, and competition among Moro leaders for control of the movement produced a threeway split in the MNLF during the late 1970s. The first break occurred in 1977 when Hashim Salamat, supported by ethnic Maguindanaos from Mindanao, formed the Moro Islamic Liberation Front, which advocated a more moderate and conciliatory approach toward the government. Misuari's larger and more militant MNLF was further weakened during that period when rival leaders formed the Bangsa Moro Liberation Organization, drawing many Mindanao Maranaos away from the MNLF, dominated by Misuari's Sulu-based Tausug tribe. The Bangsa Moro Liberation Organization eventually collapsed, giving way to the Moro National Liberation Front/Reformist Movement. Moro factionalism, compounded by declining foreign support and general war weariness, hurt the Muslim movement both on the battlefield and at the negotiating table. (Pike, 2001)

Interestingly, despite the Moro Islamic Liberation Front's (MILF's) initial conciliatory approach, it was the MNLF that came to terms with the Filipino government in 1996 while the MILF continued the armed struggle. The splintering of warring groups, as was the case here, often has the effect of lengthening the duration of civil wars (Cunningham, Gleditsch, and Salehyan, 2006). In the above example, despite settlement with the MNLF, the war continued through the MILF.

Similarly, it has been reported that factions of warring Iraqi Kurdish clans emerged during their independence struggle against Saddam Hussein's government during the 1980s while Iraq was engaged in cross-border warfare with Iran. Some of these factions reportedly collaborated with Hussein for purposes of convenience in an effort to gain predominance in the Kurdish national movement. President Hussein in turn played these splits to his advantage in his efforts to suppress the insurgency, though he ultimately employed lethal poison gas attacks against Kurdish villages, thus alienating great portions of the Kurdish population in general. The course of a war can offer supposed opportunities or pressures that seem to compel leaders to persevere or change course, as they seek to divide their opponents and they veer among obstacles in order to stay in power and avoid losses.

Thus, although group splintering can lengthen the duration of civil wars through the creation of additional parties to the conflict, splintering also has the effect of weakening the parties involved and perhaps compromising their cause. The Philippine and Kurdish conflicts certainly continued; however, the intensity of the armed struggle and the ability of the opposition groups to fight was at least temporarily weakened. Opposition strength is a rather significant determinant of civil war duration generally. Weaker parties unable to generate effective resistance to governmental action are likely to be defeated fairly quickly. In fact, effective state bureaucracy is likely to undermine rebel coherence. The ability of an opposition or rebel group to persist and avoid defeat at the hands of the government is often a victory given the significant power imbalance present in civil war situations (DeRouen and Sobek, 2004).

Another type of splintering that can lengthen wars and weaken parties is known as rejectionism. Here, extremist elements, sensing that negotiation and compromise may be near because of hurting stalemates or leadership reconciliation, may undertake outrageous acts of violence and terror that are designed to perpetuate the war, humiliate the negotiating parties, and arouse various sectors of the population. Rejectionists may even strike directly at the leadership through assassinations, as when Yitzhak Rabin was killed by a Jewish extremist during key moments of the peace process negotiations with the Palestinians in 1995, thus seemingly derailing a pending agreement.

Conflicts can become even more difficult to resolve when warring parties become entrenched in society. This is a particularly tricky aspect to overcome when party elites begin to benefit financially from the war. The diamond and coltan (the mineral used in cellphone chips) trade in the Congo and in West Africa, opium in Afghanistan, and cocaine in Colombia have transformed civil war economies, creating a rather lucrative stream of income for wealth and armament among the parties controlling these resources, either in their entirety or even partially. Disrupted wartime economies add to the lure of such "underground" economies. Control and sales (or resales) of weaponry have had similar effects creating constituencies for continued war. Although, generally speaking, civil wars can make the nation-state very weak economically, control of exploitable resources can make individuals or groups of elites very rich. Those that are benefiting from warring environment are unlikely to see the value of bringing that war to its conclusion. Through the exploitation of such resources, rebel groups are better able to finance their struggle against the government, thus leading to extended and longer wars (Fearon, 2004). This rather unfortunate civil war dynamic creates additional conflict issues, including economic pressures and cross-border fighting, that must be addressed if a warring society is going to move toward post-war stability.

As conflict progresses, party goals can change as well. Issues of grievance, for example, may lead opposition groups to advocate for political autonomy or fair representation. If, however, those calls go unheeded and armed struggle ensues, in the interest of gaining more certain security, party members may begin to advocate for a more permanent solution to their grievances in the form of secession (i.e., a complete territorial and governmental separation from the former state). Separatist wars can be more intense than less extreme forms of civil war if the parties believe they can attract international intervention through chaos and disruption (Fearon, 2004). Intensity also increases in separatist wars as the central authority struggles to maintain the state's territorial integrity, resulting in wars of longer duration (Balch-Lindsay and Enterline, 2000).

Further, the progression of war in and of itself can lead to additional conflict issues. In Israel, conflict over territory has become even more complicated as scores of additional Jewish settlements have been created on land considered by the Palestinians to be theirs, and as more and more Palestinian prisoners have been detained by Israel. The Israeli settlement policy has sometimes been referred to in Israel (see Aronson, 1990) as "creating facts" i.e., establishing changed circumstances that would make it more difficult for Palestinians to win concessions. Each expansion of an issue such as land settlement involves an additional element, even including resource (water) scarcities, that will need to be negotiated and resolved in order for conflict resolution to occur. As issues and conflict intensity escalate, further destructive interaction between the parties becomes more likely.

In addition to the phenomenon of group splintering discussed above, the proportion and number of parties to a civil conflict may expand through outside intervention. As civil war intensifies, there are a number of ways that neighboring states may find themselves drawn into the conflict. The anticolonial war of 1972–79 in the former state of Rhodesia (now Zimbabwe) resulted in the creation of rebel bases in neighboring countries of Zambia and Mozambique. Although neither state became actively engaged in the Rhodesian war, the white-led Rhodesian government frequently crossed borders to attack rebel camps, even to the extent that a bombing campaign ensued inside Mozambique. More recently in the post-colonial era, we have seen that the spread of violence from war-ravaged states can transcend internationally recognized boundaries. For example, Rwanda's fighting found its way into neighboring states, notably the Democratic Republic of the Congo next door, as former ruling Rwandan Hutus fled from the new Tutsi-dominated Rwandan government, generating "the widest interstate war in modern African history": nine African nations and various armed groups, after 1998. The Hutu refugees even succeeded in destabilizing the corrupt former Congo government of Joseph Mobutu by backing his successor, Laurent Kabila (see Globalsecurity.org, "Congo Civil War"). These developments led to intervention by states, either sympathetic or opposed to the Hutus and/or the new Congolese state, including Uganda, Rwanda, and Burundi on the anti-Hutu (or pro-Tutsi) side, and Namibia, Zimbabwe, Angola, and Chad on the pro-Hutu (or anti-Mobutu) side. This type of interaction is exacerbated when neighboring states contain kindred-group support for a warring faction. In Rwanda, for example, war and genocide against the Tutsis and moderate Hutus also created similar conflict in neighboring Burundi, which likewise has had a historical Hutu-Tutsi divide.

BOX 5.1: A CASE IN POINT: INTERNATIONALIZED CIVIL WAR IN YEMEN

The Yemeni civil war, beginning in 1962 with the republican revolution ousting the royal regime of Muhammad al-Badr (see http://www.onwar.com), was another case with significant and recurring military intervention and party expansion. Early on in the republican/royalist battle for control over the nation, several external players became involved. As the parties engaged in a larger regional struggle for power, Egypt, and to a lesser extent the Soviet Union, intervened on behalf of the more modernistic Yemeni republicans, while Saudi Arabia (along with Iran, under the shah, and Jordan) supported the traditional royalists. Yemen, as a result, became the battleground for a larger regional war, to the extent that the original civil war struggle over the structure and makeup of the Yemeni government was temporarily eclipsed.

By 1970 the Yemeni factions recognized this to be the case and began a process that resulted in a nominally reunited state, with the expulsion of the Egyptian and Saudi forces (but not all of their influence) and by alternating negotiations with renewed warfare over the next twenty years. Another civil war broke out in 1994, involving ambitious factional leaders in the south, but it was put down with the support of outside powers including the United States. Subsequently, the US suffered effective terror attacks—on its naval forces visiting Yemen's port of Aden—carried out by al-Qaeda extremists. While a reunited Yemeni government structure along protodemocratic lines was developed, discord remained in evidence even into the new millennium (see US Department of State, December 2007).

As seen in the Yemeni example (Box 5.1), not all military intervention in civil wars is committed by neighboring states. Cold War interventions occurred fairly frequently in states suffering civil war, which led them to become embroiled in the supposedly zero-sum game between the United States and the Soviet Union. In the post-Cold War period, civil war recurred in Afghanistan following NATO involvement (involving cross-border issues in Pakistan as well), and civil war was spawned by the US intervention in Iraq. These cases of intervention were motivated almost entirely by strategic interest in a larger geopolitical struggle within the international system.

Statistics show an increase in multilateral interventions since 1990 by world or regional organizations such as the UN and NATO for purportedly and largely humanitarian reasons to quell fighting and safeguard civilian populations in places such as Bosnia and Sudan (see Talentino, 2006). Indeed, the end of the Cold War eased the way for more multilateral actions of this type, since one superpower no longer necessarily exercised or threatened to veto proposals for such moves, or to oppose them by force.

Civil wars can also expand and change due to intergovernmental and/or nongovernmental intervention. The 1974 war on the island of Cyprus led to unilateral Turkish intervention and, subsequently, peacekeeping intervention by the UN. As a result, the island has been effectively divided between the northern Turkish Cypriot controlled territory and the southern Greek Cypriot controlled territory. A peace and reunification plan was put to public plebiscite in 2004 and was accepted by the Turkish region but rejected by the Greek side as legitimizing the Turkish presence. Yet, the rejectionist Greek Cypriot "state" was allowed into the European Union (EU) in 2004, while the Turkish side was denied EU entry despite its willingness to reunify under a federal structure.

Sometimes parties in stalemated situations can be enticed to cooperate by an outside inducement, such as EU membership, with its promise of economic benefits and expanded markets; this proved to be the case in the Northern Irish conflict. However, sometimes politics gets the better of such prospects, reviving old antagonisms, as with European suspicions and opposition to Turkey's (and Turkish Cypriot) membership in the EU. Of course, not all external involvement or intervention of this sort is bad. In fact, in Cyprus as well as in Bosnia the violence for the most part has stopped, and multinational forces provide a rationale for the war-weary parties to leave each other alone despite the elusiveness of a more comprehensive resolution. Nevertheless, any form of intervention has the effect of bringing an additional party to the conflict and additional issues or pressures with which to contend.

Although it appears that *military* intervention, for the most part, has led to civil wars of longer duration (Regan, 2002), other forms of intervention can have a rather different impact. International organizations and states external to the conflict sometimes seek to influence wars through the use of economic or diplomatic sanctions, thus avoiding potentially lengthy military commitments. Sanctions normally take the form of economic trade or arms embargoes (refusal to supply or sell) on the warring state in an effort to make continued participation in the war too financially difficult to maintain. Economic sanctions were placed against South Africa for much of its later apartheid period, for example. Such measures were aimed at encouraging a more rapid transition to majority rule.

Economic embargoes have been heavily criticized both for the negative impact they can have on the populations forced to go without necessary provisions and for the perceived length of time such sanctions must be in place in order to render the desired effect (see Smith, 2004; Lopez and Cortright, 1995, 2000). This criticism has led to the implementation of "smart sanctions" aimed particularly at ruling elites rather than at general populations, and involving such measures as limiting access to weaponry or other resources used specifically for purposes of war. All forms of sanctions and embargoes are notoriously leaky, however, making such tools rather unreliable and imprecise in bringing about a quick resolution to any civil war (Pearson, Olson Lounsbery, and Grillot, 2007). As an additional impact, arms embargoes also tend to create rather lucrative black markets for weaponry, thereby driving up prices and profits. This creates an incentive for governments and private dealers to trade in arms, as well as for the development of an indigenous arms industry in embargoed states.

However, in combination with effective measures to stifle smuggling, patrol borders, and embed embargoes in larger multifaceted sanctions, sanctions can have a telling effect in ending some wars. South Africa's largely British economic elite felt the brunt of banking and financial sanctions against the country beginning in the mid-1980s and evidently helped bring pressure to bear on the white minority regime to open a dialogue and transitional reforms with African National Congress leader Nelson Mandela. Indeed, economic embargoes have been found to shorten the duration of a civil war when used in combination with diplomatic efforts to resolve the conflict (Regan and Aydin, 2006). Continued diplomatic efforts over time tend to increase the odds of bringing about a resolution through a negotiated outcome (Olson and Pearson, 2002). When a combination of approaches is used, the duration of civil war is likely decreased: it becomes clear to warring parties that external actors have a commitment to seeing resolution come about.

DYNAMIC RELATIONSHIPS AND EVOLVING RIVALRIES

Clearly, the changing circumstances of war have a significant impact on how parties relate and interact with one another. In one form or another, the psychological changes that result from individual and group dynamics in civil war create, perpetuate, or resolve situations of rivalry. As conflict progresses, parties engaged in the conflict become ever more focused on the enemy as the level of threat intensifies, thus transforming the relationship between the parties and individuals involved, and making resolution, or even conciliatory action, difficult. Rivalries, both domestic and international, have been characterized as "enduring" and persistent (Goertz and Diehl, 1992). The longer a civil war endures or the more intense (bloody) a war becomes, the more parties become caught up in each other's fate. As in the Yemen example contained in Box 5.1, a nation experiencing a civil war once is likely to experience another war that involves either the same or newly emergent parties (Licklider, 1995), and typically, over similar or the same issues.

Some civil wars are essentially "one-off" affairs, as in the US North-South struggle during the American Civil War. Even here, however, the former antagonists remained nonbelligerent but resentful and sometimes violent rivals for a long period of time while the wounds of war slowly healed. Other instances of internal violence recur, sometimes at the level of repeated full-scale civil war or repeated skirmishes. Israel continues to be plagued by episodes of fighting and resistance on the part of the politically subordinate Palestinians. The politically dominant Sinhalese population in Sri Lanka has been engaged in civil war with the minority Sri Lankan Tamils since 1983, although the roots of the conflict date back as far as the late 1950s.

Such enduring, recurring, and volatile conflict relationships can give the appearance of being "intractable" and unsolvable, leaving observers and participants alike to make references to "ancient hatreds" and unremitting hostility. In reality, these relationships are often characterized by periods of thawing and refreezing hostility. Often as well, constructive visionary leadership, such as that shown by President Mandela and his South African government counterparts, can turn the tide of hostility and break its cycle relatively quickly. Recognizing that rivalry does exist within states, however, is important conceptually because it allows us to track significant shifts and dynamics in the relationship between warring rivals.

By focusing on rivalry, we move beyond seeing civil wars, or even episodes within the same war, as isolated events. Parties learn lessons from their previous interactions, which helps to inform their likely reactions to enemy actions in the future. In fact, the existence of prior fighting influences the probability of future fighting, just as parties that were able to work out their differences successfully through dialogue are more prone to turn to dialogue again as conflict arises. Kriesberg (1998) has described conflict, generally speaking, using a cyclical framework beginning from its origins (or bases) through conflict manifestation and leading toward a destructive phase—recognizing that conflicts change through the influence of external intervention well. Kriesberg also recognizes that "a protracted conflict often has many escalating and de-escalating periods of varying magnitude" (1998: 23). Scholars exploring so-called intractable disputes have specifically contributed to the discussion of intrastate conflict persistence (see Crocker et al., 2004).

Policy-makers and resolution practitioners have long been perplexed and stymied by prolonged seemingly unresolvable conflicts, as well as by the ferocity and intensity these types of intrastate wars can engender. Yet, by focusing on the dynamics of the relationships involved and viewing at least some civil wars as wars of rivalry, we improve our understanding of a war's progression from an isolated event, or series of isolated events, to the set of action-reaction sequences, complete with building resentments, competition, and opportunism, that they actually are.

In order to understand the implications of an enduring intrastate rivalry, it is important to understand what such a rivalry entails conceptually. Scholars of civil war, to this point, have tended to focus much of their analyses on characteristics relating to the parties involved, the state itself, or the system in which the conflict occurs. Rivalry (i.e., the dyads of actors who are locked together in deadly action-reaction sequences over time), however, has not been the focus of civil war analyses for the most part, despite the influence that action-reaction processes appear to have on the parties and the course a conflict may take. As a result, we place our understanding of civil war in the context of rivalry by borrowing heavily from the *interstate* rivalry literature (i.e., wars between states), which looks at interacting rivals as a form of conflict system in which the parties become attuned to and respond most readily to each other's moves.

Diehl and Goertz (2000) identify three dimensions of an interstate rivalry. The first dimension involves spatial consistency. A rivalry is said to contain "the same pair of states competing with one another, and the expectation of a future conflict relationship with the same specific opponent" (2000: 19). Spatial consistency is also an important dimension in intrastate rivalry, although potentially more complicated at the state level. Civil war, by at least one definition, involves the state as a party to the conflict (Small and Singer, 1982), thus distinguishing civil wars from intergroup violence as we discussed in Chapter 1.

It can be argued, however, that the state in many situations also includes an identity (ethnic or otherwise). Different identity groups may come to dominate the state at different times (see the shift, for example, in the South American state of Guyana's mainly Afro- to its mainly Indo-Guyanese ruling party during the 1990s). Violence in post-Saddam Iraq rose as a reaction both to US occupation and to the prospect of a mainly Shi'a-dominated state emerging under the new constitution in a Baghdad previously ruled by Sunnis and secular Ba'athist Party bosses. In many states, a particular identity group or set of groups finds itself in opposition to another politically dominant identity group within the state over a long period of time. The state's political structure, as well as political dominance and subordination patterns among identity groups within the state, can change and become attuned to long-lasting rivalry, fear, and resentment.

Regimes can shift, becoming more or less democratic; politically dominant groups can shift as well. What typically does not change (at least very quickly), however, are identity-group demographic divisions (both political and cultural) within the state (immigration, of course, can be a source of fairly rapid change). This is not to say that cultural or political identity is fixed, but rather that politically salient identities are slow to change: thus the ability to sustain a rivalry over time despite potential changes in government or political structures and despite some geographic movement and attempts at reform. As a result, intrastate rivalries are thought to be reasonably spatially consistent because they involve the same actors, who are potentially dominant or seeking dominance over the same regions or neighborhoods, over time. Generally, one of those actors is the state, which includes the cultural or political identity of the politically dominant group.

As we know, civil wars can sometimes be categorized by the primary identity of the parties involved in the struggle: typically they can be ideological, territorial, political, or identity-based wars. It is thus argued here that ideological, territorial, political, and identity-based rivalries can exist, sometimes with more than one factor simultaneously at work. Thus, ideological, territorial, or political rivalries (such as the Northern Irish dispute) may also involve elements of identity (e.g., religion and nationalism). In Southeast Asia, leftist opposition groups, at some points predominantly Chinese, have found themselves engaged at times in intrastate rivalries with more centrist or rightist regimes reflective of other populations, spawning ethno-political attacks and, on occasion, massacres, as in Indonesia and Malaysia during the 1960s. Given hopeful political and economic developments (such as more equity of opportunity and decision-making authority), such rivalries can be negotiated and transformed into livable relationships, even in the light of massive historical bloodletting. Yet, there always remains the potential for recurring rivalry if socio-economic conditions worsen or if a more hostile leadership emerges to stir up bitter memories.

The second dimension of interstate rivalry identified by Diehl and Goertz (2000: 21) deals with time and duration. It is argued that in order for rivalry to exist, "militarized competition must last long enough for the states involved to adjust their behavior and long-term strategy because of the competition." As a result, rivalries can be distinguished from isolated events and from events that fall somewhere in the middle (protorivalry) between isolated and enduring. Thus, the concept of intrastate rivalry presented here also includes the elements of time and duration. Isolated rivalries are thought to be short in duration, even if within that time period the conflict is particularly intense. Enduring rivalries, on the other hand, are more than sporadic outbreaks involving armed or repeated struggles of varying intensity over longer periods of time. Protorivalries involving recurrent clashes are not as lengthy as their enduring counterparts, but are more persistent than isolated rivalries. Depending upon how one views the American civil rights struggles and violent backlash of the 1960s, one might argue that they were a manifestation of "unfinished business" left over from the actual civil war and reconstruction of the nineteenth century, and they reflected lingering bitterness and North-South rivalry. Each type of intrastate rivalry carries with it different implications as to the duration and intensity of any particular civil war.

The third dimension of interstate rivalry according to Diehl and

Goertz (2000) is militarized competitiveness. This dimension distinguishes protest events from events involving armed violence, but also adds the element of competition over particular issues. Civil wars, by definition, involve armed struggle and, hence, easily satisfy the third rivalry dimension.

We begin to recognize through this approach that conflicts have histories and that these histories involve experiences wherein one set of events impacts the next set of interactions. As the conflict becomes entrenched, the parties involved become subjected to selective perception, sometimes taking on hideous and odious forms as in the case of the Hutu-Tutsi hatred. In other words, as a party to a conflict "gets to know" their enemy, they will see and dwell on the myths and actions that they expect to find. Conciliatory actions and words are less likely to be recognized than are volatile and aggressive actions and words. The more families that are impacted by the violence perpetrated by the "other," the more the resentment and preoccupation with the "other" endures, which leads to the placing of blame for negative outcomes. Fixation on the enemy's moves can lead to mutual arms races and weapons-spending (see Sislin and Pearson, 2006). In fact, any efforts to compromise or come to terms with their opponent will become inconsistent with what is expected of them, a form of what psychologists refer to as "cognitive dissonance" (Kriesberg, 1998).

As a result, enduring rivalries are more prone to recurring violent outbreaks or future war, unless the cycles of fear, insecurity, and resentment can be broken, either through reconciliation (e.g., tit-for-tat) processes, or by third party peacekeeping where the parties are separated and isolated (e.g., Cyprus). Over time, as passions and memories cool and fade, or as new external preoccupations arise (such as the prospect of joining an organization such as the EU), the potential for renewed beneficial relations, as in trade and commerce, can be revived. Until that happens, however, the severity of enduring rivalries, as opposed to those that are isolated in occurrence, is likely to be high. In a study of civil conflict in Southeast Asia, Olson Lounsbery (2005) found not only that proto- and enduring rivalry dominates the intrastate violence landscape but also that some ongoing protorivalries are especially likely to become enduring in nature. Enduring rivals are also likely to experience full-scale civil war as opposed to lower levels of violence, which confirm the impact of changing party relations discussed above. Rivalry patterns are illustrated in Box 5.2.

BOX 5.2: A CASE IN POINT: THE PHILIPPINES

In the southern Philippines conflict involving the government and the various Muslim separatist groups predates Filipino independence, as is the case in many contemporary intrastate conflicts. During the period of colonial rule, both Spain and the United States attempted to subdue the predominately Muslim populations in the regions of Mindanao and the Sulu Archipelago, but both met with heavy resistance. Prior to the arrival of the Spanish, governance in the region had been established in the form of Islamic Sultanates, and thus the population had experienced and benefited from self-rule. Despite Muslim resistance and requests for independence, Mindanao and Sulu were passed to the Philippine legislature under US administration, allowing the Philippines to claim sovereignty over the region upon independence in 1946.

The government of the Philippines sought to better integrate the southern region of the country and created the Commission on National Integration in 1957, which identified Muslims as a national minority, thus providing scholarships to Muslim students. Muslims, however, resented being considered a minority and considered integration efforts a threat to their identity. The region remained, for the most part, determined to resist the government's efforts and claimed autonomy over its political, social, and cultural identity. Despite the government's interest in incorporating the southern Muslims into the Philippine nation, it did little to address issues of economic development. Compared to the north, the southern part of the country remained almost entirely underdeveloped.

During the period 1948–60, a significant population shift occurred. Large movements of settlers, predominately Christian, pushed south. Muslim claims to demographic dominance in the region became tenuous. This migration would continue throughout the 1960s, complicating later efforts by the government to provide some form of autonomy that would satisfy the Muslim population without threatening the security of the growing Christian population. By the end of the 1960s, the region was experiencing communal violence as these populations became involved in both land and political disputes.

Communal violence gave way to armed factional violence, which involved the government of the Philippines and its army in the wake of the Jabidah massacre of 1968, and was exacerbated by President Ferdinand Marcos's declaration of martial law in 1972 as Muslims refused government demands to turn in their firearms. The complexities of the conflict lay in the various rebel groups that emerged, all of which began their opposition to the government with secessionist claims. Further, these groups retained connections to the Malaysian region of Sabah (also predominately Muslim), through which Filipino armed factions were both trained and supplied weaponry, although these connections were later revoked when Sabah leaders made declarations against supporting secessionist movements. Other international actors such as Libya, led by Mu'ammer Qaddafi, objected to the Philippines' treatment of the Muslims in the south and began to apply pressure under the auspices of the Organization of the Islamic Conference, even to the point of threatening to place an oil embargo on the Philippines.

In addition to population and diplomatic support shifts, the strength of the rebel groups' resolve appears to have been challenged in the late 1970s as the Moro National Liberation Front (MNLF) became weakened by a large number of surrenders and splintering of groups, as discussed earlier in the chapter. At the onset of conflict, MNLF had enjoyed something of a strategic advantage over the governmental forces, which did not appear to be very organized or well motivated.

The Moro insurgency has formally involved four different identifiable armed factions. The original Moro opposition emerged in the form of the Muslim Independence Movement (MIM) calling for secession for Mindanao. MIM later became defunct when its leader, Datu Udtog Matalam, once governor of Cotabato province in Mindanao, became Marcos's presidential advisor on Muslim affairs, but not before young recruits from MIM branched off to form MNLF, claiming armed struggle to gain independence as their motivation. The actual date of MNLF's formation is not agreed upon (Buendia, 2005).

In the late 1970s, when MNLF began to discuss options for autonomy with the Philippine government, MNLF splintered. Led by Salamat Hashim, the "new MNLF" was formed, later to be called the Moro Islamic Liberation Front (MILF). In 1991 the Moro rebellion experienced yet another splinter group in the form of the Abu Sayyaf group (ASG). By 1996 Nur Misuari's original MNLF reached a negotiated settlement with the government of President Fidel Ramos, thus ending conflict with one faction of the Moro insurgency, although even Misuari would reappear later, first as a government negotiator for MILF and later as a belligerent when his position as governor of the "Autonomous Region in Muslim Mindanao" became threatened.

Population and power shifts, group splintering, various external actors, as well as various Filipino administrations have characterized the Filipino Mindanao insurgency, demonstrating how complex civil wars can become.

CIVIL WAR DURATION

Groups engaged in civil wars within a state are unavoidably prone to the potential for rivalry. The domestic players involved often come to have a relative familiarity and even share cultural similarities (e.g., Serbs and Croats, Sunnis and Shi'a), albeit with abundant misunderstandings and miscommunications. On the personal level, civil wars and civil disputes are already more intense, generally speaking, than their interstate counterparts (Miall, 1992), echoing the famous adage that fights *within* a family are the most severe fights. Those that persist and become enduring rivalries reach an even higher level of intensity (Olson Lounsbery, 2005). Given patterns of exploitation and further division between parties during the course of conflict, civil wars are likely to persist and endure. Indeed, the growth of global markets starting in the 1980s has fueled the arms and contraband trade, which has helped rebel groups maintain the funding they need to survive (Collier, Hoeffler, and Soderborn, 2004). Arms flow from one war to another through patterns of re-export via black markets, smuggling, and the exchange or capture of used equipment.

Thus, the average civil war duration has increased from below five years to almost 16 years for the period of 1945 to 1999 (Fearon, 2004), although a small subset of post-Cold War civil wars occurring in Eastern Europe tended to be shorter in duration (Collier, Hoeffler, and Soderborn, 2004). The factors that extend civil war duration, due to the many processes we have noted in this chapter, can be quite different from the factors that contribute to the onset of civil war (Elbadawi and Sambanis, 2000). Like initiating factors, however, several state, conflict, and international factors have been found to be linked to longer wars as well.

State Factors and Duration

As we have noted, the duration of civil war has been steadily increasing since World War II, coinciding with a rather dramatic increase in the number of civil war occurrences particularly beginning in the 1970s. It should be clear by now that rebel groups, at least in "nonfailing" states, face a distinct disadvantage relative to the power wielded by governments. As a result, a rebel group's ability to survive the first few months of war significantly influences the potential duration of that conflict, as well as the chances that such a group will prevail in the long run. The group's strategy, as in the use of guerrilla tactics, is simply to survive, or "avoid losing for a long enough period of time so that the accumulated costs of conflict for the government undermine its level of popular support and its ability to wage war" (Mason and Fett, 1996: 552). Rough or mountainous terrain has been thought to foster rebel groups' staying power (recall Fidel Castro's tactics while gaining power in Cuba in the 1950s and more recent Pakistani difficulties uprooting militants from the Afghan border region) by providing a physical environment conducive to attack and concealment. At times though, leadership and tactics, rather than terrain, will tell the tale, as government forces miss their chances to capture fleeing insurgents (note President Lincoln's chagrin at the repeated failures of Union army generals to follow up on their few battle successes in the early years of the US civil war).

The availability of resources has also been linked to longer civil wars (Fearon, 2004; Ross, 2004). For example, once rebel groups are able to capture or loot valuable economic resources, such as diamond mines, oil fields, or weapon stockpiles, their ability not only to survive but also to fund conflict escalation is dramatically improved, as has been seen in West and Central Africa.

Two other economic factors have been identified as impacting civil war duration as well. Kaufman (1996) has argued that it is very difficult to convince economically satisfied people to rebel against their government, presumably even in light of ethnic imbalances in political access or power. Aspects of "fiscal federalism" were identified by Yongo-Bure (2007) as leading to Sudan's long and bloody north-south civil war because certain parts of the country were systematically disadvantaged by government spending and investment patterns. This might have been true of the American north-south struggle as well.

On the whole, countries with extremely unequal distributions of wealth as measured by the Gini inequality coefficient (see the World Bank website at http://go.worldbank.org/3SLYUTVY00 for an explanation of this measure) have been prone to longer civil wars (Collier, Hoeffler, and Soderborn, 2004). Presumably, in such situations rebel groups engaged in the fight are not only economically dissatisfied but significantly so, thereby making the fight not only worth pursuing but pushing those involved to persist when, under more equitable conditions, others might resign. Similarly, states with higher per capita incomes tend to have shorter wars (Collier, Hoeffler, and Soderborn,

2004). This may have much to do with the state's capacity to carry the fight to the opposition, but it could also be related to the level of economic satisfaction influencing the persistence of the conflict.

We might further expect that a state's *regime type* would influence conflict duration. Autocratic regimes might be likely to come down hard on rising opposition, thus bringing about a swift end to rebellions. Whereas, we might also expect democratic regimes to engage in negotiation or dialogue more so than other regime types, potentially averting conflict escalation, or potentially dragging out the entire process of resolving the war (as electoral audiences must also be satisfied with the terms of settlement, for example). Elbadawi and Sambanis (2000) find that extremely autocratic regimes have civil wars of shorter duration, but the same cannot be said for democracies (Fearon, 2004).

The size of a state's population and other demographic patterns have also been linked to duration, with larger states experiencing longer wars (Collier, Hoeffler, and Soderborn, 2004). Yet, this finding is not supported when other factors are included in the analysis (Fearon, 2004). More populous states, such as India, can potentially have multiple armed rebellions occurring simultaneously, which might help to explain the discrepancy in findings regarding population (Collier, Hoeffler, and Soderborn, 2004). Certainly, civil war in the world's most populous state, between communist and nationalist forces in China, lasted some two decades in the 1930s and '40s, interrupted by the Japanese invasion before and during World War II, which saw the two sides turn to fight the outsiders (though not in a unified front). The civil war resumed after World War II with the communist side prevailing.

The composition of a state's population also needs to be considered in explaining civil war duration. When states are particularly polarized along ethnic dimensions, civil wars tend to last longer (Elbadawi and Sambanis, 2000). This finding, of course, is not surprising given our earlier discussion of conflict polarization tendencies once wars have begun. We might therefore expect that so-called ethnic wars, or those being fought along identity-based lines, have the tendency to last longer. Although Elbadawi and Sambanis (2000) found this to be the case, Fearon (2004) did not, suggesting that other factors are potentially more important predictors of civil war duration. However, Fearon (2004) did find that in ethnically heterogeneous (diverse) states, there is a slight tendency for civil wars to be lengthy. Others have found that states that are ranked in the middle between fully homogeneous and heterogeneous (i.e., receiving a score of 50 on a scale of 1 to 100) have longer civil wars (Collier, Hoeffler, and Soderborn, 2004), unless outside intervention snuffs out the war (Elbadawi and Sambanis, 2000).

Based on this and previous discussions, it appears that state societal composition can be exploited and can become increasingly polarized, thus making civil war both possible and potentially very lengthy (as has been seen in Sri Lanka). Efforts to exploit issues of identity can run into resistance, however, when populations tend to be better educated, making for shorter wars (Collier, Hoeffler, and Soderborn, 2004), though this finding may be more a function of per capita gross domestic product (i.e., overcoming poverty and lack of economic opportunity).

We have seen that access to resources affects the duration of civil war. One key resource for fighting, of course, involves the availability of and access to armament, which in turn can depend on converting other resources (money, goods) in order to acquire the arms through illicit or legal trade. When weapons are available, armed rebellion is more likely and easier to sustain. Once a group has made a war-enabling decision and followed through with that decision with armed action, the ability to acquire a steady supply of weaponry (including spare parts, ammunition, and "dual use" equipment that can be converted from civilian to military use, such as pickup trucks) will often coincide with the willingness of the participants to continue the fight, making longer wars more likely (Sislin and Pearson, 2001).

Indeed, the ebbs and flows of civil war can frequently be explained by the availability of armament supplies. This is one of the characteristics of civil wars that makes them quite different from their interstate counterparts. Availability to arms is likely to depend mostly on irregular channels, as weapons flow from one war to another and become available for local sale or barter. International legal norms work against rebellious groups within a state, unless the group can convince world powers and arms suppliers that they are exercising a legitimate right of self-defense. In order to gain access to arms, such actors usually must make purchases through the black (or gray, i.e., skirting regulations) market, through smuggling networks, and even sale by or capture from government forces. Nonstate actors typically do not have the availability of tax revenue with which to make such purchases, although some groups, such as the Sri Lankan Tamils, reportedly did progress to that point through the capture of territory and by having their ethnic kin living and working abroad.

The role that arms play in influencing civil war duration is not limited simply to their availability. The type of weapons utilized during the course of war appears to have an impact as well (Sislin and Pearson, 2001). Civil wars, for the most part, tend to involve more small or light ("man-portable") arms as opposed to major weapons such as heavy artillery, planes, ships, and tanks. Small arms and light weapons are likely to be sufficient for insurgents to sustain their struggles utilizing hit-and-run tactics. On the other hand, the war may end quickly when major weapons are used, usually by the government side under propitious circumstances. More likely in such situations, however, the government will be able to take advantage of their initial power and military advantage, but the insurgents can fight back through unconventional methods such as terror attacks against installations and high-value targets such as urban populations. Interestingly, Sislin and Pearson (2001) also found in their research on arms and civil war that the more a government imports arms, the longer the war will be. This may have to do with the longer wars requiring governments to replace diminishing weapons caches, and with complex arms races in enduring rivalries, such as in Sri Lanka.

Conflict Characteristics

The type of conflict or the goals of the rebellion appears to impact the duration of civil war. Conflicts involving separatist demands tend to be lengthy drawn-out affairs as nation-states struggle to maintain their territorial integrity (Balch-Lindsay and Enterline, 2000). These types of wars, as we have discussed, also tend to be more intense for the same reason. On the other hand, military coups (as when an army takes over a government) that result in civil war tend to end rather quickly, as do popular revolutions (Fearon, 2004). Both of these forms of war, if successful, result in a change in government rather than the potential creation of a new state.

Popular revolutions tend to involve "mass demonstrations in the capital city in favor of deposing the regime in power" (Fearon, 2004: 280). Such demonstrations, because they begin localized in or near the government center, can be put down rather quickly compared to a separatist-type conflict typically occurring in more distant and remote parts of the country. Successful popular revolutions may also be short in duration given the factor of mass participation coupled with the proximity of the conflict to the major power center of the nation's government, as the government itself crumbles.

Although coups and popular revolutions tend to be associated with shorter civil wars, conflicts involving what Weiner (1978) has termed "sons of the soil" tend to be longer (Fearon, 2004), much like separatist wars. Such conflicts involve ethnic minorities on the periphery of a state engaged in armed conflict against ethnic, politically dominant, majority groups encroaching upon their land and resources (e.g, the Philippines). The geographic location of the conflict can influence the length and pace of fighting in such situations. "Sons of the soil" wars are only responsible for a portion of what we call "identity-based" or "ethnic" wars. Although it may appear that ethnic or identity wars are longer in duration than ideological wars because rebel leaders are better able to maintain mobilization among their ethnic kin, Fearon was unable to confirm this expectation when controlling for other factors, including whether such wars could be considered "sons of the soil" wars (Fearon, 2004: 288).

International Factors

It should be clear at this point that civil wars are very much linked to their environment. Although some civil war participants view themselves as engaged in issues of domestic concern, various aspects of civil wars transcend borders to the extent that some have argued a "new class" of war has emerged involving transnational actors, as in the Iranian-Syrian linkage to the Hezbollah forces in Lebanon and the latter's ties to Hamas in Gaza (although this is certainly debated, see Kaldor, 2006; and Henderson and Singer, 2002). Regional and international influences on civil wars and civil war states, not surprisingly, have a significant impact on the dynamics of a conflict, and hence, its duration. As we know from our discussion in Chapter 4, civil wars frequently attract intervention by neighbors, major powers, or other interested parties. Many civil war researchers have explored the impact of intervention on the duration of conflict. As we would expect, the impact tends to vary depending on the conditions of the intervention, which parties are involved, and on whose behalf the intervention occurs. Questions of viability of the state's government (i.e., the potential for a "failed state") will also work to the advantage of international interveners supporting rebels or opposition groups.

First and foremost, civil wars that involve outside military and/or economic intervention tend to last longer in duration and are more intense (Regan, 2002). The majority of civil war interventions (95 per cent) tend to be military in nature or involve a mixed military and economic strategy (Regan, 2002: 29). The very act of another party intervening in a conflict, particularly in the case of military intervention, has the effect of expanding the conflict. Conflict expansion, a significant conflict dynamic, means that the intervener becomes a party and potential target in the dispute; thus there is at least one additional party that will need to be considered and consulted should attempts to resolve the dispute occur. It is unclear, however, whether intervention actually "causes" longer wars. Longer wars themselves may attract outside intervention as the international community becomes either drawn into the struggle for strategic purposes or intervenes in an effort to bring about an end to a long intense battle (Elbadawi and Sambanis, 2000; Regan, 2001).

Of course, we would expect that the target of the intervention would affect war duration (Olsson and Fors, 2004). In the initial stages of a full-fledged war, when the government typically holds the power advantage, an intervention on its behalf could potentially bring about a swift end to the fighting through a military victory over the less powerful rebels. We would also expect that interventions on behalf of rebel groups would lengthen wars, giving the rebellious actors a chance to maintain their struggle long enough to overcome their initial power disadvantages. The presence of a diaspora (i.e., a kindred identity group of a party to the conflict located in another country) has been known to increase rebel-group viability as well (DeRouen and Sobek, 2004).

On the other hand, systematic research efforts have not entirely supported such theoretical assumptions (Regan, 2001; Collier, Hoeffler, and Soderborn, 2004). For one thing, it matters whether pro-government interventions back popular or unpopular regimes. The latter would seem to be doomed to have disadvantages in war-making. It is also possible that countermeasures, such as counterintervention by the intervener's international rival, interfere with the linkage between intervention on behalf of one party and the predicted impact on the other party and on war duration. The USSR assisted North Vietnam to resist American intervention with arms such as improved anti-aircraft missiles, and the US returned the favor in Afghanistan by backing the rebels against the Soviet-backed government, thus prolonging the struggles in both cases. In fact, both intervention countermeasures (Balch-Lindsay and Enterline, 2000) and multiple interveners (Regan, 2001) have been associated with longer wars. Once again, such actions have the effect of adding additional parties to the conflict generally, making resolution more difficult (i.e., through conflict expansion). A further effect of these actions is to continue to fuel the conflict by supporting and maintaining parties that might otherwise suffer defeat (e.g., American clients in Afghanistan in the wars after 2001 had already suffered defeat in the prior Afghani civil war of the 1990s).

Intervention is not the only external factor to consider when exploring civil war duration. Other regional and international influences can play a significant role in deterring continued war, or escalating a conflict that may otherwise have ended. One of these influences is the presence of other wars in the region. When a civil war state has a neighbor that is also experiencing civil war, a lengthy conflict is likely (Balch-Lindsay and Enterline, 2000). In such a situation, conflicts tend to fuel one another. Arms traffic tends to be active, and neighboring countries have a difficult time assisting governments in the pursuit of fleeing guerrillas, thus creating safe havens and rebel camps. This is also the case when a neighbor to a civil war state is experiencing an interstate war or a militarized interstate dispute. The civil war at issue is likely to be longer in duration (Balch-Lindsay and Enterline, 2000) for much the same reasons. Wars are contagious and expansive, making resolution more difficult when larger regions are unstable.

When, on the other hand, the civil war state itself becomes the target of a militarized interstate dispute, the civil war will likely end sooner (Balch-Lindsay and Enterline, 2000), even if it involves only temporary accords to fight against the outside invaders, such as Japan in China. We might attribute this finding to something of a "rally around the flag" effect. Although internal groups may still feel disgruntled and belligerent, support for the cause may diminish as the external threat becomes temporarily more significant. As a corollary to these findings, hard-pressed civil war parties may try to seize on a foreign dispute to reunite the country. In 1865 the South sought to convince President Lincoln that the US civil war should be shelved in order to jointly attack the French in Mexico, a proposal that Lincoln firmly refused.

Clearly, civil wars are dynamic events and those dynamics have significant and varied impacts on how long any particular war may last. Parties change over time, as does the environment of the conflict itself. Individual leaders may come and go, some more confirmed to fight to the death ("risk-acceptant," or confirmed/entrapped), others more prone to negotiate ("risk-averse," or confident/conciliatory). The processes of conflict produce many anticipated and unanticipated consequences, making resolution both interesting and challenging.

CONCLUSION

As we discuss the processes and consequences of civil war, it is clear that attention must be focused on preventing them, shortening them, and on reconstruction in their wake. This means that early-warning measures may be necessary to promote negotiation on hastening the pace of reforms that may satisfy minority and ethnic identity group concerns before the situation gets out of control (see Figure 5.1). Such measures during war must deal with and offset the escalatory factors we have discussed that tend to lengthen the conflict, measures such as restricting arms flows, denying illegal trade in commodities such as diamonds and drugs, and restraining potential interveners and turning them instead into promoters and guarantors of peace initiatives (gestures) and accords. Mediation and other third party assistance (in the form of security guarantees, financial assistance, and membership in trade blocs, for example) can be offered as incentives to parties to put down their arms. Timely assistance given to enlightened governments may help in the processes of reform and negotiation. Certainly, there must be threats of international sanctions (e.g., military intervention, nonrecognition, or trade embargoes) against parties that commit excesses and atrocities such as genocidal attacks and "ethnic cleansing." We consider these and other approaches taken to ameliorate the probability and effects of civil war in the next chapter.

NOTES

1. Even an authoritarian type of democracy such as Pakistan moved to stabilize its domestic politics by negotiating a ceasefire and a relative autonomy arrangement with militant Pushtun tribal groups operating in the western border area with Afghanistan in 2008, much to the displeasure of the United States, which wanted harsh repressive tactics used to avert cross-border Islamist raids and support for Taliban forces in Afghanistan (see Khan and Gall, 2008).

2   The question of individual "agency" in accounting for war is, of course,

hotly debated among historians. Some question whether large social and economic forces, such as those of the 1850s in pre-civil-war America, largely condition the outcomes and the "descent" into war, or whether individual leaders can have decisive effects in averting or turning the tide away from war. Certainly, for a long period in the early- to mid-1800s, notable "compromisers" prevailed in creating bargains and averting bloodshed over the extension of slavery. It could be that institutional conditions, such as the breakdown of one major political party, the Whigs, swamped such compromisers in a tide toward secession and war by 1860. Did it matter whether Abraham Lincoln moved to fortify and regain Fort Sumpter as war approached, or whether a Democratic president might have struck yet another accommodation with Southern leaders? Was the Union on irredeemably shaky ground by that time or could a leader of "vision" have made a difference? Such debates are discussed by Wood (2008). We structure our action-reaction model on the premise that leaders nearly always have choices—some perhaps quite unpalatable—and that the conditions they face do condition both the "occasion for decision" and the range of choice perceived to be available, as well as the expected consequences.

3   Using the Vietnam War as an example, although postconflict experiences varied among the war's veterans, those who witnessed or committed acts of abusive violence seemed to experience higher levels of PTSD (Laufer, Gallops, and Frey-Wouters, 1984).

4   The Jordanian-Israeli working relationship included the so-called Black September Jordanian army attacks on Palestinians in Jordan in 1970 with Israel's commitment to protect Jordan from Syrian or other Arab reprisals. The result was a spread of new civil wars and violence. There occurred a mass expulsion of Palestinians from Jordan to Lebanon, thus straining the political capacity of that divided nation, fomenting both the Lebanese civil war and Palestinian resort to global terrorism (i.e., airline hijacking) in order to gain influence against the Israelis. Israel responded with the eventual Israeli occupation of southern Lebanon, and finally to an all-out Israeli invasion of Lebanon in 1982. A bloody US Marine intervention in Lebanon took place to separate the combatants and facilitate the Palestinian Liberation Organization's (PLO) transfer to Tunisia, opening the door to Lebanese terror attacks on the American Marine barracks. Thus, as we have noted previously, the effects of one civil war can have far-ranging effects on regional politics and can spark both other civil wars and outside interventions.

CHAPTER SIX

The Resolution of Civil Wars

"The quickest way of ending a war is to lose it."

—George Orwell

Wars, whether international or civil, tend to end in certain patterns: a nearly complete military victory by one side (the government or rebellious group); or a negotiated settlement short of each side's maximum demands after some degree of mutual attrition in the fighting. Civil wars can also result in inconclusive and recurring episodes of fighting, stalemate, or exhaustion, sometimes even within what we have come to know as tragically "failed states" with no coherent governing authority (e.g., for long periods in Somalia). It is interesting to note when one sort of ending, or nonending in the case of recurring warfare, is most likely, under what circumstances, and with what probable implication for subsequent social relations.

The American Civil War ended in a harassed Confederacy finally throwing in the towel in surrender at Appomattox Courthouse, Virginia, in 1865. A series of decisive battles and widespread military destruction of Southern towns and farms had finally disrupted and exhausted Southern resources and available manpower after five grueling years of war. There is little indication that serious efforts were made to negotiate a peace that would have left the Confederacy intact. The surrender was basically unconditional, though, except for slavery, President Abraham Lincoln had indicated that the peace would be a forgiving one (he, of course, did not survive to keep that promise). Similarly, in our own time in another former British colony, an overwhelmed regional Biafran army in Nigeria, having fought for independence for three years and gaining only limited outside backing from one major state—France (which had provided only enough aid to prolong the war in the hopes of pressuring a negotiated settlement)—surrendered abruptly to Nigerian government forces (backed with arms from Britain, the Soviet Union, and Italy) in January 1970 (O'Connell, 1993).

Some wars end short of such decisive outcomes. Parties may explore peace terms with each other tentatively or diligently either once or repeatedly over time. Third parties may exert pressure on the warring sides to settle, might offer "good offices" to help mediate the outcome, or may even offer to underwrite the settlement in the form of security guarantees and aid to one or both sides. In addition, a *lack* of third party intervention can also be decisive, as seen in Biafra's lonely fate and in Britain and France's decision not to support the Confederacy in the American Civil War; nonintervention may have foreordained the ultimate outcomes and defeats in these struggles.[1]

Another form of outside intervention is support for a "peace process," and this too might, given proper timing, facilitate negotiated outcomes, especially if significant international opinion is represented. In the 2002–04 negotiations to end Sudan's decades old north-south war, Kenya offered timely "good offices" and hosted the talks, while Norwegian, British, and American observers added to the international encouragement. Among the topics crucial to the war's settlement that had to be treated at length in the talks were the government's attempts to impose Islamic law on the whole nation; integrating rebel leaders into the government structure; arranging the sharing of resources and wealth; and providing security through the protection of human rights and a ceasefire (Globalsecurity.org, "Sudan People's Liberation Army [SPLA], Sudan People's Liberation Movement [SPLM]"). Clearly, the positive or negative outcome of talks can depend on the complexity and priority of issues to be resolved.

Ironically and sadly, once a north-south agreement was reached in Sudan, certain western groups in the country evidently felt short-changed and initiated a rebellion in Darfur that was then opposed with brutal force by the Sudanese government and associated Janjaweed militia forces, thus extending the country's and the region's misery several more years and leading to outside humanitarian intervention attempts by regional and world organizations (i.e., both governmental and nongovernmental organizations—see Chapter 4).

Thus, a variety of factors can cohere in determining which path a war takes toward conclusion. Civil war seems to be an especially "tough nut to crack" when it comes to finding settlements. For one thing, as we saw in the last chapter, such wars tend to last considerably longer than international wars. In US congressional testimony in 2006, political scientist James Fearon noted, "For civil wars since 1945, the average duration has been greater than 10 years, with fully half ending in more than seven years (the median)" (Fearon, 2006). Indeed, the last chapter showed that the trajectory of conflicts over such long periods are difficult to predict, as for example factions may be "co-opted" or given a place in the ruling circles, thus being induced to give up on a relatively small-scale revolt. In another scenario, the revolt could be crushed and the rebels dispersed within the country or abroad. Funding and the availability of armament or ammunition from abroad may also dry up with the occasional effective embargo.

In this chapter we will explore some of the factors most important to civil war outcomes. We will also explore the types of conflict resolution measures and peace processes that seem to best withstand the test of time, and offer some possible policy suggestions about conclusively ending wars.

PATTERNS OF CIVIL WAR SETTLEMENT: VICTORY VERSUS NEGOTIATION

In his initial empirical study of civil war conclusions, Licklider (1995) found that the vast majority appeared to be settled by conclusive military victories, much like the US civil war demonstrated.[2] Negotiated settlements were much rarer. Walter (1997: 335) concurs, noting that, "between 1940 and 1990 55 percent of interstate wars were resolved at the bargaining table, whereas only 20 percent of civil wars reached similar solutions" (Walter cites support for this finding from other analysts as well).

Fearon (2006) sustains these findings while distinguishing between struggles for control of the central state and struggles for ethnic separation or secession. Indeed, "fully three quarters of civil wars fought for control of the state end with a decisive military victory," a figure even higher than for civil wars as a whole. Power-sharing arrangements dividing up control of the central government were uncommon, coming in at only about 17 per cent for wars fought over central state control (as in El Salvador, 1992, South Africa, 1994, and Tajikistan, 1998). According to Fearon (2006), negotiated outcomes rise to about a third in cases involving a struggle over secession or greater autonomy. Thus, it appears easier for warring parties to contemplate agreement if it involves a form of divorce from each other than if they are meant to remain under the same roof.

When civil wars do end, therefore, the pronounced tendency has been for military victories by either the government or the insurgents, often, as Walter notes, involving "the extermination, expulsion, or capitulation of the losing side" (1997: 335). Fearon (2006) maintains that these decisive victories are frequently (about 50 per cent of the time) due to the provision or withdrawal of support (diplomatic and perhaps military) to one side or the other by key foreign powers or patrons.

Despite these stark figures and developments, the post-Cold War era has seen an increase in both the number of attempts to negotiate outcomes to civil wars. With the relaxing of bipolar tensions, the international system has been better able to avoid zero-sum (all or nothing) struggles, spurred on by outside powers, in civil war states that tended to interfere with resolution efforts. Achieving a negotiated outcome, however, continues to remain elusive in many cases and a precarious task in others.

If we look to the question of what best predicts military versus negotiated outcomes,[3] we find that both the structure of the international environment and also the type of regime in the country appear to have much to do with the outcome (Pearson et al., 2006: 123). Civil wars that began during the Cold War seemed considerably more likely to end in military victory than in negotiated settlements, as compared to post-Cold War civil strife. This reflects Fearon's findings of some relative decline in military victories after 1989 for the reasons noted above. When the most recent government in a civil war state was reasonably democratic as opposed to authoritarian, the conflict was also more likely to end in a negotiated settlement.

The roles of conflict duration and intensity appear to be significant for predicting not necessarily the success rate of settlements but rather the tendency toward either military or negotiated outcomes themselves; higher conflict intensity tends to correlate with military outcomes, and longer duration, perhaps reflecting time for repeated talks, relates to an increased prospect of negotiated outcomes. Hartzell's work (2001) also shows that lower intensity and drawn-out conflicts may be more amenable to negotiation.

Controversy still persists about these patterns and also about the role of third parties in conflict outcomes. Indeed, Walter (1997) puts her finger on a paradox in the politics of ending civil wars: *attempts* to find solutions short of fighting to the bitter end are not as rare as *success* in negotiations. For one reason or another, warring parties frequently attempt to settle their disputes, even overcoming ethnic hatreds and bitterness and reaching at least limited or temporary agreement. Between 1940 and 1990, Walters notes that 42 per cent of the 41 civil wars she studied saw some formal peace negotiations, and that 94 per cent of these agreed on at least one ceasefire accord (Walter 1997: 337). Fearon (2006) agrees that, "negotiations on power-sharing are common in the midst of civil war, as are failed attempts to implement such agreements, often with the help of outside intervention by states or international institutions." Licklider (1995) found that military victories are more likely than negotiated outcomes to result in genocide or politicide (i.e., the elimination of political leaders or governments).

What then impedes a greater success rate? Both Fearon and Walter cite distrust within and between the warring factions, especially over whether principles agreed on paper will actually be observed. Walter (1997: 358) goes on to highlight her case findings about the importance of third party security guarantees in facilitating successes: "In every case in which a guarantee was offered, the two sides managed to reach and implement a lasting negotiated settlement. When no guarantee was offered, negotiations almost always broke down." This puts a great onus on third party guarantors for peace pacts. Walter attributes the frequent failure of negotiated settlements not so much to an unwillingness to compromise, but rather to a distrust regarding the outcomes when no enforceable security guarantees exist. Why else would parties balk at laying down their arms and entering the country's political process? Negotiation success, she argues, has far less to do with the parties' relative strengths or stalemates (as proposed by scholars such as Zartman) or the relative skill of mediators as it has to do with finding ways to enforce the peace.

In terms of Walter's pertinent points about security guarantees, note that depending on the conditions in the state itself, peace enforcement may strain the capabilities of even the greatest military powers (witness the US, British, and NATO struggles in Iraq and Afghanistan). Not only may Walter's suggested solution require sustained commitment to intervene on a relatively large scale in a supposedly "sovereign" state and involve some form of occupation among hostile populations but it also appears to downplay the role of other issues related to peace and trust-building: (1) the substance of the conflict; (2) the characteristics of the warring sides, including the capacity of the government to govern; (3) the sustainability of the combat; (4) economic and political power-seeking behavior; and (5) the agenda of issues on the negotiating table.

Research findings have varied on the question of why accords fail so frequently and why parties so often resume fighting. Walter's (1997) answer is quite clearly connected to relational insecurities as reflected in distrust and the lack of firm enforceable guarantees. Others, however, note that ceasefire agreements themselves, rather than serious attempts to reach peace, can at times be purely tactical moves designed to buy time to regroup, replenish arms, heal wounds, and renew the struggle. Policy-makers have noted varied prerequisites for successful accords, including going beyond merely violence cessation to other considerations such as developing reliable national institutions, especially in the area of administration of justice and the police. This may be particularly problematic for poorer countries. Thus, it appears that the answer to why negotiations fail may be more complicated than merely third party guarantees, and may include characteristics such as national and group scarcities, poverty levels and prior war disruption, along with lack of state capabilities. Indeed, the factors underlying civil war settlement can be grouped into three main headings:

- the nature of the conflict itself;
- domestic conditions in the disrupted state, such as the state of the police and justice system; and
- the nature of the end of hostilities, whether by victory or negotiation (see Pearson et al., 2006), and the degree of issue resolution.

Various data "recounts" and studies over different numbers of years and types of internal wars have shown many nuances regarding the propensity to negotiate and success in doing so, sometimes resulting in contrary findings on these matters. Although security guarantees appear very important, one may need to understand other issues in accounting for negotiated settlements, such as the identity and characteristics of the warring parties, their capabilities, available wealth, the degree of the government's repressive policies (which can spur ongoing civil unrest), armament and resources, and the broad role of outside interveners in stimulating or retarding the combat. As certain analysts have noted, each war is somewhat unique in the combination of factors and forces at work, and thus so too are the requirements and circumstances for a viable peace.

Nature of the Conflict

Among the main determining factors of civil war outcomes are conflict characteristics such as the war's duration or intensity. King (1997) notes that the structure of conflict itself, apart from the parties' emotions, beliefs, or goals, helps account for the persistence of a civil war beyond the point where it would appear reasonable and necessary to settle. The conflict structure would entail the political issues and factional array of the parties, such as Fearon's distinctions between government control and secession motives, thus alerting would-be interveners to the complications they may encounter in trying to sort things out and guarantee security, for instance.

Similar to duration and issue or factional complication, analysts have looked at the killing rate or "intensity" of violence in order to predict how and when civil wars end. Apparently, low-intensity fighting over a long duration, as opposed to very bloody fighting, has a more conducive effect on reaching ultimately successful negotiations. Regan (2001) notes that intensity tends to predict third party intervention success. Certainly, the American Civil War, which ended in a Confederate military defeat rather than a negotiated outcome, wrought unprecedented levels of human carnage (617,000 died, a war death toll approximately equal to all other US wars combined; see PBS, "Judgment Day") due to the mechanization and industrialization of weaponry in the nineteenth century.

Perhaps contrary to expectations, however, Mason, Weingarten, and Fett (1999) find that higher casualty rates generally tend to correspond with rebel victories, reducing the probability of governmental victory or negotiated settlements. They argue (1999: 239) that the main factors affecting settlement involve the parties' declining estimates of the likelihood of victory, the rising costs of conflict, the estimates of time required for victory, and the increased valuation of settlement versus victory.

Thus, both the type of conflict underway and its dynamic effects on the parties' perceived prospects (on dynamics, see Chapter 5) seem to affect negotiation possibilities. Conventional wisdom suggests that so-called ethnic conflicts would be more difficult to negotiate than other types, since in such disputes, groups' interests are tightly associated with their very identity, something not open to negotiation. On the other hand, ideological conflicts, though certainly challenging, would presumably leave more negotiating "room" in which to maneuver. Parties may agree to take their ideological fights to the political arena rather than the battlefield.

While it is intriguing to speculate on the effects of different types of conflict, the findings of various studies appear somewhat contradictory. DeRouen and Sobek (2004) indicate that the type of war indeed relates to the probability of rebel victories, though Mason, Weingarten, and Fett (1999) find no such relationship. It also seems plausible that the reasons for which parties go to war (see Chapters 1 and 2) will strongly affect the ease with which they can extricate themselves from the combat. Complex and ambitious goals (such as redistribution of wealth or complete independence) would appear more difficult to resolve short of total victory than would more limited and modest aspirations. An outcome that did not achieve well-advertised goals would be difficult to sell to the leaders' constituents, although we might in part expect the connection between goal achievement and conflict outcome to be a function of conflict duration. Initial goals may change over long periods of struggle, hardening or becoming less compelling. The pure length of combat and the resulting devastation may impact what participants are willing to settle for.

There is disagreement in the civil war literature on how big a role such motivational factors play in the success or failure of negotiations. While analysts such as Walter (1997, 2002) may downplay the importance of goals in settling disputes, it appears worth examining the question in some depth.[4] For example, Fearon's data, as we noted earlier, seem to indicate an important distinction between struggles for control of the central government versus secession versus local autonomy campaigns. Negotiated outcomes seem quite rare in cases of central power struggles, presumably due to distrust among the parties that their security or prosperity could be maintained if the other party controlled the government. Fearon found more frequent negotiated settlement in separation or partition struggles. However, if insurgents desire secession and a separate country, as they did in the US civil war, in Biafra, and in Sri Lanka, the prospect of successful negotiation may become rather remote. It would require either compromising on these goals or dividing the country's territory, a prospect not very palatable to many if not most ruling governments (Mikhail Gorbachev did countenance the dismemberment of the Soviet Union as preferential to potential civil war in the late 1980s). Vasquez (1993) has noted that, in general, territory is one of the key issues leading states to war.

If, again contrary to Fearon, the insurgents in a civil war campaign for local autonomy, or other forms of concessions and reforms within the single state, the fight to the finish may be less frequent. Structurally, there is more potential "common ground" for a negotiated settlement, provided that the government responds in a timely fashion with the necessary concessions. The historical record on timeliness of concessions is not especially good, however, and the more a rebellion brings harsh reprisals by the government, resulting in civilian casualties and hardships (such as forced population resettlement), the brighter the prospects might seem for the insurgents to prolong the war, provided they have the personnel, the sanctuaries, and the resources to do so. Thus, the "window of opportunity" for reform often closes and the rebels may opt instead for outright secession.

Domestic Conditions

Various theorists hypothesize that state characteristics and the type and capability of a country's government will relate to its viability, its decisiveness and effectiveness, and the final outcome of civil conflicts. Mason, Weingarten, and Fett (1999) think the size of the government's forces affect the probability of victory, as opposed to negotiated settlements. Fearon (2004), on the other hand, finds evidence that militarily stronger governments are more likely to negotiate outcomes as they can more easily live with the terms.

Other state characteristics have also been found to be either weakly or strongly related to ongoing civil wars. Based on a study of civil wars and insurgencies from 1945 to 1999 (involving 100-plus annual battle deaths cumulative to over 1,000), Fearon and Laitin question the prevailing notion that ethnic and religious diversity has made countries more prone to civil war in the post-Cold War period. Ethnic and political grievances may be linked to these wars as well as to nonwar situations; the deciding factor on whether war breaks out and continues may have more to do with the geography, topography, poverty, and political instability of the country and its environs. These environmental and underlying factors, including the overall effects of decolonization creating weak and disrupted states, condition whether, in today's world, an insurgency breaks out, whether it can be sustained (e.g., in mountain and forest hideouts or in rural guerrilla raids), and whether terms of settlement are seriously sought.

> "Grievances such as economic inequality, lack of democracy or civil liberties, or state discrimination against minority religions or languages are less effective predictors of civil conflict than weak states marked by poverty, large size and instability, Fearon and Laitin explained." (Trel, 2002)

The Nature of the End of Hostilities

In terms of negotiated outcomes, we may wonder whether the negotiations for conflict settlement in a civil war are largely spontaneous between the parties themselves, or whether they are more or less imposed by outside powers and parties. One may be able to predict a greater negotiation success rate if the parties themselves are ready for settlement—the notion that Zartman tried to capture in his concept of conflict "ripeness" for settlement. Yet, the degree to which outside parties either make it "worth the parties while" to reach agreement, by offering inducements such as foreign aid and security guarantees, or penalize the parties for nonagreement by levying sanctions and boycotts, can be crucial in swinging the balance in negotiation toward agreement. So-called coerced settlements (i.e., those involving significant third party threats or pressure for parties to come to terms) do not appear to predict either settlement duration or success (Pearson et al., 2006), although there were only a few settlement cases that could actually be considered coerced during the time period of 1945–2000.

Military intervention by individual third parties, for example, as measured by Regan (2002), has a discernable though relatively weak effect on boosting the chances for rebel victories and a more robust effect on promoting negotiated outcomes. Intervention, presumably on the government side, does not appear to consistently increase chances of government victories. Intervention itself, of course, is a complicated phenomenon, consisting of various alternative modes (military, economic, diplomatic), and replete with cases of "counterintervention" of various sorts. Under certain circumstances, timely arms shipments to governments or insurgents, for example, can tilt the outcomes. Note the failure of the US to increase the viability of the South Vietnamese government during the 1960s and 1970s, a period that also witnessed Russian and Chinese aid and *matériel* to the more successful North Vietnamese. Similarly, the Soviet failure to sustain the favored Afghani government in Kabul during the 1980s was affected by American assistance to anti-Soviet mujahadeen fighters (including Osama bin Laden). These were cases of largely unilateral governmental intervention or counterintervention. Meanwhile, multilateral intervention by the UN appears to work somewhat against decisive government victories and decidedly in line with ultimate rebel victories.

A further factor conditioning the success of settlements has to do with the role of "spoilers" or "rejectionists," i.e., those who refuse to participate in a settlement or actively work against it. In the confusing Darfur struggle that began in 2003, for example, pitting so-called Arab Sudanese herdsmen and the government against mostly settled Sudanese "African" rebels (unlike the north-south civil war in Sudan, both sides in Darfur were mainly Muslim), most of the parties came to an internationally brokered agreement at Abuja, Nigeria, in May 2006. Under the agreement, the agriculturalist rebel forces would reintegrate into Sudanese politics and the government would call off its support for marauding Janjaweed militia fighters who would demobilize. However, some few but active rebel groups (again illustrating that various sides in wars are not necessarily monolithic) refused the deal at the last minute and, fearing that they would not gain sufficient land and protection in the bargain, held up the peace accord. The situation was eventually referred to the UN Security Council, which by November 2006 had passed a peacekeeping resolution that, through additional international pressure, was finally accepted by the government (though the fighting and killing continued).

Thus, bringing all relevant factions into agreement can be a telling and difficult challenge, and even relatively small parties can, through strategic continued violence, impede settlements and rekindle warfare (on ways to manage or overcome spoilers, see Stedman, 1997). The ambiguous nature of rebel groups often makes it difficult to bring relevant parties to the table, even if those parties can be identified (see Box 6.1).

BOX 6.1: CASE IN POINT: DARFUR

Peace negotiations scheduled to take place in Sirte, Libya, in October 2007 between rebel leaders in Darfur (see Box 4.5) and the Sudanese government were impeded by factional disputes. A conflict in which two primary rebel groups (Sudan Liberation Army or Movement [SLA/M] and Justice and Equality Movement [JEM]) opposed the government, and the Janjaweed experienced significant group splintering as the opposition struggled for power; factionalism emerged in light of a vast geographical landscape coupled with tribal loyalties. The result was the proliferation of rebel groups numbering near 28 (according to a United Nations count). Getting all such groups to attend the Sirte negotiations proved unrealistic.

Although seven rebel leaders did attend the talks, those that made their way to Sirte were "dogged by questions about where the big guys are, such as Abdel Wahid el-Nur, a founding father of Darfur's rebellion, and Khalil Ibrahim, the commander of one of the strongest rebel armies" (Gettleman, 31 October 2007). Both of these leaders boycotted the talks. Regardless, it is becoming evident that with significant fractionalization, the "big guys" may not be "big" anymore. In reference to Wahid, for example, "he may still be popular in the squalid displaced-persons camps across Darfur, but he does not command mass numbers of troops anymore. Actually, because of all the factionalization, nobody does" (Gettleman, 31 October 2007).

With so many opposition leaders, it is not surprising that creating a unified front in order to engage in effective negotiations with the government became problematic. In the October 2007 talks, those leaders that did attend were stymied by their inability to put forth a cohesive message, but also by their continued marginalization. "Even more frustrating [than working with the many factions], several rebels said, was the fact that nothing they have said or done has gotten the applause or headlines that the Sudanese government scored when it announced on Saturday a unilateral cease-fire in Darfur" (Gettleman, 31 October 2007). This problem is exacerbated by the rebel groups' inability to trust the government, including any declaration of a ceasefire, given the atrocities committed in Darfur and the government's poor track record when it comes to upholding ceasefires.

The October 2007 talks demonstrated the challenge of getting rebel groups to come to the table, particularly when splintering had occurred. Further, the experience that those that did attend had was unlikely to make them the first in line in subsequent rounds of discussion.

Source: BBC (29 October 2007); see also Gettleman (31 October 2007).

FACTORS ASSOCIATED WITH SETTLEMENT SUCCESS

What then have we learned from our review of factors associated both with negotiated and military outcomes and their respective success rates? Clearly, each civil war is somewhat unique in causal factors, numbers of participants, level of fighting, issues in dispute, geography and topography, and roles of neighbors and outside parties (intervening or not). Understanding trends and commonalities among wars allows for more productive and effective policy-making. As a result, we may ask what circumstances correspond most closely to the success in reaching negotiated outcomes, as opposed to fighting to the finish, along with the ultimate consequences of negotiating the outcomes versus the occurrence of outright victories. In other words, was the country or region in question conspicuously better off and more peaceful with one form of settlement over another? By better understanding the effectiveness and consequences of negotiation we can better gauge the amount of international effort that could productively be devoted to encouraging this form of civil war settlement. Among the factors to be considered in managing the conflict "end game" are the type, degree, and timing of outside intervention; the diplomatic approach to the conflict; the methods available to promote ceasefires and translate them into viable settlements; the provisions of settlement that ultimately lead to greater stability and security in and around the state; and the prerequisites for postconflict peacebuilding measures to seal the peace.

Earlier we noted the pronounced tendency for most civil wars to end with military victories, though the pattern may be changing over time and with certain improvements in fostering peace talks. Toft (2006) has succinctly summarized the implications of tendencies toward militarily dictated rather than negotiated outcomes:

> In a negotiated settlement, warring factions agree both to end violence and to become partners in a new government. Although negotiated settlements are the most popular policy option (promising high short-term benefits and low risk), they may not be best if we want a permanent settlement to civil war. Negotiated settlements have ended about one-fifth of all civil wars since 1940 and they are two and half ... times more likely to break down than military victories. The probability of failure is even greater for identity-based civil wars ended by negotiated settlement.

Research has shown that when negotiations do produce results, certain provisions of settlement agreements can be more crucial than others in accounting for lasting success—for example in precluding a resumption of fighting a few years down the road. Hartzell, Hoddie, and Rothchild (2001) found that, at least for the large-scale conflicts they studied, provisions for territorial autonomy for ethnic minorities plus an active role for third party guarantors of the agreement were especially important provisions in fostering success.

As with factors predicting the type of conflict outcome—negotiations versus conquest—conflict characteristics, particularly conflict duration and intensity, are also likely to play a role in settlement success, i.e., the prospect that agreements will hold. Perhaps contrary to expectations about the buildup of bitterness in long wars, Doyle and Sambanis (2000) associate longer conflict duration with greater success of peacebuilding (i.e., the restoration of positive and trusting relations and institutions) and fewer war recurrences after the conflict. The parties involved presumably have suffered more losses and higher costs over time and are readier to accept terms of settlement and rebuilding.

Hartzell, Hoddie, and Rothchild (2001) tend to confirm the importance of duration in predicting at least the short-term success of peace agreements for full-scale civil wars over a five-year span after the fighting has ceased. These results for longer wars may themselves relate to the tendency for military victory by one side or the other to finally emerge over time, which, as Toft mentioned, is correlated with more lasting settlements. However, Mason, Weingarten, and Fett (1999) reported finding no such consistent duration effect. DeRouen and Sobek (2004), using the Doyle-Sambanis data, found that the longer the conflict, the less probability of a clear-cut government victory (at least the type seen at Appomattox Courthouse during the American Civil War), or of treaty-based outcomes, and the more likely the chance of ongoing conflict. Conversely, Pearson et al. (2006) found that the prospect of clear-cut military victory is increased in longer-term conflicts. Aside from measurement differences, conflicting results among these studies seem to indicate that factors other than mere duration play a significant role in determining conflict outcome.

Turning to the effect of the ravages of war and the intensity of fighting and killing, Hartzell, Hoddie, and Rothchild (2001) find that, perhaps due to bitterness and motives of revenge, higher intensity wars (in terms of average numbers of battle deaths over the war's duration) have a greater chance of resuming in the short run. Further, type of conflict has also been explored as a predictor of whether or not a war will end in negotiation and of how long the settlement will last. Hartzell, Hoddie, and Rothchild (2001) examine the importance of a conflict typology, including ethnic-based as opposed to political-economic motives. Again, they find only a relatively small relationship between these categories and successful peace agreements. Likewise, Doyle and Sambanis (2000) and Pearson et al. (2006) have tended to downplay the importance of factors such as states' ethnic diversity in accounting for settlement success, finding no correlation with sustained peace after wars. However, Collier and Hoeffler (2001) and Collier, Hoeffler, and Soderborn (2001) did indeed report finding such a statistical relationship.

Regan (1996) and Licklider (1995) also found that ethnic, religious, or ideological conflict issues can influence settlements and outcomes. Licklider asserts that ethnic, religious, or other forms of identity disputes tend to recur within five years more frequently than do other types of disputes such as socio-economic struggles. Evidently the embers of ethnic suspicion or hatred die hard even under the best of circumstances. Yet, Regan (along with Doyle and Sambanis [2000]), also notes that ethnic and religious conflicts may be relatively easier to resolve by outside intervention than other types such as ideological disputes, though Regan uses a shorter postconflict time period than Licklider's five-year range. Doyle and Sambanis (2000), on the other hand, find that peacekeeping efforts, such as multilateral forces dispatched by intergovernmental organizations (e.g., the UN), tend to be less successful in cases of identity disputes apart from the issues of ethnicity and religion.

It appears then that identifying a relationship between type of conflict and settlement success tends to be a function of both operational definitions and the time period under study, leading us to question the presence of a general relationship. Certainly, however, particular civil wars appear to be stymied in part due to the characteristics of the parties and their disagreements.

In addition to exploring type of conflict, others have also looked at domestic conditions related to settlement success, focusing on the pre-war or wartime regime status. Hartzell, Hoddie, and Rothchild (2001) highlight the importance of domestic regime type, finding that negotiated settlements are more successful (lasting) in countries where the pre-war regime or political tradition was largely democratic as opposed to authoritarian. Perhaps familiarity with the rule of law, human rights protections, and popular sovereignty help cushion the blows in settling violent disputes.

Pearson et al. (2006) find that democracies, as opposed to autocracies, are somewhat more likely to negotiate conflict termination rather than fight on to the bitter end. This would appear to correspond with historian Niall Ferguson's (2005) assertion that because the world is becoming more democratic, we are witnessing an actual decline in both international and "societal" (internal) wars over time (Ferguson's assertion is based on information obtained from the University of Maryland's Center for International Development and Conflict Management, which lists only eight societal wars as ongoing in the past 10 years). Yet, the events of 1865, along with the decades-long conflict in Sri Lanka and recurrent violence in Lebanon, as well as the empirical findings of DeRouen and Sobek (2004), cast doubt on the pivotal role of democracy in easing the negotiated end of civil war (remember that the extent of American "democracy" in 1865 was debatable, given a constitution leaving the majority of human inhabitants out of the political process in both the North and the South). As Lebanon shows, no matter what the regime type, civil war settlement agreements can also be jeopardized by disruptive interference in the state from neighboring states and foreign powers.

Ferguson himself (2005) posed an alternate explanation for the somewhat declining numbers and extent of civil wars in recent years (with a different slant than Fearon, he noted that very few of the post-1989 wars have lasted longer than seven years): "Many local people, regardless of foreign intervention, are simply opting for peace because they're sick of war." However, again such an impressionistic conclusion runs into contradictions. For example, in 1864–65 Americans were quite war-weary and sick of the carnage (Ayers, 2005), and yet no widespread grassroots or governmental peace initiative (discounting the mainly immigrant draft riots seen in New York and other Northern cities) of any substance emerged on either side. A contrary tendency has been noted by conflict theorists, namely a tendency toward overcommitment or "entrapment," as prior "sunken costs" (i.e., blood and treasure already invested in the conflict) lead the parties, essentially irrationally, to invest more (Pruitt, Rubin, and Kim 1994). This appears to be partly the case in Sri Lanka.

The post-1989 picture that Ferguson sees may therefore be an aberration, since Fearon showed that civil wars generally last longer than the War between the States and longer than the average interstate war. Thus, one may find the crucial effects of fatigue and disillusionment occurring much later on in the fighting than a mere five years after first engagement. It is also important to keep in mind the psychological changes occurring over generations of war, as noted in Chapters 2 and 5. Although populations may grow weary, the difficulties and conditions of living in situations of continual violence over a long period of time can result in spiraling violent action-reaction processes.[5]

A state's economic development or poverty levels are also arguably related to peacebuilding success. A state must have sufficient resources to satisfy the security and welfare demands of various segments of the population, as well as the political will to devote resources to those requirements as opposed to, for example, military pursuits. Empirical findings on the role of economic development and resources in the success of peacemaking are rather mixed. Jett (1999: 124) finds little effect, while Doyle and Sambanis (2000) find that economic development (measured by per capita electricity consumption) does facilitate post-war settlement success.

As might be expected, Doyle and Sambanis report that the fewer natural resources a state possesses, the less chance it has of successful peacekeeping. Yet, Jett (1999) argues, based on two African conflicts in Angola and Mozambique, that significant natural resources combined with extensive outside military intervention diminish successful outcomes, while fewer resources and less intervention improve the prospect of peace. African resources have proven to be a tempting and disruptive source of outside intervention and manipulation in civil wars, perhaps because African states themselves have been so weak and subject to corruption.

Therefore, to determine whether resources and wealth are wasted to a great extent one may want to add a measure of state corruption. Certainly, we know from civil wars and insurgencies, such as those in Lebanon, Afghanistan, Colombia and Burma, that corruption and black market economies (e.g., the drug trade) increase in disrupted conditions. Interveners attracted by potentially lucrative resource trade can severely hinder a state's recovery from war, as private and regional factions or warlords, arms dealers, and militia come to struggle over control of such trade, whether legal or through smuggling and black markets (a scene witnessed at various times in Afghanistan, for example). This trade may enable parties to buy arms and sustain their struggles longer. In fact, in such situations there is a noticeable and significant lack of what can be termed a "constituency for peace." If an end to war is to be achieved, major players have to buy into the resolution process. If, however, some players find a continuation of the war to be too lucrative to pass up, or too closely entwined with their own political survival and power, conflict resolution "spoilers" are likely to emerge. Hence, the "greed" theory put forth by Collier and Hoeffler (2001) and discussed in Chapter 2 can be very telling.

Another line of thought looks more closely at the circumstances surrounding the end of the conflict and the nature of those settlements. For example, Licklider (1995) investigated the relative staying power of peace through military victory as opposed to negotiated outcomes, generally finding, as Toft (2006) indicated, greater sustained effect for military outcomes. Yet, military outcomes are also more prone to genocide and mass murder than occurs in wars that are shortened by successful negotiation. Licklider also noted that ethno-political and identity wars more frequently reached lasting final military outcomes, while war tended to recur more often, despite military victories, in the small number of political and economic civil wars he examined.

Negotiation is often a delicate process because too heavy a hand, either by warring parties or by prospective mediators, can bring parties or factions to balk against what is seen as a dictated solution and to renew fighting in the near future. Indeed, it was reportedly the shah of Iran's pressure on Saddam Hussein in their border dispute of 1975—offering to withdraw Iranian support for rebellious Kurdish tribesmen in northern Iraq in return for Iraqi territorial concession on the Iran-Iraq border (the Shatt al'Arab waterway)—that led Saddam Hussein to launch war against Iran in 1979, following the fall of the shah, in order to regain that territory. That war also led to further bloodshed and atrocities between Baghdad and the Kurdish rebels within Iraq, including the famous poison gassing incidents.

In looking at the nature of settlement agreements, Hartzell, Hoddie, and Rothchild (2001) distinguished between substantive versus merely symbolic or rhetorical agreements, and they stressed the importance of building in provisions for territorial autonomy in bringing cases of factional or ethnic fighting to a successful conclusion. This relates to making groups feel safer and more secure in the outcomes, a point made by Walter (2002) in her "credible commitment theory" of settlement success, which identifies both third party security guarantees and power-sharing provisions. Hartzell (1999) also examined the question of formal power-sharing arrangements or power-balancing in fostering negotiation success. Controlling for other factors, Hartzell concluded that power-sharing and territorial autonomy were both important. Pearson et al. (2006), however, found a good deal less conclusive support for these provisions when using a more stringent definition of settlement and a lower battle death threshold. And as we have seen elsewhere in this book, there is some doubt about the efficacy of institutional arrangements such as federalism and formal power-sharing when it comes to averting civil war renewal. As part of the Dayton Peace Accords for Bosnia, there was supposed to be a functional revolving Bosnian presidency, with each ethnic community taking its turn. This arrangement, which has been nominally observed, has hardly resolved the problem of coming up with a government that could survive the withdrawal of foreign peacekeeping forces.

NATURE OF PEACE ENFORCEMENT

As noted, a number of scholars, and especially Walter (1997), stress the importance of third party peace enforcement or security guarantees. The success of agreements among wary parties can hinge on such reassurances. Indeed, Hartzell, Hoddie, and Rothchild (2001) found that the inclusion of third party enforcement provisions in negotiated agreements reduces the subsequent failure rate by some 98 per cent. Walter adds that the third party must not only be willing to support the provisions but must guarantee a commitment. The intervener's commitments and capabilities to carry them out, therefore, are thought to be crucial.

Pearson et al. (2006: 119–24) retested the Hartzell model of settlement success when applied to data on both large- and small-scale civil wars ending in either military victory or negotiated settlement, distinguishing between agreements that were essentially dictated by occupying powers as opposed to those reached by the parties themselves (i.e., coerced versus noncoerced). Their findings indicate that the only variable still statistically significant in predicting five-year success rates is third party guarantees or enforcement of the negotiated agreements. In fact, all cases with such a guarantor were rated as successes (meaning there was little or no violence over five years following the settlement). On the other hand, no effect could be gauged for the other variables that Hartzell found significant, such as conflict duration, intensity, or the presence of territorial autonomy provisions in settlements. Democratic regime status had only a relatively weak effect on the success of settlements. Hartzell's overall findings appear to be limited to full-scale civil wars (1,000-plus battle deaths) and to negotiated outcomes, as opposed to all internal wars (200-plus deaths) and military outcomes.

Getting back to negotiated outcome successes as related to third party guarantees, we do not yet know precisely who the best guarantors would be in any given circumstance: parties close to, or indeed involved in, the conflict or distant states; great powers or smaller neutral states; individual states or multilateral forces; or combinations of the above. For example, a regional intergovernmental organization, the Africa Union (AU), agreed to send troops to maintain a peace agreement in the Darfur region of Sudan in 2006 but lacked the capacity to send more than a few thousand forces—not nearly enough to cover the territory the size of the American state of Oregon. Urgent requests for additional UN troops followed as the ethno-political killing resumed, but these were met with resistance by the host Sudanese government, which feared too much intrusion on its sovereignty. The needed security arrangements were thus delayed and hindered for months while the killing continued.

Therefore, some parties may prefer the more decisive intervention commitments of individual nation-states to the improvised consensus arrangements of multilateral councils, but in doing so, they also open themselves up to potentially more intrusion by great powers, as well as to disagreements *among* the various powers. Employing regional guarantors also opens the state up to the foreign policy motives of their neighbors, motives that may seem less than altruistic as compared to those of distant neutral guarantors. Yet, neighbors as opposed to relative strangers may be more trusted by the various parties to the dispute, because of kinship ties or common culture. Thus, there is always a trade-off between enforcement and intrusion, between security, sovereignty, and dependence, between cultural cohorts and strangers.

This trade-off became evident in the civil conflict in Somalia in 2006 as Ethiopian troops were dispatched across the border to roust so-called Islamic Court forces from their strongholds in Mogadishu, the Somali capital; the titular Somali "government" (also composed of Islamic clans) had failed to display the ability to defend itself against the "Islamists." Somalia had been without effective governance for over a decade, and its people had suffered greatly. In fact, the Islamist parties reportedly had provided the first stable rule and relief for the citizens in years, though with a potential intent to impose strict Islamic law on the country (National Public Radio, 29 December 2006).

As the United States learned in 1993, when its UN-committed troops had to be withdrawn under fire, Somalia's civil wars tend to involve ethnic clans as much as well-developed political parties and ideologies, including any so-called Islamist ideology. However, the specter of a potential Islamic state on its border alarmed Christian Ethiopian rulers, whose own country was roughly 50 per cent Islamic with many of the Muslims living adjacent to Somalia or potentially sympathetic to Ethiopia's breakaway rival, Eritrea. Thus, Ethiopia chose to intervene in force to oust the Somali Islamists regardless of whether the titular government was fit to rule. In doing so, Ethiopia was supplied and encouraged by Washington, which also saw an alarming potential for another North African Islamist state to become linked to international terrorist organizations.

Thus, the complications of third party involvement become evident, on the one hand fostering certain outcomes, either military victories, stalemates, or negotiated settlements, while on the other hand reflecting potentially divisive regional and global interests and interference, often with uncertain prospects as to a lasting peace. Indeed, Ethiopia's neighbors and frequent opponents, Eritrea and Kenya, were also reportedly concerned by the Somali events in 2006, fearing potential Ethiopian expansion (prior regional wars had involved all of these states). The threat of a wider war loomed, while retreating Islamist clans sought to regroup and renew the civil war, deciding to now target Ethiopia if not the United States as well (National Public Radio, 29 December 2006).

Clearly, the empirical evidence associated with what brings about a negotiated settlement versus a military victory, as well as what it takes to achieve settlement durability, is contradictory. In an attempt to reconcile these contradictions, Suzuki has analyzed data on violent internal conflicts from 1946 to 2000, focusing specifically on the role of intervention, conflict characteristics, and state capacity (see endnote 2). His study and findings are presented in Box 6.2.

BOX 6.2: TESTING A UNIFIED MODEL OF CIVIL WAR OUTCOMES

Query: What factors are associated with particular civil war outcomes?

Spatial-Temporal Domain: 148 internal violent conflicts between 1946 and 2000.

Variables:

Outcomes: armed conflict outcome (government victory or rebel victory; negotiated settlement lasting at least six months; and ongoing conflict)

Predictors: Intervention Characteristics
  (1) third party intervention
  (2) UN intervention
    Conflict Characteristics
  (3) duration
  (4) intensity
  (5) conflict type
    State Capacity
  (6) regime type
  (7) army size

Data Sources: Data on internal conflicts compiled by Regan (2002, with a 200 battle-related death threshold) and supplemented by Pearson et al. (2006)

were used. The data on internal conflict outcomes were also checked against data compiled by Walter (2002) and Doyle and Sambanis (2006), as well as Fearon and Laitin's (2003) data.

Data Operations: In any given period, an armed internal conflict has one of three outcomes: victory by the government, victory by the rebels, and negotiated settlements. The comparison category is ongoing conflict. Conflicts were coded based on *Keesing's Contemporary Archive Reports* and compared against the dataset on civil war outcomes compiled by Walter (2002) and Doyle and Sambanis (2006).

Regarding third party intervention (predictor 1) and UN intervention (predictor 2), if an intervention in a conflict was observed within a given period, it was coded one; if it was not, it was coded zero. The data on third party intervention were taken from Regan (2002) and the data on United Nations intervention were based on Doyle and Sambanis (2006).

Conflict duration (predictor 3) was measured by combat months. The last month of observation was December 1999. The data were taken from Regan (2002). Intensity or cost of conflict (predictor 4) was calculated as the average number of battle deaths over the entire duration of fighting. The data were taken from Regan (2002). Type of conflict (predictor 5) was coded as a dichotomy. If a conflict was ethnic/identity-based conflict, it was coded one; if it was not, it was coded zero. The data were taken from Regan (2002).

Previous regime type (predictor 6) was coded as a dichotomy. If the previous regime was an autocracy, it was coded zero; if the regime was a semidemocracy or democracy, it was coded one. The data were taken from Pearson et al. (2006). Following Balch-Lindsay and Enterline (2000), as well as Mason, Weingarten, and Fett (1999), army size for the government (predictor 7) was calculated by the total number of military personnel divided by the total population. The data were taken from the Correlates of War Project's National Material Capability data, version 3.02 (Singer, Bremer, and Stuckey, 1972).

Data Analysis: Multinomial Logit Analysis was used. This is a statistical technique of multiple binary logistic-regression analyses appropriate for multiple dichotomous outcome variables (Long, 1997).

Findings: According to Table 6.1, the duration of conflict is the most significant and consistent predictor of the outcome of armed internal conflicts. This suggests that longer conflict duration is less likely to lead to conflict resolution, either through victories or negotiations. Third party intervention seems quite strongly related to negotiated settlements, perhaps substantiating the findings in the literature about third party guarantors of agreements. As also indicated, UN intervention in the dispute seems (because of the negative or inverse sign in the statistical relationship) to work against rebel victories, while other forms of third party interventions seem to promote either such rebel victories or negotiated settlements. The UN has been noted as an organization that strongly observes norms of state sovereignty, even as it takes up human rights concerns. Similarly, as might be expected, the greater the government's capacity and capability, the less chance for rebel victories. The occurrence of a democratic regime type prior to the conflict does not generally seem to enhance prospects for either governmental or rebel victories.

TABLE 6.1 MULTINOMIAL LOGIT ANALYSIS OF INTERNAL CONFLICT OUTCOMES, 1946–2000

Variables	Government Victory vs. Ongoing Conflict	Rebel Victory vs. Ongoing Conflict	Negotiated Settlement vs. Ongoing Conflict
Intervention Characteristics			
Third Party Intervention	1.11 (0.65)*	1.62 (0.82)*	1.99 (0.72)**
UN Intervention	-1.39 (0.79)	-41.45 (0.92)***	-0.14 (0.60)
Conflict Characteristics			
Duration	-0.02 (0.00)***	-0.02 (0.00)*	-0.01 (0.01)**
Intensity	0.08 (0.00)	0.03 (0.00)	-0.03 (0.00)
Ethnic Conflict	-0.37 (0.53)	-1.51 (0.82)*	-0.233 (0.55)
State Capacity			
Army Size	-85.23 (49.75)	-198.80 (83.34)**	-34.10 (43.34)
Regime Type	-1.36 (0.63)**	-2.34 (0.83)**	0.010 (0.59)
Constant	3. 36 (0.88)***	3.15 (1.17)**	0.27 (0.77)

Number of Observations = 140
Wald X^2 (21) = 10,812***
Pseudo R^2 = 0.2633
Log Pseudo-Likelihood = -134.07445

Note: Models were estimated with Stata Release 9.2. Robust standard errors (numbers in parentheses) are heteroskedastic-robust. Significance levels are based on two-tailed tests. Ongoing Conflict is the baseline of this estimation.
Significant Level: *$p < 0.10$; **$p < 0.05$; *** $p < 0.001$.

Based on the findings reported in Table 6.1, Suzuki also conducted a series of scenario analyses on intervention characteristics. The results are presented in Table 6.2. According to Suzuki's analyses, the chance of a government victory in a civil war is 46.4 per cent without any intervention, while the probability of a rebel victory is 33.1 per cent without any intervention. The chance of a successful negotiated settlement in a civil war without any intervention is only 6.7 per cent.

Interestingly, however, the chance of a successful negotiated settlement with either third party or UN intervention is dramatically increased. For third party intervention in an ethnic war, the probability of a successful negotiated settlement increased from 6.7 per cent to 51.8 per cent (a difference of 45.1 per cent). UN intervention in an ethnic civil war raises the probability of a successful negotiated settlement by 16.4 per cent (from 6.7 per cent to 23.1 per cent). On the contrary, the chance of either a government or rebel victory significantly declines with third party or UN intervention. These preliminary findings can be argued as being consistent with the literature on the duration of civil war, which shows that outside military intervention, while it may extend the duration of civil wars, also tends to bring on more definitive outcomes, often in increased prospect of negotiated settlements. To explain the more complex phenomena of internal conflict outcomes, scholars need to conduct further vigorous investigation, both theoretically and empirically.

TABLE 6.2 MARGINAL EFFECT OF THIRD PARTY INTERVENTIONS ON INTERNAL CONFLICT OUTCOMES

Scenario	Government Victory	Rebel Victory	Negotiated Settlement
Baseline with No Third Party Intervention (Nature)	46.4%	33.1%	6.7%
Third Party Intervention	37.8% (-8.6)	45.2% (+12.1)	13.3% (+6.6)
UN Intervention	39.3% (-7.1)	0.00% (-33.1)	18.1% (+11.4)
Third Party Intervention in Ethnic War	26.2% (-20.)	4.0% (-29.1)	51.8% (+45.1)
UN Intervention in Ethnic War	9.0% (-37.4)	0.00% (-33.1)	23.1% (+16.4)

Note: Each scenario was estimated with S-post based on the coefficients reported in Source: Suzuki (2007).

THE VARIED CONTENT OF NEGOTIATIONS

In order to determine why some civil war negotiations succeed better than others, both in ending warfare and promoting stable conditions of peace, it would be well to review the nature of peace negotiations themselves and what was on the bargaining table at various phases of talks. Phases can include initial feelers, substantive plenary and working group sessions, and implementation reviews. It matters whether the settlement dealt effectively with all the major grievances on the two or more sides of the conflict and whether it opened the way to constructive or destructive third party involvement and enforcement.

Negotiated settlements can range from the purely local agreements, made between factions and governments engaged in warfare, to broad international agreements, such as the one described in Box 6.3. The latter resemble formal treaties and are negotiated by countries surrounding or involved in the fighting and are aimed at stabilizing the situation. Often actual negotiations involve both local and international actors, as in the Sudanese agreement to end the 21-year-old north-south civil war in 2005. The government and southern rebel leaders met directly, and numerous interested outside parties, including the UN Security Council, drawn in by such a long and destructive war, offered to underwrite and support the agreement. As we have seen, outside actors become involved not simply for humanitarian reasons but also to secure interests of their own. In the case of Sudan, for example, the disrupted and weakened state had several times become a target and refuge for opportunistic extremist and terrorist groups and thus drew considerable attention from major powers such as the United States. Oil had been found in the area, to the intense and special interest of powers such as China, and Sudan had always been a key Egyptian interest, given its strategic location astride the Nile River.

> **BOX 6.3: A CASE IN POINT: A FRAMEWORK FOR ENDING CENTRAL AFRICAN CIVIL WARS**
>
> In 2006 leaders and representatives from 11 African countries in the Great Lakes region met to discuss the ending of interstate and civil wars and promoting economic growth. Although some of the countries involved

in the talks had either fought wars against each other or had assisted neighboring rebels in their fights, those present agreed to the Protocol on Non-Aggression and Mutual Defence in the Great Lakes Region. By signing the protocol, member states agreed to deal with acts of aggression collectively to the extent that "any armed attack against one or more of them shall be considered an attack against them all" (Protocol Article 6, Section 2).[6] Acts of aggression were said to include cross-border attacks or invasion, as well as bombing campaigns or the blockading of ports. Also included as acts of aggression, and therefore in violation of the pact, are the support or encouragement of armed rebel or terrorist groups in another member state. Collectively, security measures were aimed at reducing and ultimately eliminating threats to peace and security in the region. In addition to collective security measures, member states also agreed to create a Special Fund for Reconstruction and Development. Contributions to the fund were mandatory.

Source: International Conference on the Great Lakes Region (2006), and United Nations News Centre (15 December 2006).

Negotiated agreements also range from ceasefires, prisoner exchanges, and terms for dialogue, to full-scale settlements including disarmament and reconciliation provisions. Along the way, the issues on the table might include the following:

- the cessation of hostilities (to be effective, ceasefires must be quickly followed up with more substantial progress on key conflict issues);
- prenegotiation terms defining how the peace will be negotiated, including procedural questions such as schedules, agendas, invited participants and observers, location, the role of peacemakers, and even the shape of the negotiating table (as in Vietnam);
- interim or preliminary agreements on such matters as ceasefires (sometimes these are all that the parties can bear to complete at a given time) that may set the stage for fuller agreements later, especially if the parties display good faith and good behavior in the interim;
- framework and comprehensive agreements, the former outlining a sketch, framework or basic process toward a comprehensive peace

in general terms—such as the so-called US Roadmap principles for Israeli-Palestinian negotiations under the George W. Bush administration;

- implementation agreements outlining what has to happen when and how the adherence to the agreement will be monitored and conceivably enforced, including potential penalties and sanctions for noncompliance (see Yawanarajah and Ouellet, 2003).

Merely a glance at the chapter topics that Stedman, Rothchild, and Cousens include in their 2002 study of the different ways to end civil war alerts us to the variety of peace "implementation tasks" that exist: disarmament and demobilization; economic priorities; role of postsettlement elections; human rights and the role of law; refugee repatriation; civilian security; and building local capacity.

A spate of specific and often thorny issues, then, will be included in the various phases of peace talks, depending on the nature of the conflict in the specific country. Among these are: the terms of surrender; movement or exchange of populations; release of prisoners; withdrawal of foreign forces; disarmament and reintegration of militia into society or into the national army; power-sharing in government; resource-sharing; security guarantees; amnesty or trials for those accused of crimes; new elections and plebiscites; verification and monitoring; third party peacekeeping; nonintervention by neighbors; external financial or military assistance; a neutral or trusted process to resolve future procedural or substantive grievances and complaints; improved governmental services; accountability; and human rights observance (Yawanarajah and Ouellett, 2003). Taking a look at the multiparty multistate accord outlined in Box 6.3 concerning the "Great Lakes" region of central Africa, one sees that much work still remained in order to transform the broad outlines or framework of the accord into accountable comprehensive undertakings on which the parties could specifically rely.

If we recall the importance of "good governance" in avoiding and settling civil wars, and the conspicuously deficient record on this score in many of the most recent wars, we can deduce that, "peace agreements that bring these conflicts to an end often focus ... on rebuilding governance mechanisms," as opposed to peace agreements signed in interstate wars, which more often focus on enhanced security and territorial issues (Yawanarajah and Oullet, 2003: 2). Thus, a focus on rebuilding a viable state and laying conditions for continued peace becomes crucial, and is part and parcel of what we often refer to as "peacebuilding" (as distinct from "peacekeeping"—the imposition of forces to separate the sides and promote a ceasefire, and "peacemaking"—negotiations to achieve an agreement to formally end the fighting).

The comprehensive multilateral arrangements of 1991 that restored the Cambodian state after decades of civil war, after the defeat of Pol Pot's forces and the discovery of a domestic genocide fomented by the state, in a sense constituted a classic peacebuilding model. The country was essentially delegated to international administration under UN auspices so that public functions and governance could be restored under international supervision, and security and justice could be re-established (see the UN's "Peace Agreements Digital Collection: Cambodia," 2000). Thus, a "failed" state whose population had suffered one of the world's most horrifying genocidal fates was effectively restored to viability and stability, at least across a span of over 15 years.

Stedman (2001), Jones (2001), O'Toole (1997), and the United States Institute of Peace (1996) have gone on to investigate the qualitative factors evident in making or breaking agreements across different cases of civil war. They, too, note the importance of linking negotiation to implementation and peacebuilding, along with the often haphazard way in which third party actors come to achieve crucial coordination in seeking and facilitating solutions. Rothchild (2002) points out that security guarantees and provisions must apply to both the elites and the masses, to both groups and individuals, all of whom have different concerns and needs. It is not enough simply to hold elections and re-establish political parties; individual citizens must be protected and given jobs and hope; group rights and interests must be recognized.

O'Toole (1997) notes that,

> For some people sometimes, war is safer than peace. Starting with that premise helps one understand why the United Nations, the United States and others so often fail to implement the peace treaties they help others negotiate. Add to that the incompetence, inconsistency and bickering of the would-be peacemakers and you get a better idea of why civil war seems to flare up in the headlines not long after the formal announcement that peace has broken out.

Reviewing the findings of a 1997 Stanford University conference among scholars and diplomats (eight of whom had negotiated key peace agreements in the past, both successes and failures), O'Toole (1997) went on to discuss the challenges encountered regarding the success or failure of peace agreements.

Despite the success of achieving negotiated outcomes in Angola, Cambodia, and Rwanda, a significantly larger number of people died after the signing of these accords than those that died prior to the agreements. This is not to say that all peace agreements fall victim to near term renewed violence. Zimbabwe, Namibia, and El Salvador were able to end their civil wars through settlement without experiencing significant near term renewed violence. When civil war agreements do fail, additional efforts become even more costly in terms of time, money, and lives. As a result, it seems evident that more attention needs to be placed on the implementation of such agreements as opposed to focusing solely on the act of mediation.

In order to effectively implement agreements, it may be necessary to make use of both carrots and sticks to ensure compliance by those that are hesitant. Further, other implementation obstacles may need to be overcome, such as the vagueness of agreements and bureaucratic turf wars among peacemaking organizations. Peace agreement implementation may also be challenged by the very factors that helped to bring about resolution. For example, the 1991 Angolan agreement was designed to be enforced by the United Nations, yet the UN had no involvement in the crafting of the agreement, which was a product of US, Russia, and Portugal brokering. In addition, the Angolan agreement was negotiated under the assumption by both major factions that they would win the September 1992 elections; therefore, they agreed to "winner-take-all" elections. When UNITA lost with 40 percent of the vote, however, the group backed out of the agreement and chose to return to armed conflict. [7]

Reflecting the latter point in congressional testimony regarding the "civil war" in Iraq in 2006, Stedman (2001: 4) noted the frequent failure of elaborate power-sharing formulas in negotiated settlements, sometimes with outside intervention. In fact, he characterized the Rwandan genocide and the subsequent internal fighting that replaced the government as arising from a prior failure to implement a complicated power-sharing arrangement involving Rwanda's government, opposition Hutu parties, and insurgents. A kind of "security dilemma" exists in such internal struggles (seen as well in Bosnia and, to a certain extent, Lebanon), where fear and distrust rule.

> If one militia fears that another will try to use force to grab control of the army, or a city, then it has a strong incentive to use force to prevent this. The other militia understands this incentive, which gives it a good reason to act exactly as the first militia feared. In the face of these mutual fears and temptations, agreements on paper about dividing up or sharing control of political offices or tax revenues are often just that—paper. (Fearon, 2006)

Each side acts to promote its perceived security interests with the result that all sides feel less secure.

THINKING AHEAD

If one is looking to outside guarantors in a civil war to relieve the security dilemma and reassure the distrustful parties, there are many complications. Part of the problem relates to credible commitments. It appears to many that Western powers, for example, have been more willing to intervene, despite admitted reluctance at times in European- or Middle Eastern-related disputes (e.g., Bosnia, Afghanistan, Lebanon) than in African or East Asian conflagrations. Some charge a form of racism on this score. Others put it down to fewer defined "strategic interests" (e.g., less oil) in Africa or parts of Asia; to disillusionment about being sucked into collapsing domestic situations; to disillusionment with prior failed interventions (e.g., Vietnam, Somalia); or to outright neglect.

This pattern of intervention on the part of Western powers may change over time as more resource deposits are discovered or as resource markets become competitive in Africa and East Asia, and as the international security situation continues to center on failed states as breeding grounds for terrorists. The interests of powers such as the United States, China, and France could be engaged in a variety of regions, but then again, their preference could be for the use of regional security organizations where they exist (Africa's newly developing AU, for example), or favored states (e.g., Nigeria, Ethiopia) to undertake the interventions. Sometimes these states and organizations lack the capabilities or training to undertake effective peacekeeping missions, and sometimes they have been accused of becoming parties to the disputes. Theoretically, guarantors must be willing to use force, although in some circumstances where the warring parties have reached "ripeness" for settlement, not much force is needed. In a sense there must already be a peace to keep. In El Salvador, for example, the UN missions from 1991 to 1995 were successful in patrolling the country, with about 368 observers and 631 police observers (see United Nations, "Facts and Figures").

In addition to the use of states as proxy interveners, we have seen in prior chapters that the international system has witnessed increased multilateral intervention in domestic conflicts, particularly those involving human rights abuses, since the end of the Cold War. There had previously been considerable official international reluctance to intervene in "domestic" disputes in order to preserve the pivotal agreement of the Treaty of Westphalia (1648), which had ended wars among religious princes in Europe and had thus established a "peaceful" international system of "live and let live." Such noninterventionist norms were especially prevalent in post-colonial Africa. Since 1990, however, a slow erosion of noninterventionist norms has emerged, with the AU beginning to take on a more ubiquitous, if still not fully effective, role, backed, sometimes to an awkward extent, by the technical and military assistance of powers such as the United States (e.g., Washington moved under both the administrations of Bill Clinton and George W. Bush to establish a greater military training mission on the continent).

We have seen that analysts have identified economic growth and opportunity as key factors leading groups and individuals away from civil war. For Africa and worldwide, Collier (2003) posed three indicators of a country's proneness to civil war: low per capita income; economic decline; and high dependence on natural resources. Collier downplayed the roles of regime type and ethnic division in comparison to these three factors (in fact, he and others have indicated that more ethnically diverse states may be less prone to civil war, though the example of India's periodic hostilities gives pause to this conclusion). Given these criteria, Africa has been in a particularly war-prone situation, since many African states tend to rank highly on all three of Collier's danger signs.

In dealing with the war-proneness of some African states, Collier (2003) suggested that the "international community" adopt a mix of approaches, almost a cocktail of remedies dealing with the goals of preventing, shortening, and forestalling resumptions of fighting. Collier's "policy coherence" strategy would combine and synchronize aid, trade, and military policy, coordinated in such a way as to relieve the most poverty-stricken or declining African economies, if possible by boosting both their self-sufficiency and their exports, and to address poor governance and the control of natural resources by rebel groups. Some have also called for the World Bank and other global financial institutions to pointedly aim their relief and loans at wartorn societies needing new incentives and to foster improved legal systems and police performance. As reflected in most of the studies and indicators reviewed in this chapter, this is all sound advice, but one must also bear in mind and expect the patterns of instability, as discussed, in Chapter 3 when states begin to transition from subsistence to developed economies and from authoritarian to more open political systems.

We have seen that Collier (2003) put a different "spin" on the trend in civil war duration as contrasted with Fearon's (2004) claim that civil wars have been shorter in length since 1990 (see Chapter 5). Collier detects a trend toward longer duration conflicts, lasting up to 20–30 years, largely because they are easier and more lucrative to sustain financially. Thus, in order to shorten ongoing wars, he suggests undercutting the prices paid for illicit shipments of goods such as "blood" diamonds and gold. Some international agreements requiring certification to forestall the purchase of questionably traded goods have been reached in recent years, but enforcement has been problematic since shipments can go through and be "laundered" by third parties as there is so much money to be made in the process. Thus, bolstering legal economies is doubly important, not only to directly preclude violence but also to short-circuit the illicit trade that feeds violence.

On the question of "breaking the conflict trap" in postconflict settlements, Collier (2003) also notes that perhaps 50 per cent of all civil wars result from failed postconflict settlement situations. Thus, despite the best efforts of negotiators, parties revert to war when the resolution of prior conflict falls through. Here, Collier suggests that the phenomenon of recurrence could be lessened by (1) concentrating more aid on economic recovery; (2) phasing in aid to allow the wartorn state to build up over five to six years as its "absorption capability" is restored, including all social groups in the aid structure; and (3) reducing portions of budgets and aid going to the military. Collier cites Mozambique as a state where a decrease in military spending was combined with a conspicuous increase in social spending (one would want to carefully gauge the capacity and training of the police to keep order) to signal to the population, former war winners and losers alike, that they could begin to trust the conditions for peace and security. These changes can be usefully combined with the involvement of external, trusted guarantors sending military contingents, as in Australia's dispatch of troops to the Solomon Islands in the Pacific in 2003.

We have seen that another key set of policy debates, especially regarding ethnic wars, has to do with the wisdom of partition versus unified state models, incorporating such various forms of governance as central state dominance, confederations, federations, local autonomy or group entitlement, and power-sharing.[8] Ever since India and Pakistan were separated in 1947 in the midst of violence and skepticism about whether Muslims and Hindus could coexist in the same state, those favoring or opposing partition as a general solution have had their say. Indeed, we have seen evidence (see Chapter 3) that partitioned states may fare better than decentralized states in averting civil war.

After the Indo-Pakistani partition of 1947, Pakistan was a bizonal state, consisting of East and West Pakistan, separated by hundreds of miles across northern India. That proved an unstable solution, in that Bengali nationalism grew in Eastern Pakistan against a government dominated by Western Punjabi ethnic parties, leading, along with conditions of poverty and natural hardships (e.g., floods), to Bengali moves toward secession. With Bengali refugees flooding into India in 1971, taxing that state's capacities, New Delhi threw its weight behind the Bengali separatists, who succeeded in a military campaign for independence, thus dismembering India's Pakistani rival. Some might consider Pakistan's later support for Islamic insurgents in the long-simmering Indian Kashmir territorial conflict as a form of "payback" for that dismemberment.

In the case of India and Pakistan, instead of potential civil wars (though both states suffer internal turmoil), one could argue that the greater danger is that an international war will explode between the two states, now with nuclear potential. At the same time, large numbers of Muslims (perhaps the second-largest Muslim population in the world after Indonesia) continue to reside inside India, which has been periodically wracked by bloody communal violence between the religious communities, which in turn has often involved the public authorities.

A similar debate has raged about the potential solutions to the Palestinian-Israeli conflict. Pre-World War II colonial Palestine was to have been partitioned by the UN in 1947 into separate Jewish and Arab states. The latter Palestinian state has yet to come into existence and the Jewish state has subsequently been territorially enlarged as the result of several wars. The question remains: Can these two peoples coexist in a "two-state" solution, or, as the UN's 1947 "minority report" suggested, would the better solution be a single "binational" secular state? The consensus appears to rest with the former solution, but the provision for a viable pair of states that would leave each other in relative peace has been very elusive, in part because both the Palestinians and the Israelis continue to value much of the same territory. Proposals for a Palestinian state, including those put forward by US President Bill Clinton at the Camp David negotiations of 2000, have generally included the Gaza and West Bank areas on either side of Israel. However, maintaining a bifurcated Palestinian state would be difficult and challenging because of requirements for a connecting road surrounded by Israeli territory, and forces and potential for Israeli security interventions in both territories. Clear outside security guarantees, given, for example, by NATO forces, may be necessary for the two states to feel secure enough to live in peace.

Pro-partition views tend to emphasize the benefits of keeping warring parties separated so they can recover on their own, find and preserve their own communities, and potentially re-establish tentative relations with each other later on. This has been roughly the case in the states that fought the Bosnian wars of the 1990s, which were frozen by NATO and UN peacekeeping efforts into relatively distinct Muslim, Croat, and Serb territories. Similar arguments are made about Cyprus, which seems further along the path toward reconciliation. Some see this separation strategy as a tragedy, as individuals and families had to abandon their traditional homelands, neighborhoods, and houses. Others see it as a necessary step that allows a cooling off of vengeful passions and resentment, a time of opportunity for democratic institutions to take root and normal economic activities to take hold. In theory, a single Bosnian state still exists with diverse ethnic components, and it should have a joint ethnic presidency and a joint multi-ethnic army. In reality, these provisions are hardly implemented and the ethnic communities remain largely estranged.

Critics of partition see it as a surrender to the "baser instincts" of human society, an admission that, to paraphrase Rodney King, "we cannot all just get along."[9] Advocates consider it a "realist" solution since clearly in many cases groups do not get along. Partition can lead either to new and workable borders or toward the building of insurmountable walls (sometimes literally) between neighbors. It can also be a slippery slope toward a further subdivision of states. One secession can encourage others, as the history of the former Yugoslavia after 1990 has shown. Indeed, the resultant newly divided states are generally not themselves ethnically pure or homogeneous either, so that additional groups may want their own autonomy down the road due to what has been termed the "minority within a minority" problem. Macedonia and Montenegro have now both opted out of their federation with Serbia, and the province of Kosovo, with its ethnic Albanian majority, has sought violently to do the same.

How do we determine which groups are entitled to secede and form their own states or control separate territories? There is no international forum to which groups can reliably bring their claims for adjudication and legitimacy. Unfortunately, the force of arms often remains the only recourse to prove the intention and capability for self-rule.

CONCLUSION

In this chapter we have reviewed the challenges and possibilities for successful conclusions of civil wars, either through military or negotiated outcomes, noting of course that military tussles are themselves a form of "bargaining" give and take, push or shove, through force. The importance of factors such as security guarantees, partition, targeted economic assistance, better governance, and democracy have been noted and debated.

In part the question of effective settlements depends on what we mean by "peace." If it is defined as "the process of carrying out a specific peace agreement," focusing on the "narrow, relatively short term efforts.... to get warring parties to comply with their written commitments to peace," one set of remedies may apply, such as pressure from major powers (Stedman, Rothchild, and Cousens, 2002; see also Reeder, 2006). If "peace" means a long-term cessation of hostilities over many years, another set of remedies may apply, such as third party guarantees and forms of territorial division. If it implies rebuilding a viable society and governance structure in one or more states or territories, additional requirements might pertain (e.g., major economic reconstruction and development programs and significant institutional reforms, especially in national budgeting and the administration of justice). Of course, each of the various definitions of "peace" relates to the others; one does not necessarily acquire long-term peace without the observance of agreements or without institutional rebuilding and reform.

Stedman, Rothchild, and Cousens (2002) also alert us to two basic contexts for peace: the conflict environment, and the willingness of international actors to uphold or underwrite settlement agreements and their necessary conditions. They note that civil wars differ in environmental characteristics. In some civil wars, such as in Guatemala (1992–98), violence effectively ended before talks began. Perhaps this reflects the international community's encouragement of, or tragically belated response to, the fighting in the first place. However, it means that a negotiated agreement may be easier in cases like Guatemala than in cases where the fighting rages on unabated; even 25,000 US Marines could not readily subdue relatively primitively armed clan militia in Somalia in 1991 (Reeder, 2006). United Nations peacekeeping has also experienced varied demands and roles, ranging from election or ceasefire monitoring to performing the tasks of failed state governments. UN mission statements have also ranged from merely buffering between previous combatants, thus risking the possible resumption of warfare, to actual combat against parties violating the truce or endangering populations. In the most complicated cases, such factors as a clear division of labor, coordination between and among intergovernment organizations and private relief agencies, and timing of initiatives, together with constant communication and messaging between UN agencies and local governmental or military officials are crucial.

As Professor Michael Doyle of Princeton University highlighted as special advisor to UN Secretary-General Kofi Annan in 2002: "Ending war can be as destabilizing as war itself." War disrupts societies and undermines democratic structures, with power devolving to the hands of the military while media and economic functions are disrupted. People and their livelihoods become dependent on war itself, and peace therefore becomes a near revolutionary process of dismantling the "war-based society." (UN Department of Public Information and Department of Political Affairs, 2002).

In the case studies included by Stedman, Rothchild, and Cousens in *Ending Civil Wars*, three main factors are seen to worsen the peacemaking environment: domestic spoilers; neighboring and regional states that undermine or oppose the peace; and valuable resources and the spoils of war that tempt fighters to persist. Again, these factors also intermix, as when unfriendly or opportunistic neighboring governments supply or harbor spoiler insurgents from across the border, or when spoilers finance their operations on ill-gained spoils of war through supply networks in neighboring states. Conversely, neighbors agreeing and able to uphold the peace process and to stop the flow of illegal trade and arms can go a long way toward impeding spoilers, denying them supplies and refuge and enforcing borders effectively against smuggling.

Stedman, Rothchild, and Cousens (2002) especially note that the will of international actors to uphold internal peace agreements depends on their political calculations of perceived self-interest, cost, and benefit. The international community pulled out of Rwanda as the ethno-political fighting worsened, evidently because the country was perceived as marginal in strategic importance, not worth even the relatively low cost of staying and opposing the violent parties, especially in light of the setbacks sustained by international interveners in Somalia. Calculations and commitments can change over time, with one historical "lesson" affecting a state's willingness to repeat policies the next time. Administrations can change in the capitals of powerful state actors, increasing or decreasing their willingness to help uphold peace agreements, or in some cases their zealousness to intervene abroad, either in resource-rich or resource-poor regions, or in strategically interesting or marginal locations. Interest groups, such as multinational corporations engaged in varied forms of global commerce (e.g., oil firms interested in establishing business in the disrupted former Soviet republics of Central Asia) or nongovernmental organizations concerned about matters such as human rights, poverty, and political prisoners, can also affect these calculations.

Stedman, Rothchild, and Cousens (2002) conclude, perhaps ominously, that peace implementation strategies by the UN or other international organizations should only be attempted—except in the most forgiving and "easy" of environments—if and only if major and regional powers are fully supportive, committed, and operationally coordinated. Otherwise, the needed resources (including military troops) for provision of security and aid guarantees will not be forthcoming. Unfortunately, this may mean that so-called strategic locations will continue to enjoy a better prospect of international involvement and underwriting than more remote locations. The role of the media in highlighting human rights abuses can somewhat affect this calculus, however, bringing more attention to remote areas as they did in parts of Southeast Asia and the Pacific, leading to Australia's multilateral dispatch of troops and police units to the Solomons beginning in 2003, for example.

Of course, in some strategic locations, such as Iraq in the first decade of the twenty-first century, international and multilateral support for peace processes has been limited both by ongoing violence, civil war, and insurgency, and also by the rather intense commitment of one major power: the United States. Those actors who coordinate their approaches to ending the civil war risk association with the outside power and its priorities, a politically risky stance in regional terms. Regional actors may exact a price for their cooperation from the heavily invested major power, as was seen with the demands made by Syria for progress against Israel, the demands by Turkey for restraint on the Iraqi Kurds, or the demands by Iran for its emerging regional and nuclear status. All of these international priorities tend to complicate the achievement of stability in the country in question, namely Iraq, where antagonistic domestic actors also tend to resent the whole process of outside interference.

Those who would make peace must have their priorities, both local and regional, in order. They must value culturally appropriate solutions as well as the implementation of so-called subgoals in the agreement process (Stedman, Rothchild, and Cousens, 2002), ranging from demobilizing military forces in or around the wartorn state, to rebuilding local police and justice institutions, to establishing "civil society" organizations such as labor groups, service clubs, and women's organizations. This means that civil war peacemaking must paraphrase the adage about war-making in the nuclear era, a maxim supposedly written on a sign over the door of the special executive committee (Excom) that hammered out American policy during the Cuban Missile Crisis of 1962: "One makes peace like porcupines make love—very carefully," and, one might add, painstakingly.

NOTES

1 In the American case, the Northern Army benefited from a larger population and significantly more resources. The Confederate president, Jefferson Davis, sought external aid to counter this power

disadvantage. Despite England's reliance on cotton, however, Davis was unable to convince London to support his cause. This was in part due to Lincoln's Secretary of State William H. Seward's diplomatic maneuvering, but it was also due to Britain's divided sentiments, the long awaited Northern battlefield victories by Generals George B. McClellan and Ulysses S. Grant, and the Emancipation Proclamation in September 1862 (which was popular with British liberals). By 1863 concerns over European intervention appeared to have dissipated (LaFeber, 1994: 149–52). Outside support can at least increase the chances of a stalemate and thus result in a much different outcome and negotiation process.

2　Various readings associating war characteristics with war outcomes are nicely summarized by Susumu Suzuki, "All Armed Internal Conflicts Must End: Rethinking the Empirical Models of Internal Armed Conflict Outcomes," preliminary draft, Wayne State University, December 2006. Data compilations by Suzuki are also employed in this chapter, with great appreciation.

3　One additional test of these alternate outcomes, on data from 1946 to 2000, was carried out by Suzuki (2006, see Box 6.2). He utilized various studies and augmented them from news sources to compile a list of armed internal conflicts (each involving 100-plus battle-related deaths) in the latter half of the twentieth century. Once again, Licklider's (1995) and Walter's (2002) findings were basically confirmed in noting a decided tendency toward armed victories, mostly by the government side. Over 50 per cent of the civil wars (1,000-plus battle deaths) and near-wars ended in this way. The nearly 30 per cent proportion of negotiated settlements, however, was somewhat higher than Licklider and Walters recorded for their more limited lists of cases. Thus, we have more numerous examples of successfully negotiated civil war outcomes to study in determining circumstances that might lead to cutting the fighting short. On the other hand, of course, slightly more than 20 per cent of the cases Suzuki studied persisted in unresolved, ongoing conflict. Nearly identical percentages emerged from Suzuki's checkup study comparing his findings with those of Fearon and Laitin (2003)—the checkup study showed 48 per cent ended in victories, 38 per cent by governments; and 29 per cent ended with negotiated settlements.

4　Among the distinctions analysts make in dealing with different types of civil wars is a contrast between "old" and "new" forms, a contrast that may be quite invalid. Kalyvas (2001) argues that there is little evidence that today's wars are, as Kaldor (2006) would maintain, more matters of privatized criminality involving either plain greed or gratuitous violence as compared to the supposedly calculated political or ideological power struggles of the past, which some even characterize as more noble, popular, and strategic. Looting and banditry have existed in civil wars throughout history; warlords exist in contemporary Africa or Afghanistan just as they existed in ancient China; and conflict goals have always been complex, involving various combinations of individual, group, and national interests and gains.

5   Further, we should also note that determining a war's "end" can itself be problematic. As our discussion of intrastate rivalry made clear (see Chapter 5), civil wars have the tendency to ebb and flow, or to recur, even after fairly lengthy periods of time. It may be a bit too optimistic, or at least premature, to say that intrastate wars are both declining in number and becoming shorter in duration due to, or in spite of, democratization

6   The full text of the protocol can be found on the International Conference on the Great Lakes Region website at http://www.icglr.org/common/docs/docs_repository/protocol_nonaggression.pdf.

7   For more information on peace agreements in a particular country, see the International Conflict Research (INCORE) Peace Agreement website at http://www.incore.ulst.ac.uk/services/cds/agreements/.

8   This issue is reflected, for example, in some of the conclusions by Preston (2004).

9   On March 3, 1991, Rodney King, an African American, was pulled over for a traffic violation and was subsequently beaten by Los Angeles police officers. The incident was caught on video tape and was quickly labeled evidence of police brutality in the media and by citizen groups. The officers in the case, however, were acquitted, sparking days of rioting in the city. The quote provided here was made in response to the riots.

CHAPTER SEVEN

The Aftermath of Civil War

"I'm for peace—I've yet to see a man wake up in the morning
and say, 'I've just had a good war.'"

—Mae West

When the decades old north-south civil war in the Sudan appeared
to have ended in a negotiated settlement in 2005 with diplomatic
pressure from outside third parties, people expected that the country
would finally be able to get back on its feet, move toward reconciliation and reconstruction, and begin to enjoy the benefits of newly discovered oil deposits. There was even something of an economic boom
in Juba, the formerly wartorn main city of the south, a region which
was granted a good deal of local autonomy under the provisions of the
peace agreement. Juba's population swelled from 65,000 to almost one
million in two years. American consultants for the fledgling regional
government reportedly paid up to $300 a night to sleep in a tent. How-
ever, despite some of the encouraging economic news, reality proved
a rude awakening:

> [Juba's] streets are piled high with stinking garbage.
> Thousands of refugees who survived unspeakable
> horrors during Sudan's north-south civil war have

trudged back home, hoping for work, opportunity and a lasting peace.

Instead, even many of the educated Sudanese live in little grass huts behind government ministries being built with oil money, waiting for jobs that may never come.

The government here [in the south] has been struggling, partly because it is led by former bush fighters who had to become administrators almost over night.

The United Nations World Food Program has already built 1,300 miles of road in South Sudan. The abundant opportunity for manual labor (skilled jobs are fewer) has put wads of cash into countless young men's pockets.

But much of it is going toward beer and motorcycles.

While there are plenty of low-paid workers here, there is still no centralized water or electricity or even good cellphone service which has stymied efforts to develop more lucrative businesses.

(Gettleman, 29 November 2007:4)

Thus, not only did a second civil war break out with tragic consequences in Sudan's western Darfur region, but those who had returned to their homes in the "peaceful" portions of the country continued to confront hardships. The description of Juba, as set down by Gettleman above, is, in fact, somewhat reminiscent of the chaos and corruption of the immediate reconstruction in the American South, so pointedly portrayed in Margaret Mitchell's *Gone with the Wind*.

One of the most immediate and obvious consequences of civil war is the death of the combatants. In fact, in order for a civil conflict to be considered a "war" by some analysts, at least 1,000 battle-related deaths need to have occurred. As we have discussed, civil wars tend to be much more intense (deaths per unit of time) than their interstate counterparts (Miall, 1992). Lengthy battles within a country have led to significantly diminished adult male populations in several civil war countries, often leaving women and children to survive on their own. Women and children have been described as the main casualties of recent civil wars. In Bosnia, for example, mass rape was used as a weapon to demoralize and humiliate the ethnic enemy. Such wanton and psychotic episodes tend to coincide with other tactics designed to rid a territory or state of a particular identity group. Though killing, rape, and enslavement certainly have been seen in large-scale international wars (note, for example, Japan's record on these issues in World War II), and although international wars can spark domestic atrocities and revolutions (e.g., the Russian Revolution), so-called killing fields and genocides seem to be a direct response to domestic politics or domestic fighting.

Death may seem to be the ultimate consequence of civil war, but generally there are many more injuries than deaths. Typically, survivors of war, blinded or missing limbs, are casualties of the ubiquitous small arms and light weapons that tend to characterize fighting in civil war, their range from land mines to machetes. The scars of fighting, not always physically apparent, are certainly psychologically damaging as well. Post-traumatic stress disorder strikes both soldiers and civilians who are caught in the web of war.

Mass rape and mass killing are considered genocidal acts, which Harff (2003: 3) has defined as a "deliberate and sustained effort by authorities aimed at destroying a collectivity in whole or in part." The most obvious example of genocide involved the systematic killing of Jews, Roma ("Gypsies"), and other prisoners by Hitler and his followers during World War II. Civil wars in the post-World War II era have produced significant genocidal episodes. Although not all civil wars degenerate into genocide, those that end in military victory appear more likely to do so (Licklider, 1995).

Intense and prolonged civil wars, whether they involve mass killing or not, are likely to lead to large numbers of people fleeing the conflict for either their safety or in search of food or work. These individuals can become internally displaced, moving to other parts of the country, or internationally displaced as refugees. In fact, the number of global refugees tends to mirror the amount of civil conflict occurring in the system, as indicated in Figures 7.1 and 7.2. Refugee number appear to have peaked in the years 1992 and 1993 at around 17 million; the number of civil conflicts occurring in the system peaking in the years 1991 and 1992 at around 49. These figures do not include the people relocating away from the conflict occurring within their state (i.e., internal refugees).

With global refugee figures so high, often as a direct result of civil wars, it is not surprising that these wars destabilize entire regions. In addition to the availability of arms that such wars generate, neighbors often feel compelled to act when they experience significant and economically costly refugee flows into their territories, as India did during the Bangladesh war (see Chapter 6). The economic costs for the neighboring state can be enough to destabilize a region politically, but certainly violence contagion becomes an issue if the neighbor becomes militarily drawn into the conflict (as the Democratic Republic of the Congo was after the Rwandan fighting).

Figure 7.1 Global Refugee Population, 1980–2005

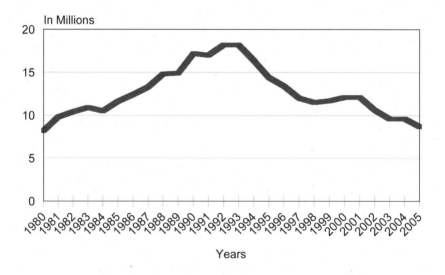

Years

Source: UN High Commissioner for Refugees, UNHCR Statistical Yearbook (2005); Weiner (1996)

Civil wars leave significant long-term consequences beyond the immediate threat of death and violence. Economically, civil war states will suffer from lower tax ratios (Theis, 2005) and significantly lower state gross domestic product (GDP) (Murdoch and Sandler, 2002). Post-civil war states have been known to recover from the costs of war, but the road to rebuilding society is challenging and can involve several setbacks even to the point of renewed warfare. The predictable pattern of arms proliferation brings the cost of surplus armament down, making renewed war a more affordable option (Sislin and Pearson, 2001; Weiner, 1996). As a result, the long-term effects of a civil war at any point in time could evolve into renewed civil violence at a later date, either in the same state or other states receiving the arms sell-offs. People, in fact, can become conditioned to war and violence. Re-educating a child or youth who has witnessed, experienced, and committed horrific violence is no easy task. The risk of not doing so, however, is immense.

Figure 7.2 Amount of Civil Conflict and Civil War in the System, 1980–2005

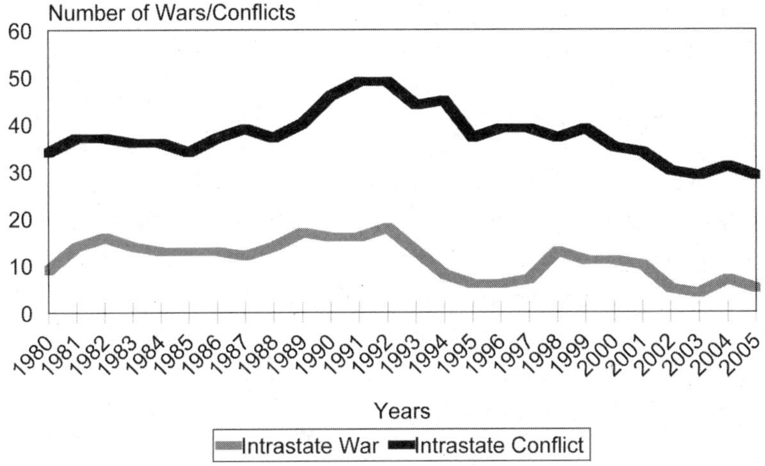

Number of Wars/Conflicts

Years

Intrastate War Intrastate Conflict

Source: PRIO Armed Conflict Data

Civil wars, as all wars do, involve environmental consequences. Wars, particularly those involving major weapons, are destructive. Villages, towns, and general state infrastructure are destroyed, requiring costly reconstruction. Depending on the tactics used by war participants, other environmental consequences may involve drought and agricultural dislocation, and therefore famine. Such consequences disrupt the provision of water and electricity, as well as market processes. Landmines have become a persistent legacy of civil war, resulting in the death or maiming of civilians well after the war has concluded. Former UN Secretary-General Boutros Boutros-Ghali (1994) estimated that there were more than 100 million landmines in 62 countries as of 1994 when the amount of civil war in the system was near its peak. Since that time, while many states have signed a treaty to ban landmines (conspicuously without the signatures of the US and other major powers¹), efforts to clean up landmine-laden regions are slow, arduous, and expensive, which impedes the repatriation of refugees and delaying economic and public health measures.

"Peacebuilding," as a phase of political, social, and economic recovery that ensures a lasting end to war, has also proven to be a phase that is delayed and complicated by a number of post-war factors, including the need to feed, house, and provide hope and opportunity for returning refugees and the youths who may or may not have been caught up in the winds of war, in some cases losing families, foregoing education, and becoming child soldiers. Even with significant resources and revenues, such as from Sudan's oil in the case discussed above, and with massive outside aid, it remains difficult to rebuild a country in the face of regional disparities, crime, sporadic violence, and corruption.

The Russian and Spanish civil wars of 1918 and 1936 respectively ended with the upheavals of entire political systems that reverberated around the world. The Russian war, sparked by the Bolshevik revolution, ended (though with lingering resentments and insecurities in Moscow) with a new state, the Soviet Union, which eventually rose to and maintained superpower status over some 70 years. The Spanish Civil War resulted in a fascist authoritarian regime under General Francisco Franco, which lasted from World War II (Spain was an ally of Germany but remained essentially out of the war and retained a large degree of autonomy) on into the 1970s until, under the aegis of the European Community, the country reverted to democratic rule and the restoration of a titular monarchy. Still, the threat of regional secession and terrorism has continued to hang over the head of the Madrid government. Clearly, not all civil wars have such far-reaching consequences, but nearly all have long-persisting effects on coming generations.

It is true that some civil wars have ended on a relatively hopeful and optimistic note and that the states at issue have sustained that optimism perhaps more so than, for example, the Sudan. The Northern Irish "Troubles,"² complete with their bitter and bloody history of terror and counterterror going back to the 1916 Easter Rising, seem to have been resolved in a joint parliamentary government structure that includes if not complete reconciliation between the Republican (pro-Irish) and Unionist (pro-British) populations, then at least significant disarmament of the warring sides and a conversion to political means of competition. The outside inducements of the European Union and the role of outside powers such as the Irish Republic, the US, and

Great Britain may have conditioned this progress; populations on all sides of the conflict were undoubtedly weary of war. For every success, though, one can point to a disappointing and frustrating case, such as the chaos and prolonged civil war that occurred in the Democratic Republic of the Congo following the genocidal killing in Rwanda during the 1990s.

What then is likely to be the path of post-war peace settlements? What are the conditions that make for a soft as opposed to a hard landing for states emerging from civil war? We will explore some of these factors in this chapter as we seek to identify policies for effective peacebuilding. Chen, Loayza, and Reynal-Querol found a hint of relevant answers to these questions in their 2007 World Bank study of the aftermath of civil war. They analyzed the economic, political, social, and demographic situation in 41 post-civil war countries between 1960 and 2003, concluding that "even though war has devastating effects and its aftermath can be immensely difficult, when the end of war marks the beginning of lasting peace, recovery and improvement are indeed achieved" (Chen, Loayza, and Reynal-Querol, 2007). Thus, preserving the peace itself, i.e., avoiding the renewal of violence, is a prime factor allowing for a cumulative healing, rebuilding, and reconciliation to take place, even if it takes a long period of time. Of course, the problem is cyclical since the rate of progress with reconstruction will affect the prospect for continued peace. In this sense, a wide variety of factors—economic, political, and demographic—must also fall into line for a positive outcome to civil war.

FACTORS IN SUCCESSFUL RECONSTRUCTION

As with the causal structure leading to civil wars, we can trace key factors in their aftermath at the individual, state, and international levels. For individuals, both adults and children (e.g., orphans and refugees), depending on their personal experiences during the war, the aftermath can be one of horror in overcoming effects of physical injury and post-traumatic stress. Of course, not every individual will be affected by such traumas in the same way, but warfare's damaging and long-lasting psychological scars are major impediments to healing and effective reunification (see, for example, the topics related to grief, victimization, healing, and reintegration covered in the workshop concerning the aftermath of war in Angola and Mozambique, "No War, No Peace: Coping with the Aftermath of Wars," sponsored by the Watson Institute for International Studies at Brown University and the University of Lisbon in March 2007). Tactics such as reconciliation processes ("truth and reconciliation") where victims can confront aggressors have been shown to provide some degree of "closure," allowing people to move forward in places such as South Africa and Rwanda. Yet, soldiers and refugees who have spent years in the field or in exile must be reintegrated into a peaceful society; this includes child soldiers who may not know any other sort of life. They will lack skills and education and may end up, as in Juba, Sudan, (see p. 197) immersed in aimless pursuits—beer and motorcycles.[3] They must be convinced to surrender their arms and trust in the government to provide security and hope.

States and governments that emerge from civil wars—if indeed they do emerge, since sometimes, as in Somalia, a power vacuum or "failed state" persists—face the prospect of reorganizing and reintegrating society; providing for basic human needs such as the restoration of health care, electricity, water, housing, and employment; securing the borders; and rejoining the international community of nations. One study of the effects of civil war (Ghobarah, Huth, and Russett, 2003), for example, found the spread of contagion and disease, leaving many a public health menace to remedy. Another chronic difficulty at the national level attends the environmental and infrastructural damage that civil war wreaks on such dimensions as toxic waste level, deforestation, despoiling of farmland, pollution, and water contamination.

A further looming question, as seen in the Soviet and Spanish examples, is what type of regime will emerge in the post-war state, since the roots of effective democracy, if they had existed at all prior to the conflict (in the form of a functioning civil society, middle class, and rule of law), may have been damaged to such an extent that long periods of authoritarian rule may instead prevail. Local autonomy provisions may, on the other hand, severely weaken central governing authorities, leaving power effectively in the hands of local leaders, whether of the traditional clan or ethnic type (e.g., Somalia, Iraq, Afghanistan), or of rival political "warlords" (such as between the forces of Nationalist Party leader Chiang Kai-shek and Communist Party chief Mao Tze Dong during China's civil war before and after World War II). Indeed, the outcome of China's civil war left one ruling authority in power on the mainland (People's Republic) and another holding refuge on the adjacent island of Taiwan (Nationalist China). This has led to all sorts of international complications, with the United States somewhat reluctantly drawn into a security alliance with Taiwan, and the latter sparring with Beijing over whether Taiwan is to be part of China or to become a separate state.

Thus, the international system must also adjust to the new regime and the new situation inside the formerly warring state, which may mean coming to terms with newly emergent or prominent leaders and ethnic groups (e.g., the Shi'a in Iraq). States must determine when and whether to diplomatically recognize a newly emergent government, as well as the extent to which the formerly disrupted state can and will be assisted back to health. These are all daunting tasks under the best of circumstances. However, we have seen in the last chapter, and in examples such as Cambodia, the crucial importance of international security, economic guarantees, and multinational assistance in helping put wartorn countries back on their feet, and in sustaining peace agreements.

Many of these factors that come into play were evident in the early positive returns on the prospects for Tajikistan after its wartime experience (see Box 7.1). With more than 50 per cent of the Tajik population under 14 years old, again indicating the importance of youth in dislocated and post-war societies, and while the country was pressured by the nearby Afghani civil conflict (e.g., drug and gun smuggling) and was still led by somewhat authoritarian leaders intent on squelching Islamic militancy, the population enjoyed some measure of stability after years of fighting (BBC, 21 August 2007).

BOX 7.1: A CASE IN POINT: POST-WAR TAJIKISTAN

While much international attention was paid to conflicts in such places as Somalia, Rwanda, and Bosnia Herzegovina, Tajikistan, located in central Asia, was experiencing its own civil war. In 1992 the United Tajik Opposition (UTO) took up arms against the neo-Communist government. UTO was an umbrella organization comprising both democratic forces, as well as Islamic militants interested in establishing an Islamic state in Tajikistan. The war was fairly brief, raging from 1992 to 1996, with additional hostilities occurring again in 1998, but it was destructive. By the end of the war, over 50,000 people had died and approximately 1.2 million had become refugees or internally displaced persons, according to the United Nations.

Despite the ravages of war, a peace agreement was negotiated, moving Tajikistan along the path toward reconciliation. The UN proved instrumental in the process, working to bring about resolution over a period of 12 years. Beginning with a fact-finding mission in December 1992, followed quickly by a goodwill mission, the UN sought to provide the tools for reconciliation and rehabilitation of the wartorn country. Negotiations between the warring factions began in 1994 with the cooperation of eight countries in the region resulting in a peace agreement. The United Nations Mission of Observers of Tajikistan (UNMOT) was established in December 1994 to monitor the peace. After a brief period of conflict resurgence, the peace agreement was concluded in 1997.

The post-war activities aimed at reconciliation illustrate just how much UN peacekeeping has transformed since its inception. The UN Tajikistan Office of Peace-building (UNTOP) has been involved in helping "mobilize international support for programmes promoting demobilization, voluntary arms collection and employment creation for former irregular fighters" (United Nations News Centre, 2004). With the assistance of 12 aid agencies, the UN hopes to see Tajikistan continue to transform itself from a war-ravaged state to a fully stable and functioning member of the international system.

Source: United Nations News Centre (2004); Project Ploughshares.

In their study of the aftermath of civil war, Chen, Loayza, and Reynal-Querol (2007) take off from the findings of Prezeworski et al. (2000) that post-civil war economic growth tends to be greater under dictatorships than in democracies (even though wars are deadlier under dictatorships), and that post-war growth is generally quite rapid, with an average growth rate across the countries they studied of nearly 6 per cent in the first five years after conflict, a pattern we saw in the Sudan account. In part, such respectable growth could be due to the very low economic level to which most wartorn states are reduced (i.e., quite literally, there is nowhere to go but up), but other factors such as renewed foreign investment and resource discoveries (e.g., oil) can boost economies and create at least temporary economic booms. Whether such growth can be sustained, or whether the growth itself causes new dislocations (such as housing shortages in boom towns like Juba) is another question.

As with economic growth per se, Chen, Loayza, and Reynal-Querol

(2007: 4) found, by comparing a cross-section of states' pre-war and post-war levels, that median levels of nearly all economic, political, and social development indicators improve gradually following civil wars as compared to pre-war levels, especially as budgetary expenditures are transferred from military to social spending and as per capita income tends to rise. Thus, without saying that civil wars are in any sense good for nations (in fact, wartorn states tend to do worse than comparable nonwar states in the Chen, Loayza, and Reynal-Querol analysis), wars' conclusion does seem to engender movement and changes that often surpass the pre-war conditions in areas as varied as school enrollment, and female and infant survival. Some of this improvement appears to be due to external humanitarian relief, to the replacement of repressive regimes, or to the end of wartime atrocities. However, some also appears to be due to a shift in government priorities away from war and toward domestic reconstruction.

Still, certain aspects of life appear to become only marginally better, or decline. For example, the increasing ratio of old to young in the population as war-age cohorts are killed represents growing economic imbalances, which are also sometimes seen in nonwar states (this pattern is somewhat at odds with other civil war examples such as Tajikistan's very young cohort). Post-war political and human rights observance can fluctuate and lead to temporarily increased terrorism (a factor not statistically significant in the Chen, Loayza, and Reynal-Querol study). In some growth categories the trend in conflict-ridden states was lower than for a comparable group of states that did not experience civil war, and in some cases (e.g., mortality and education rates) the growth only continued a pattern already underway before the war.

In reference to the earlier point about peace itself motivating improvement, Chen, Loayza, and Reynal-Querol (2007: 11) found that, in terms of median levels across nations up to seven years after the end of hostilities, and in comparison to the control group of nonconflict states, "there were no clear or significant signs of worsening conditions after the onset of peace," even if conditions did not always match the levels of the control group. After peace, countries generally reduce their overall governmental expenditures and slash their military spending (2007: 12), at least for a time; per capita income levels tend to rise and then sink back down over the seven year period. While political rights might be relatively slow to advance, police and law and order functions tend to improve markedly following peace (2007: 13).

As we have noted in recounting these studies, post-war progress seems dependent on a variety of factors at the personal, national, and international levels. If any one of these breaks down, the post-conflict state could revert to conditions of chaos and warfare. This seems especially true of the law and order and administration of justice factors that improve after peace. A tenuous example, at least according to a UN report in 2005 reproduced in Box 7.2, was Sierra Leone, the scene of horrific internal fighting from 1991 to 2000, whose progress seemed to be dependent on continued outside military peacekeeping, with the mission itself coming to an end. Recovering states must be able eventually to stand on their own, but the time necessary for that to happen can vary greatly and depend on the readiness of educated and qualified leaders to take over.

BOX 7.2: A CASE IN POINT: SIERRA LEONE

Sierra Leone gained independence from Britain in 1961. The country lacked effective governance early on, which ultimately led to a corrupt patrimonial system that benefited a few political and economic elites. Despite the availability of diamond and timber resources, Sierra Leone did not develop economically, resorting instead to an extractive economic system with "plenty of opportunities for illicit natural resource extraction and hordes of unemployed and frustrated youth" (Uppsala Conflict Data Program, Sudan Conflict Summary). The civil war began with the invasion by the Revolutionary United Front (RUF) from neighboring Liberia (see Box 7.3) in 1991. Liberia's Charles Taylor "was a primary driving force in the creation and the sustenance of the RUF" (Uppsala Conflict Data Program, Sudan Conflict Summary). Diamonds, arms, and soldiers flowed freely across the Sierra Leone-Liberian border during this time. Although RUF's stated goals involved democratic rule and "freeing the peasantry," it soon became clear that capturing the wealth of the diamond mines topped its list.

After nearly a decade of civil war and human rights abuses, with the civilian population experiencing the bulk of the conflict, the Lomé Peace Agreement was signed on July 7, 1999. The agreement called for the integration of RUF rebels into the government, as well as the development of a truth and reconciliation committee to deal with the atrocities committed during the conflict. Given the level of abuse perpetuated at the hands of both the RUF rebels—including cutting off limbs—and the government soldiers, the terms of the agreement were controversial. Maintaining the peace has proven to be a difficult task, involving a follow-up ceasefire agreement, as well as the creation of the United Nations Mission in Sierra Leone (UNAMSIL), which completely took over third party enforcement from the Economic Community of West African States (ECOWAS) in 2000.

Despite the challenges posed, the United Nations considers UNAMSIL "one of [its] most visible successes, having deployed in the wake of a brutal civil conflict that left at least 75,000 dead and many more maimed" (United Nations News Centre, 2005). As a part of this process, the UN has been able to disarm more than 72,500 combatants and assist in the creation of a new government, as well as help "regularize the nation's diamond-mining ... for the benefit of the entire country" (United Nations News Centre, 2005). UNAMSIL completed its mandate in December 2005. At the time, the country still suffered from widespread unemployment and poverty, conditions that helped to lead the country into war initially. As a result, UNAMSIL was replaced by the United Nations Integrated Office in Sierra Leone (UNIOSIL). Along with the International Military and Training Team led by the United Kingdom, peace has been maintained, though clearly this third party support is largely responsible.

Source: United Nations New Centre (2005).

In terms of the enlightened leadership factor, many observers also found hope in the emergence of free elections in Liberia following its agonizingly prolonged and destructive civil wars during the 1980s and '90s. The winner of the election was a Harvard-educated woman, Ellen Johnson-Sirleaf, Africa's first female head of state (other leaders, such as Graça Machel-Mandela of Mozambique and South Africa, have been quite influential as first ladies and in other capacities), who promised an end to corruption and a focus on rebuilding the devastated countryside.

Notwithstanding the aggregate indications of overall progress in post-war recovery that Chen, Loayza, and Reynal-Querol (2007) and other researchers have found, the stark conditions facing many individual countries, including staggering foreign debt (which can also affect states without civil wars), displaced populations, and the destruction of infrastructure as described in the Liberian case, are daunting, indeed, for any leader. The challenge of rebuilding Liberia and effectively transitioning from war to peace is the subject of the 2006 UN report referred to in Box 7.3.

BOX 7.3: A CASE IN POINT: LIBERIA: POST-WAR DEVELOPMENT CHALLENGES

In 2006 Liberia emerged from 14 years of civil war, including conditions of ethnic hatred, mass killing, and corruption. Liberia became an independent state during the nineteenth century as American slaves were returned to begin a colony in Africa. Americo-Liberian and indigenous Liberian ethnic communities remained in a state of tension, with the former coming to dominate the state. Through the years, the Liberian economy, largely centering on its rubber plantations and shipping, came to depend on major powers such as the United States and later Japan.

The American-educated militia leader Charles Taylor carried on a guerrilla campaign beginning in 1989 against the regime of former Sergeant Samuel Doe (who had come to power violently). Following Doe's overthrow and assassination and a period of internecine warfare among Liberian factions throughout the 1990s, Taylor gained power in 1997 and was ousted in 2003. Subsequently turned over to an international human rights tribunal at the Hague, Taylor was indicted on war crimes charges; he had established a West African network of arms smuggling and resource pillaging (e.g., in the diamond trade) through the spread of civil wars in Liberia and its neighboring states.

Liberia's major post-Taylor challenge was to rebuild its infrastructure and economy and heal the wounds of war. In the words of United Nations envoy Alan Doss, special representative of the Secretary-General: "Experience has taught us that an incomplete effort in consolidating the peace is often a prelude to renewed conflict" (United Nations News Centre, 2006). In addition to the now familiar demands of reintegrating youth and ex-combatants; providing jobs and education; resettling returning internal and external refugees (numbering over 600,000 in Liberia's case); and reforming the armed forces, the moribund judiciary, and the police, President Ellen Johnson-Sirleaf also had to provide honest government and an effective central authority in which people could believe in order to rekindle respect for human rights, law and order, and to preside over some sort of reconciliation process. External powers also had to be satisfied so that they could lift the UN embargoes on Liberia's exports (e.g., diamonds and timber) so that legitimate income could once again be generated.

The context for reconstruction was a stark post-war scene of desolation and lost hope typical of many civil-war-ravaged states:

Liberia is staggering under an external debt of $3.7 billion, a per capita GDP that is estimated to have declined 90 per cent from US$1,269 in 1980 to $163 in 2005, and an unemployment rate of over 80 per cent. There are no functioning public utilities, and the vast majority of Liberians have no access to electricity, water and basic sanitation facilities, or health care. Almost all medical services are provided by international non-governmental organizations and UN agencies. Roads and bridges, which are needed to open up markets, increase employment, sustain humanitarian access to rural areas and expand the overall protection environment, are in dire need of repairs ... The education system is dilapidated, with a dearth of qualified teachers and available resources to rehabilitate school buildings. (United Nations News Centre, 2006)

The United Nations Mission in Liberia (UNMIL) came to play a vital role in stabilizing the country and in meeting many of these peacebuilding tasks. For example, UNMIL engineers and country team members helped organize significant road-building projects. Clearly, though, Liberians, including those returning to the country, would have to shoulder the major responsibilities for reshaping their government and national institutions. It will be necessary to overcome the impact of a "brain drain" and the demographic losses suffered as people fled or were killed in large numbers during the war.

Source: United Nations News Centre (2006).

In their 2002 compilation of approaches to ending civil wars and implementing peace agreements, Stedman, Rothchild, and Cousens include chapters that cover the many aspects necessary to preserve peace and stability in post-war societies. At least in the early period after hostilities cease, much rests on the quality and type of support systems built into "transitional authorities" to move societies from a footing of war to that of peace. This was seen most vividly in the Cambodian reconstruction, in which international authorities came in to help staff all key administrative departments; the interveners also had to be cognizant of the delicate balance among formerly warring sides in the country in a postgenocidal situation. Such near total access by interveners is unusual, however, as the "normal" transitional phase, as in Liberia, involves complicated and delicate relationship-building between domestic factions vying for power in the newly re-emergent state, and involves external actors offering typically more limited assistance, advice, or intervention (both positive and negative).

Much depends on positive forms of coordination and understanding painstakingly negotiated among the actors involved in post-war recovery, and on bringing all relevant parties into the governing authority, so that each has something to gain by adhering to the agreements. In some sense this process, though attempted in a series of traditional intertribal councils, was short-circuited in the American and then NATO intervention to overthrow the Taliban forces and empower the "Northern Alliance" of ethnic groups and parties fighting in Afghanistan after 2001. The result was that the central government never fully established authority throughout the country, and gradually, as US forces were preoccupied in Iraq and as various NATO allies limited their roles to noncombat support, the Taliban reasserted itself, particularly in areas near the Pakistan border (where Taliban and reportedly al-Qaeda forces had taken refuge).

Clearly then, despite the encouraging reports in places such as Sierra Leone, the UN and other external interveners have not always been fully successful in their humanitarian missions to end civil wars and re-establish order. In fact, of some 16 peace implementation cases identified by Downs and Stedman (2002: 59), six are rated as successes and an additional four, including Cambodia, as partial successes. This is a reasonably good ratio of avoiding complete failure (six cases), but it still leaves a good deal of room for improvement.

The balance between success and failure in the 16 cases seems to rest on such factors as the degree of difficulty (perhaps including factional complexity and the substance of the agreement terms) in the implementation of the peace settlements and the extent to which great and regional power interests saw the task through successfully. Unfortunately, these factors do not always jibe, but in the successful cases they clearly did (Downs and Stedman, 2002: 59). In Sierra Leone it took the UN and a major power (the UK) to follow up on the peacemaking failure of ECOWAS in order to finally halt the war and open up the way for positive developments. Generally, Downs and Stedman conclude that significant enough major and regional power interest could overcome complications and difficulties inside the host country, at least often enough to achieve partial success (e.g., Bosnia, Liberia); however, in cases such as Sri Lanka, India's major interest and military intervention ended in abject failure. One wonders what the ultimate outcome of the US coalition interventions in Iraq and Afghanistan will turn out to be, as factions in those centres conclude they can or cannot live with the new system.[4]

Among the more persistent sources of post-war difficulties are the nonreconciled hostilities between the distrustful and bitter former warring populations. It is one thing for armies to kill each other; wars have seen such carnage for millennia. It is quite another, however, for violence to be brought to people's doorsteps, in wanton attacks on families, women, and children—the innocent populations—along with forced migrations and ethnic cleansing. Such atrocities are age-old, but the bitterness they engender dies the hardest. If wars go on long enough, as in Northern Ireland's nearly century-long "Troubles," or Israel's over-40-year occupation of Palestinian territories, grievances, past and present, and vengeance become part of the folklore with which people grow up. Given sufficient economic and international support, the society can recover in a reasonable time, but distrust takes generations to overcome in such circumstances, even if the institutions are reformed and the economy restored. Some of the pitfalls in the crucial processes of reconciliation can be seen in the account of just one of Indonesia's numerous domestic conflict outcomes, presented in Box 7.4.

BOX 7.4: A CASE STUDY: INDONESIA AND THE NORTH MALUKU CONFLICT

The province of North Maluku in eastern Indonesia is still recovering from a period of communal violence that swept the region from August 1999 and through July 2000. Now reconciliation and reconstruction are the tasks ahead for the people of North Maluku. More than 220,000 internally displaced persons (IDPs) have had to return home, dozens of villages have had to be completely rebuilt, and regional infrastructure has had to be repaired.

Formed in October of 1999, the province of North Maluku includes the island of Halmahera and surrounding islands, such as Ternate and Tidore, as well as the Sula Archipelago to the southwest. As the fighting raged in Ambon further south in early 1999, North Maluku remained peaceful. However, in mid-August 1999 violence erupted in Halmahera, in the sub-district of Kao, between Makian migrants and indigenous populations. These clashes focused on plans by the regional government to create a new sub-district of Makian Daratan from the southern half of the Kao sub-district. This new sub-district would consist of all of the Makian villages that were established in 1975 when the Indonesian government moved the Makian from their homes on Makian Island and resettled them in Kao to protect them from a predicted volcanic eruption.

The argument revolved around the inclusion of several villages in the new sub-district that were inhabited by indigenous Pagu people. Government regulations insist on a minimum number of villages per sub-district. The Pagu villagers had no desire to be separated from their indigenous brethren, nor to be ruled over by the Makian. The resulting tension led to violence on the day the new sub-district was to be formally inaugurated. Another factor that has been cited as a cause of the violence was the economic benefits associated with an Australian-owned gold mine in the region.

This violence was short-lived, but the problem remained unresolved. Disturbances broke out again in October, this time resulting in the total defeat of the Makian by the indigenous population (both Muslim and Christian). Approximately 15,000 IDPs fled to Ternate and Tidore. Although the fighting started as an ethnic conflict, it soon took on the character of a religious war when the violence spread to Ternate and Tidore in November, since the Makian are Muslim, and many of the people of Kao are Christian.

The violence in Tidore began with the appearance of a false letter calling for Christians to cleanse the region of Muslims. This letter infuriated Muslims, particularly the Makian IDPs who were still resentful for having been chased from their homes on Halmahera the previous month. Once all the Christians had fled from Tidore, the violence spread to Ternate. As a result approximately 13,000 largely Christian IDPs fled to North Sulawesi and Halmahera. This was followed by Muslim attacks on the western and southern regions of Halmahera, sending thousands of Christian IDPs to North Sulawesi and northern Halmahera.

At the end of 1999, after months of tension, fighting broke out in Tobelo in north Halmahera. It resulted in the deaths of several hundred Muslims and the complete destruction of their homes and mosques. Accounts of this violence, made worse by media exaggeration, created a national uproar. This led to the creation of the Laskar Jihad, a group of self-proclaimed Muslim holy warriors who flooded into Ambon and Maluku several months later to help their religious brethren. In North Maluku, a few of these Jihad troops joined local Muslim militia and, supported by some army personnel, destroyed virtually every Christian village in the sub-district of Galela, as well as several villages on the islands of Morotai, Obi and Bacan.

By the time the conflict slowly came to a halt in July of 2000, few areas were unaffected by the violence. Several thousand people were killed and over 220,000 people (roughly 25% of the province's population) were displaced by the violence.

RECONCILIATION

Although many on both sides would like to move on with the process of reconciliation, mistrust and animosity remain. Many say they will never again be able to trust the other side. Government efforts at facilitating reconciliation have been half-hearted at best. Officials seem to believe that once IDPs have gone home reconciliation is complete. They fail to realize that the process will take a long time and extended effort.

Numerous non-governmental organizations have sprung up in the region to deal with this challenge, but with mixed success. Efforts by international aid groups were largely unsuccessful. They often brought open-minded "leaders" from North Maluku to Manado for meetings and then sent them home with little if any follow-up. People in North Maluku criticized these efforts arguing that any attempts at reconciliation had to start from the bottom up, and be made in North Maluku. Furthermore, these efforts focused on those who are already willing to reconcile, as opposed to the hardliners who refuse to attend these meetings. Although many IDPs have returned, it has been a case of [accepting] the inevitable rather than true reconciliation. Where reconciliation has begun, it is the exception rather than the rule. For example, most Muslims have returned to Tobelo, but the Christian population greeted their return with mixed feelings. Many are eager to put the past behind them, while others are still mistrustful and would rather the Muslims had not returned. Dealing with the latter group will be the challenge for the local government. Along these lines, several high-ranking government officials in the Tobelo region have made reconciliation a priority and are hoping that a revival of customary tradition will aid this effort.

In addition to reconciliation, the people of North Maluku have had to rebuild. During the fighting an estimated 20,000 homes were destroyed, along with numerous churches, mosques, schools, and government buildings. Dozens of villages were completely razed to the ground. Many people had their gardens partially destroyed, and other means of livelihood, such as fishing boats, were burnt or stolen, hampering economic recovery. The flight of civil servants and schoolteachers from the region also slowed recovery efforts. Several efforts addressed the destruction, including donations of material from USAID and World Vision Indonesia. Unfortunately these programs were only for IDPs who returned to their place of origin. They did not help people who had no desire to, or could not, return home. Furthermore, the aid programs were hampered by corruption at the local level.

Source: Duncan, *Inside Indonesia* (2007). Reprinted with permission.

Reconciliation is always a challenge, but it is compounded under conditions of economic stagnation and underdevelopment. If factional groups cannot establish useful and constructive cross-linkages with each other, for example in economic and occupational roles or in civil society organizations of professionals and service providers, the task of overcoming polarization is very difficult.[5] Much depends on the role of the government in vigorously pushing to overcome people's prejudices and hatreds, in dispelling negative stereotypes and the dehumanization of opponents that often accompanies civil wars.

The ultimate test of post-civil war peacebuilding comes in both sustained nonviolent political relations and in the fate of the nation-state in question. This brings up a debatable set of issues; we saw in the last chapter that peace may be more effectively promoted in some cases if states actually disintegrate into more homogeneous constituent parts, parts in which people, at least in the near-term, can get along with each other better. For example, Chapman and Roeder (2007) contend that post-civil war institutional structures affect peace prospects, and that following civil wars, where the nation-state or secession were called into question, partition into separate states seemed to work better in promoting peace and democratization than attempts to reform the unitary government or provisions for modified separation such as local autonomy. Of course, partition, too, is no panacea or guarantee of peaceful relations, as shown by the experience on the Indian subcontinent since 1947. Political authorities both within partitioned states and in the international regions surrounding them must always pay serious attention to reducing policies that exacerbate social tensions.

Among others who have speculated on the best way to promote and maintain the peace and the state are writers such as Etzioni (2007), who has argued in reference to Iraq that in the absence of a viable central Iraqi authority under American occupation, order may best be restored, at least in the short term, by allowing ethnic militias to patrol and keep order in their own neighborhoods and precincts. Of course, allowing this to happen often also results in the expulsion of other ethnicities from these neighborhoods and precincts. Etzioni posits that eventually such groups would work out relationships and come to terms, either to rebuild a federated state or to devolve further into separate areas. This is controversial, however, in that regional peace and stability may or may not be enhanced by empowering nongovernmental armed groups or by dissolving or weakening the state, especially a state as potentially wealthy and strategically located as Iraq (partition or dissolution would inevitably mean implications for Kurdish-Turkish, Sunni-Shi'a, and Arab-Iranian relations, as well as the flow of oil).

A crucial and arguably underappreciated factor leading to the creation of a viable or nonviable post-civil war state is the degree of groups' identity with that state. After civil wars end, a crucial question for reconciliation is whether and under what conditions the winners or losers (if any) or the previous contestants and various warring groups can live together again under the same proverbial roof. Elkins and Sides (2007) have carefully examined the types of state structures and governing institutions that have the potential to win the "hearts and minds" of constituent minority and majority groups, who may then choose to jointly profess themselves to be Iraqis, or Liberians, or whatever common political identity group the state encompasses.[6] A state's stability appears to depend on "large majorities of both majority and minority citizens express[ing] attachment to the state" (Elkins and Sides, 2007: 705). Research tends to show weaker attachment in post-war situations by newly arrived minority groups (immigrants) or those with "active grievances related to autonomy [e.g., territorial] and the economy" (Elkins and Sides, 2007: 706).

Thus, governing authorities face the challenge of promoting institutions and conditions that make it possible and desirable for group members to profess common loyalties. Interestingly, however, Elkins and Sides have found that factors such as regime type (democracy), institutional structure (federalism, power-sharing arrangements, proportional representation, etc.), and even economic development and prosperity (which could, given local desires to control wealth, actually work against unity) have relatively little evident effect on building such identities or keeping groups together. One might note, for example, that the wealthier segment of the Cypriot community, the Greek sector, rejected the unity accords for the divided island in 2006 (while still achieving European Union membership for their zone), while the poorer Turkish sector opted for federal reunification. At best, it seems that economic, institutional, and regime factors may allow factions to coexist in uneasy truces, but to cohere in a truly common society and state evidently requires far more.

It could be that the old-fashioned mechanisms of building identities and nationalism through communication channels (see Deutsch, 1953) and such factors as language education, as well as the need for common markets and the common perception of an outside threat, might correlate more closely with the formation of a common identity. The best predictors might still be common cultural norms and traditions (related to extended family identification), though we have seen in Bosnia and elsewhere that cultural similarities are no guarantee of state coherence. It is also possible for societies to cohere, at least above a minimum threshold, even if groups do not co-identify with the state in the same ways. Lebanon is a state that has been troubled, throughout its relatively short history during the twentieth and twenty-first centuries, by its constituent ethnic communities' uncertain attachment to the state (i.e., groups frequently appear to identify more with regional, ethnic, and clan or family communities), which, along with uneven distribution of wealth and the impact of foreign interventions, has been a formula for repeated tragic decline into civil war. These cleavages have not been solved by formal constitutional provisions for power-sharing and have been exacerbated by outside interveners taking advantage of the country's divisions. Yet, the country persists and, in large part due to public pressure, the various parties continue to seek solutions that will allow them to restore the peace.

CONCLUSION

It seems we conclude our discussion of civil war on a rather pessimistic note. In doing so, however, we are able to stress a number of key points.

First, it is important that we continue to explore the causes, processes, and resolution of civil wars so as to improve our ability to deal more effectively with them. To sugar-coat the consequences of civil wars is to do ourselves and those who have suffered through them a disservice. It is through additional attention, resources, and research that we will build our knowledge of civil wars to the extent that we may confidently discuss, rather than debate, a real drop in their occurrence and their accompanying damage.

Second, by underscoring the severe consequences of civil wars and the difficulties in transitioning post-civil war societies, we can stress the point that early warning of such conflicts should be heeded. Intervening constructively (and legally) through such means as concerted diplomatic pressure and assistance programs early on in a potentially volatile situation may be costly, both politically and economically, but once civil war is underway, the costs escalate exponentially for war participants, and for the international community, whether through spillover, military intervention, or post-war reconstructive aid.

An additional challenge for international political actors will be to determine how and to what extent to punish the transgressions and misdeeds that frequently occur in civil wars. International wars present one degree of difficulty in assessing war crimes; the American government's reluctance to join the International Criminal Court at the Hague reflects its misgivings about exposing its service and government personnel overseas or in Washington to potential international prosecution. It is even more difficult to achieve consensus on war crimes in internal wars, since these are by their very nature subject to debate about jurisdiction, sovereignty, and the right of individual governments to adjudicate crimes within their jurisdiction.

International and domestic war crimes tribunals have existed and do exist, beginning with the famous World War II Nuremberg trials of Nazi war criminals. Japanese war criminals were also prosecuted after World War II; for example, General Tomoyuki Yamashita was tried and sentenced to death for his responsibility in Japanese military crimes in the Philippines. The US Supreme Court sustained his sentence of execution by hanging, even though he had pled during his trial that the troops under his command had been out of his communication and control as events unfolded in the Philippine campaign. No such trials were held for senior American military leaders despite the atrocities committed by US troops during the Vietnam War (see Taylor, 1970).

The UN Security Council set up special war crimes tribunals for both the former Yugoslavia and Rwanda in the early 1990s. In the Yugoslav case, the tribunal was scheduled to complete its work by 2010. In the course of his lengthy trial, former Serbian president Slobodan Milosevic died before a verdict could be reached. The prosecution then noted that Serbia had not turned over two of the other major indicted leaders: Ratko Mladic and Radovan Karadzic. Although Serbia promised to comply, 12 years after the massacre of Muslims in the supposedly safe refuge of Srebrenica, these individuals were still at large. Russia, highly sympathetic to the Serbs, called for the tribunal's 2010 expiration date to be firmly observed (see Hoge, 2007). Thus, uncertainty still prevails regarding the extent of international coverage of domestic political and military crimes, making it difficult to establish expectations regarding human rights observance in and after civil wars.

A final point to be made through our discussion of civil war consequences and post-war peacebuilding has to do with the seeming shift in international concern toward the "War on Terror." To misinterpret the threat of continued civil war at its current rate of both occurrence and intensity is to misunderstand the connection between international terrorism and civil war states. The two are very much connected. Not only do nonstate actors engage in terrorist activity (recall the first suicide bombings by Tamil separatists in Sri Lanka in 1987—well before such bombings became associated with Palestinian and other groups) but civil war states tend to become training grounds for transnational terrorist organizations. It is not by accident that Afghanistan, the Sudan, and Somalia have been launched to the forefront of the "War on Terror," first with President Bill Clinton's 1998 bombing of Afghanistan and the Sudan in an effort to destroy al-Qaeda, then with President George W. Bush's invasion of Afghanistan and support for peacekeeping in the Sudan, followed more recently with US and Ethiopian involvement in Somalia. All three states have been experiencing long drawn-out civil war battles. Central authorities in these states are either unable to monitor activities within their borders or have found hosting extremist organizations and militia to be both ideologically and financially desirable (Pakistan, a state with diverse ethno-political forces but no formal civil war after its split from Bangladesh, has also been alleged to host such organizations).

Further, civil wars and terrorism, as well as states' counterterrorism efforts, such as those by the US and its allies in Iraq and Afghanistan and Israel's in Lebanon and Gaza, naturally involve the potential to create additional terrorism. Civil war, even the variety seen in the occupied Palestinian territories, inevitably leaves populations feeling desperate, frustrated, humiliated, and angry, making recruitment into terrorist organizations easier. Clearly then, the amount of destruction resulting from civil wars should be enough to motivate states and intergovernmental organizations to undertake early preventive measures or to lessen the local and regional spread and escalation of violence (e.g., through arms control and "smart sanctions"), as well as to help resolve the conflicting interests underlying ongoing civil war situations. A significant focus on terrorism should not be allowed to detract from these goals.

NOTES

1   The Clinton administration, under pressure from the US armed forces, argued that landmines were still a military necessity in places such as South Korea, but offered a technological approach to designing self-disarming mines.

2   Sutton (2002) lists 3,524 deaths that are directly linked to the conflict in Northern Ireland, and which occurred between July 1969 and December 31, 2001, though no evident consensus exists on the question of its civil war status.

3   Ironically, it has been reported that the famous Hells Angels motorcycle gang originated in the 1940s among disillusioned returning American World War II veterans in California (see Queen, 2005).

4   Additional sources for information on civil war outcomes can be found on Michael Allison's course website, "Civil War and Civil War Resolution CPO 3930–02 Special Topics," <http://www.apsanet.org/imgtest/Allison_CivilWar.pdf>.

5   Unfortunately, external efforts to foster civil society organizations through the work of outside interveners and transnational organizations are sometimes viewed with suspicion by domestic populations in the warring state; charges of "cultural imperialism" or domination by nongovernmental organizations or Western powers can result. See, with reference to Bosnia, Pickering (2007) and Hunter (2007).

6   In this way, we can perhaps understand why a lasting Sri Lankan peace seems so distant, since it would be difficult to envision militant Tamils once again identifying themselves first as Sri Lankans, though conceivably under the best of circumstances a majority of moderate Tamils may again risk such identity. We might also note that the Northern Irish also intensely hated each other and that some of this hatred still carries over today, yet a transformation to peace seems to be occurring.

A List of Intrastate Conflicts, 1946-2000

Compiled with the assistance of Susumu Suzuki, Wayne State University.

Intrastate Conflict ID	Country Name	Years of Conflict	Region
1	Cuba	1958–1959	America
2	Dominican Republic	1965	America
3	Grenada	1983	America
4	Mexico	1994	America
5	Guatemala	1954	America
6	Guatemala	1960–1995	America
7	El Salvador	1979–1991	America
8	Nicaragua	1978–1979	America
9	Nicaragua	1982–1990	America
10	Costa Rica	1948	America
11	Colombia	1948	America
12	Colombia	1949–1965	America
13	Colombia	1984–1999*	America
14	Ecuador	1985–1989	America
15	Peru	1982–1999*	America
16	Bolivia	1946	America
17	Paraguay	1947	America
18	United Kingdom	1968–1994	Europe
19	Spain	1968–1999*	Europe

Intrastate Conflict ID	Country Name	Years of Conflict	Region
20	Hungary	1956	Europe
21	Yugoslavia	1988–1999	Europe
22	Yugoslavia	1990–1992	Europe
23	Bosnia	1992–1995	Europe
24	Greece	1944–1949	Europe
25	Cyprus	1974	Europe
26	Cyprus	1963–1964	Europe
27	Moldova	1992–1997	Europe
28	Romania	1989	Europe
29	Russia	1988–1991	Europe
30	Russia	1994–1996	Europe
31	Georgia	1990–1992	Europe
32	Georgia	1992–1994	Europe
33	Georgia (Abkhazia)	1992–1994	Europe
34	Azerbaijan	1991–1999*	Europe
35	Guinea-Bissau	1998	Africa
36	Gambia	1981	Africa
37	Mali	1990–1995	Africa
38	Mauritania	1975–1979	Africa
39	Niger	1990–1995	Africa
40	Liberia	1989–1991	Africa
41	Liberia	1992–1993	Africa
42	Liberia	1989–1996	Africa
43	Sierra Leone	1991–1999*	Africa
44	Nigeria	1967–1970	Africa
45	Nigeria	1967–1970	Africa
46	Nigeria	1980–1981	Africa
47	Nigeria	1984	Africa
48	Nigeria	1986–1999*	Africa
49	Chad	1978–1982	Africa
50	Chad	1983–1988	Africa
51	Chad	1965–1972	Africa
52	Chad	1991–1995	Africa
53	Congo	1960–1965	Africa
54	Congo	1967	Africa
55	Congo	1998–1999*	Africa

Intrastate Conflict ID	Country Name	Years of Conflict	Region
56	Congo	1996–1997	Africa
57	Congo	1997	Africa
58	Zaire	1977	Africa
59	Zaire	1978–1979	Africa
60	Zaire	1992–1997	Africa
61	Uganda	1966	Africa
62	Uganda	1971–1972	Africa
63	Uganda	1978–1979	Africa
64	Uganda	1981–1986	Africa
65	Uganda	1986–1988	Africa
66	Kenya	1992–1999*	Africa
67	Burundi	1988	Africa
68	Burundi	1991–1992	Africa
69	Burundi	1972	Africa
70	Burundi	1993–1999	Africa
71	Burundi	1996–1999*	Africa
72	Rwanda	1963–1964	Africa
73	Rwanda	1990–1994	Africa
74	Somalia	1982–1991	Africa
75	Somalia	1991–1999*	Africa
76	Djibouti	1991–1994	Africa
77	Ethiopia	1962–1991	Africa
78	Ethiopia	1963–1964	Africa
79	Ethiopia	1988–1991	Africa
80	Ethiopia	1977–1986	Africa
81	Ethiopia	1992–1999*	Africa
82	Angola	1975–1991	Africa
83	Angola	1992–1999*	Africa
84	Mozambique	1979–1993	Africa
85	Zimbabwe	1972–1979	Africa
86	Zimbabwe	1980–1988	Africa
87	South Africa	1976–1994	Africa
88	Morocco	1975–1999*	Middle East
89	Algeria	1962	Middle East
90	Algeria	1992–1999*	Middle East
91	Sudan	1963–1972	Middle East

Intrastate Conflict ID	Country Name	Years of Conflict	Region
92	Sudan	1983–1999*	Middle East
93	Iran	1978–1979	Middle East
94	Iran	1979–1982	Middle East
95	Iran	1981–1983	Middle East
96	Turkey	1984–1999*	Middle East
97	Iraq	1959	Middle East
98	Iraq	1961–1966	Middle East
99	Iraq	1974–1975	Middle East
100	Iraq	1980–1999*	Middle East
101	Iraq	1991–1999*	Middle East
102	Egypt	1992–1999*	Middle East
103	Lebanon	1958	Middle East
104	Lebanon	1975–1999*	Middle East
105	Jordan	1970–1971	Middle East
106	Yemen Arab Republic	1948	Middle East
107	Yemen Arab Republic	1962–1970	Middle East
108	Yemen	1994	Middle East
109	Yemen Peoples Republic	1986	Middle East
110	Oman	1970–1975	Middle East
111	Afghanistan	1978–1992	Asia
112	Afghanistan	1992–1999	Asia
113	Tajikistan	1992–1999*	Asia
114	China	1946–1950	Asia
115	China	1947	Asia
116	China	1959	Asia
117	China	1980–1999*	Asia
118	India	1955–1964	Asia
119	India	1984–1999*	Asia
120	India	1988–1994	Asia
121	India	1989–1999*	Asia
122	Pakistan	1971	Asia
123	Pakistan	1973–1977	Asia
124	Bangladesh	1971–1998	Asia
125	Bangladesh	1972–1973	Asia
126	Burma	1948–1999*	Asia
127	Burma	1968–1980	Asia

Intrastate Conflict ID	Country Name	Years of Conflict	Region
128	Burma	1983–1992	Asia
129	Sri Lanka	1971	Asia
130	Sri Lanka	1981–1999*	Asia
131	Sri Lanka	1987–1989	Asia
132	Nepal	1996–1999*	Asia
133	Thailand	1965–1985	Asia
134	Cambodia	1970–1975	Asia
135	Cambodia	1978–1991	Asia
136	Cambodia	1992–1998	Asia
137	Laos	1959–1962	Asia
138	Laos	1963–1973	Asia
139	Republic of Vietnam	1960–1965	Asia
140	Malaysia	1948–1962	Asia
141	Philippines	1948–1954	Asia
142	Philippines	1971–1999	Asia
143	Philippines	1972–1999*	Asia
144	Indonesia	1950	Asia
145	Indonesia	1953	Asia
146	Indonesia	1956–1960	Asia
147	Indonesia	1965	Asia
148	Indonesia	1975–1999*	Asia
149	Indonesia	1975–1999	Asia

* Ongoing as of December 1999.
Source: Data compiled by Regan (2002), as modified by Pearson et al. (2006).

Readers interested in identifying the parties and circumstances involved in these wars can refer to the Correlates of War (COW) website <http://www.correlatesofwar.org>, although there are some discrepancies between this list and ours. In addition, COW identifies only those cases reaching at least 1,000 battle-related deaths in a given year. As a result, lower threshold conflicts will not appear on COW lists. For countries with multiple conflicts involving various actors, the International Peace Research Institute's (PRIO's) Centre for the Study of Civil War also maintains a dataset on their website <http://new.prio.no/CSCW-Datasets/Data-on-Armed-Conflict/UppsalaPRIO-Armed-Conflicts-Dataset/>. PRIO's threshold is well below both COW's and Regan's (2002), identifying conflicts with as few as 25 battle-related deaths. Narrative information on these and other conflicts can be found through the related Uppsala Conflict Database <http://www.pcr.uu.se/database/index.php>. Again, one will find some discrepancy between the COW and PRIO lists and the list provided here regardless of battle death threshold. Definitional differences account for some discrepancies, but not all. Efforts to generate a definitive civil war list are challenged by these discrepancies. Additional conflict descriptions can be found by using such sources as OnWar.com; *Keesings Contemporary Archives*; the bbc.co.uk; *Agence France Presse*; *Lexis-Nexis*; *Facts on File*; and *The New York Times*.

REFERENCES

American Psychological Association. 2003. "Preventing Violence by Teaching Non-Violent Problem-Solving." *Psychology Matters.* Washington, DC: APAOn Line.

Aronson, Geoffrey. 1990. *Israel, Palestinians and the Intifada: Creating Facts on the West Bank,* 2nd ed. London: Kegan Paul.

Axelrod, Robert. 1997. *The Complexity of Cooperation: Agent-Based Models of Competition and Collaboration.* Princeton, NJ: Princeton UP.

Ayers, Edward L. 2003. *In the Presence of Mine Enemies: The Civil War in the Heart of America 1859-1863.* New York, NY: W.W. Norton.

―――. 2005. *What Caused the Civil War? Reflections on the South and Southern History.* New York, NY: W.W. Norton.

Bairner, A. 1999. "Soccer, Masculinity, and Violence in Northern Ireland." *Men and Masculinities* 3: 284-301.

Balch-Lindsay, Dylan, and Andrew J. Enterline. 2000. "Killing Time: The World Politics of Civil War Duration, 1820-1992." *International Studies Quarterly* 44: 615-642.

Bandura, Albert. 1973. *Aggression: A Social Learning Analysis.* Englewood Cliff, NJ: Prentice Hall.

Banks, Arthur S., and Thomas C. Muller, eds. 1999. *Political Handbook of the World: 1999.* Binghamton, NY: CSA Publications.

Banton, Michael. 2000. "Ethnic Conflict." *Sociology* 34 (3): 481-498.

BBC. 21 August 2007. "Country Profile: Tajikistan." <http://news.bbc.co.uk/2/hi/asia-pacific/country_profiles/1296639.stm>.

―――. 29 October 2007. "Struggle to Salvage Darfur Talks." <http://news.bbc.co.uk/2/hi/africa/7066792.stm>.

BBC News. 1 April 2004. "Rwanda: How the Genocide Happened." <http://news.bbc.co.uk/2/hi/africa/1288230.stm>.

―――. 23 July 2004. "US House Calls Darfur 'Genocide.'" <http://news.bbc.co.uk/2/hi/africa/3918765.stm>.

―――. 30 July 2004. "Sudan Hails 'Softer' Darfur Draft." <http://news.bbc.co.uk/2/hi/africa/3938509.stm> (accessed 27 May 2008).

_____. 19 September 2006. "Thailand's Countdown Coup." <http://news.bbc.
co.uk/1/hi/world/asia-pacific/5361210.stm> (accessed 5 June 2008).

Bellamy, Alex J., Paul Williams, and Stuart Griffin. 2004. *Understanding Peacekeeping*. Malden, MA: Polity Press.

Bercovitch, Jacob, ed. 1996. *Resolving International Conflicts: The Theory and Practice of Mediation*. Boulder, CO: Lynne Reiner Publishers.

Besancon, Marie L. 2005. "Relative Resources: Inequality in Ethnic Wars, Revolutions, and Genocides." *Journal of Peace Research* 42 (4): 393–415.

Blainey, Geoffrey. 1988. *The Causes of War*. New York, NY: The Free Press.

Blimes, Randall J. 2006. "The Indirect Effect of Ethnic Heterogeneity on the Likelihood of Civil War Onset." *Journal of Conflict Resolution* 50 (4): 536–547.

Boutros-Ghali, Boutros. 31 January 1992. "An Agenda for Peace: Preventative Diplomacy, Peacemaking, and Peace-keeping." Report of the Secretary-General, Summit Meeting of the United Nations Security Council.

_____. 1994. "The Land Mine Crisis: A Humanitarian Disaster." *Foreign Affairs* 73 (5): 8–13.

Brancati, Dawn. 2005. "Decentralization: Fueling the Fire or Dampening the Flames of Ethnic Conflict and Secessionism." *International Organization* 60 (3): 651–685.

Brown, Michael E., et al. 1998. *Theories of War and Peace*. Cambridge, MA: MIT Press.

Buendia, Rizal G. 2005. "The State-Moro Armed Conflict in the Philippines: Unresolved National Question or Question of Governance?" *Asian Journal of Political Science* 13 (1): 109–138.

Bueno de Mesquita, Bruce. 2000. *Principles of International Politics: People's Power, Preferences, and Perceptions*. Washington, DC: Congressional Quarterly Press.

Burton, John. 1990. *Conflict: Basic Human Needs*. New York, NY: St. Martin's Press.

Caprioli, Mary. 2000. "Gendered Conflict." *Journal of Peace Research* 37 (1): 51–68.

_____. 2005. "Primed for Violence: The Role of Gender Inequality in Predicting Internal Conflict." *International Studies Quarterly* 49: 161–178.

Carment, David. 1993. "The International Dimensions of Ethnic Conflict: Concepts, Indicators, and Theory." *Journal of Peace Research* 30 (2): 137–150.

Carnegie Commission on Preventing Deadly Conflict. 1997. *Preventing Deadly Conflict, Final Report*. New York, NY: Carnegie Corporation.

Chapman, Thomas, and Philip G. Roeder. 2007. "Partition as a Solution to Wars of Nationalism: The Importance of Institutions." *American Political Science Review* 101 (7): 677.

Chasdi, Richard. 2002. *Tapestry of Terror: A Portrait of Middle East Terrorism, 1994-1999*. Lanham, MD: Lexington Books.

Chen, Siyen, Norman V. Loayza, and Marta Reynal-Querol. 2007. "The Aftermath of Civil Wars." *Post-Conflict Transitions Working Papers*, No. 4, WPS 4190, World Bank.

Chicago Council on Global Affairs. 2007. *Strengthening America: The Civic and Political Integration of Muslim Americans*. Report of the Task Force on Muslim American Civic and Political Engagement.

Christin, Thomas, and Simon Hug. April 2003. "Federalism and Conflict Resolution: Considering Selection Biases." Presented at the Midwest Political Science Association Annual Meeting, Chicago, IL.

———. September 2004. "Methodological Issues in Studies of Conflict Processes." Presented at the American Political Science Association Annual Meeting, Chicago, IL.

Clausewitz, Carl von. 1984. *On War*. Princeton, NJ: Princeton UP. Translated by Michael Howard and Peter Paret.

Collier, Paul. 2003. "From War to Wealth: Ending Africa's Conflicts." Presented at a public debate at the Royal African Society, London, UK.

Collier, Paul, and Anke Hoeffler. 1998. "On Economic Causes of Civil War." *Oxford Economic Papers* 50 (October): 563–673.

———. 2001. "Greed and Grievance in Civil War." Washington, DC: World Bank.

———. 2002. "On the Incidence of Civil War in Africa." *Journal of Conflict Resolution* 46 (1): 13–28.

———. 2004. "Greed and Grievance in Civil War." *Oxford Economic Papers* 56 (October): 563–595.

Collier, Paul, Anke Hoeffler, and Mans Soderborn. 2001. "On the Duration of Civil War." *Policy Research Working Paper Series* 2681. Washington, DC: The World Bank.

———. 2004. "On the Duration of Civil War." *Journal of Peace Research* 41 (3): 253–273.

Copeland, Miles. 1970. *The Game of Nations: The Amorality of Power Politics*. New York, NY: Simon and Schuster.

Cortright, David, and George A. Lopez. 1995. *Economic Sanctions: Panacea or Peacebuilding in a Post-Cold War World?* Boulder, CO: Westview.

———. 2000. *The Sanctions Decade: Assessing UN Strategies in the 1990s*. Boulder, CO: Lynne Rienner.

Crocker, Chester A., Fen Osler Hampson, and Pamela Aall. 2004. *Taming Intractable Conflicts: Mediation in the Hardest Cases*. Washington, DC: United States Institute of Peace.

———. 2005. *Grasping the Nettle: Analyzing Cases of Intractable Conflict*. Washington, DC: USIP Press.

Cunningham, David E. 2006. "Veto Players and Civil War Duration." *American Journal of Political Science* 50 (4): 875–892.

Cunningham, David E., Kristian Gleditsch, and Idean Salehyan. August-September 2006. "Transnational Linkages and Civil War Interactions." Presented at the American Political Science Association Annual Meeting, Philadelphia, PA.

Davies, James. 1962. "Toward a Theory of Revolution." *American Sociological Review* 27 (1): 5–19.

DeRouen, Jr., Karl R., and David Sobek. 2004. "The Dynamics of Civil War Duration and Outcome." *Journal of Peace Research* 41 (3): 303–320.

Deutsch, Karl. 1953. *Nationalism and Social Communication: An Inquiry into the Foundations of Nationality.* New York, NY: John Wiley & Sons.

Diehl, Paul F., and Gary Goertz. 2000. *War and Peace in International Rivalry.* Ann Arbor, MI: The U of Michigan P.

Dinstein, Yoram. 1977. "Law and Civil War in the Modern World." *American Political Science Review* 71 (2): 856–858.

Dollard, John, et al. 1939. *Frustration and Aggression.* New Haven, CT: Yale UP.

Doswald-Beck, Louise. 1986. "The Legal Validity of Military Intervention by Invitation of the Government." *British Yearbook of International Law* 56: 188–252.

Dougherty, James E., and Robert L. Pfaltzgraff. 1990. *Contending Theories of International Relations,* 3rd ed. New York, NY: Longman.

Downs, George, and Stephen John Stedman. 2002. "Evaluation Issues in Peace Implementation." In *Ending Civil Wars: The Implementation of Peace Agreements.* Edited by Stephen John Stedman, Donald Rothchild, and Elizabeth M. Cousens. Boulder, CO: Lynne Reinner.

Doyle, Michael W. 1986. "Liberalism and World Politics." *American Political Science Review* 80 (4): 1151–1169.

Doyle, Michael W., and Nicholas Sambanis. 2000. "International Peacebuilding: A Theoretical and Quantitative Analysis." *American Political Science Review* 94 (4): 779–801.

———. 2006. *Making War and Building Peace.* Princeton, NJ: Princeton UP.

Duncan, Christopher R. 2007. "The Aftermath of Civil War: Fighting has stopped in North Maluku, but mistrust lingers." *Inside Indonesia.* Edition 69. <http://insideindonesia.org/content/view/422/29/>.

Eberwein, Wolf-Dieter, et al. 1979. "External and Internal Conflict Behavior Among Nations, 1966–1967." *Journal of Conflict Resolution* 23 (4): 715–742.

Elbadawi, Ibrahim A., and Nicholas Sambanis. 2000. "External Interventions and the Duration of Civil Wars." The World Bank's Development Economic Research Group (DECRG).

Elkins, Zachary, and John Sides. 2007. "Can Institutions Build Unity in Multiethnic States?" *American Political Science Review* 101 (4): 1–16.

Ellingsen, Tanja. 2000. "Colorful Community or Ethnic Witches' Brew? Multieth-nicity and Domestic Conflict During and After the Cold War." *Journal of Conflict Resolution* 44 (2): 228–249.

Ellis, John. 1976. *Eye Deep in Hell: Trench Warfare in World War I.* Baltimore, MD: Johns Hopkins UP.

Etzioni, Amitai. 1996. *The New Golden Rule: Community and Morality in Democratic Society.* New York, NY: Basic Books.

——. 2007. "Plan Z: A Community Based Security Plan for Iraq." *Amitai Etzioni Notes.* Washington, DC: George Washington University. <http://blog. amitaietzioni.org/2007/11/plan-z-a-commun.html>.

Farer, Tom J. 1993. "The Paradigm of Legitimate Intervention." In *Enforcing Restraint: Collective Intervention in Internal Conflicts.* Edited by Lori Fisler Damrosch. New York, NY: Council on Foreign Relations Press.

Fearon, James D. 2004. "Why Do Some Civil Wars Last So Much Longer Than Oth-ers?" *Journal of Peace Research* 41 (3): 275–301.

——. 15 September 2006. "Iraq: Democracy or Civil War?" Testimony to US House of Representatives, Committee on Government Reform, Subcommittee on National Security, Emerging Threats, and International Relations. <http://www.stanford.edu/~jfearon/papers/fearon%20testimony.doc>.

Fearon, James D., and David D. Laitin. 1996. "Explaining Interethnic Cooperation." *American Political Science Review* 90 (4): 715–735.

——. 2003. "Ethnicity, Insurgency, and Civil War." *American Political Science Review* 97 (1): 75–90.

Fearon, James, Kimuli Kasara, and David Laitin. 2007. *"Ethnic Minority Rule and Civil War Onset." American Political Science Review* 101 (1): 187–193.

Feierabend, Ivo K., and Rosalind L. Feierabend. 1966. "Aggressive Behaviors within Polities, 1948–1962: A Cross-National Study." *Journal of Conflict Resolution* 10 (3): 249–271.

Ferguson, Niall. 2005. "Democracy: Giving Peace a Chance." *Hoover Digest.* Stanford University. <http://www.hoover.org/publications/digest/2913271.html>.

Fogelsong, David S. 1995. *America's Secret War Against Bolshevism: US Intervention in the Russian Civil War, 1917–1920.* Chapel Hill, NC: U of North Carolina P.

Forsythe, David P. 1985. "The United Nations and Human Rights, 1945–1985." *Political Science Quarterly* 100 (2): 249–269.

Freel, R., and E. Robinson. 2004. "Experience of Domestic Violence in Northern Ireland: Findings from the 2001 Northern Ireland Crime Survey. Research and Statistical Bulletin." <http://www.nio.gov.uk/experience_of_domes-tic_violence_in_northern_ireland-findings_from_2003-04_northern_ ireland_crime_survey.pdf> (accessed 3 June 2008).

Gagnon, V.P. 1994–1995. "Ethnic Nationalism and International Conflict: The Case of Serbia." *International Security* 19 (Winter): 120-150.

Gellner, Ernest. 1983. *Nations and Nationalism.* Ithaca: Cornell University Press.

Gettleman, Jeffrey. 15 September 2006. "Uganda Peace Hinges on Amnesty for Brutality." *New York Times.* <http://www.nytimes.com/2006/09/15/world/africa/15uganda.html?_r=1&oref=slogin>.

———. 31 October 2007. "Rebel Unity Is Scarce at the Darfur Talks in Libya." *New York Times.* <http://www.nytimes.com/2007/10/31/world/africa/31darfur.html> (accessed 5 June 2008).

———. 29 November 2007. "Juba Journal: The Boom Is Drowned Out by the Boys on Motorbikes." *New York Times,* sec. A, p. 4.

Ghobarah, Hazem Adam, Paul Huth, and Bruce Russett. 2003. "Civil Wars Kill and Maim People—Long After the Shooting Stops." *Leitner Working Papers* 2002-10. Zurich: Center for Security Studies, Swiss Federal Institute of Technology.

Gibney, M., Cornett, L., and Wood, R. 2008. *Political Terror Scale 1976-2006.* Political Terror Scale. <http://www.politicalterrorscale.org/> (accessed 3 June 2008).

Gilpin, Robert. 1981. *War and Change in World Politics.* Princeton: Princeton University Press.

Gissinger, Ranveig, and Nils Petter Gleditsch. 1999. "Globalization and Conflict: Welfare, Distribution, and Political Unrest." *Journal of World-Systems Research* 2: 327-365.

Gleditsch, Nils Petter, et al. 2002. "Armed Conflict 1946-2001: A New Dataset." *Journal of Peace Research* 39 (5): 615-637.

Globalsecurity.org. "Congo Civil War." <http://www.globalsecurity.org/military/world/war/congo.htm> (accessed 16 May 2008).

———. "Sudan People's Liberation Army (SPLA), Sudan People's Liberation Movement (SPLM)." <http://www.globalsecurity.org/military/world/para/spla.htm> (accessed 17 May 2008).

Goertz, Gary, and Paul F. Diehl. 1992. "The Empirical Importance of Enduring Rivalries." *International Interactions* 18 (2): 151-163.

Goodwin, Jeff. 1988. "Revolutionary Movements in Central America: A Comparative Analysis." Working Paper 7, Centre for Research on Politics and Social Organization. Reprinted in *The State: Critical Concepts.* Edited by John A. Hall. London: Routledge, 1994.

Gurr, Ted Robert. 1970. *Why Men Rebel.* Princeton, NJ: Princeton UP.

———. 1993. *Minorities at Risk: A Global View of Ethnopolitical Conflicts.* Washington, DC: United States Institute of Peace Press.

_____. 1997. "Ethnopolitical Rebellion: A Cross-Sectional Analysis of the 1980s with Risk Assessments for the 1990s." *American Journal of Political Science* 41(4): 1079–1103.

_____. 2000a. "Ethnic Warfare on the Wane." *Foreign Affairs* 79 (3): 51–73.

_____. 2000b. *People Versus States: Minorities at Risk in the New Century.* Washington, DC: United States Institute of Peace.

Gurr, Ted Robert, and Barbara Harff. 1994. *Ethnic Conflict in World Politics.* Boulder, CO: Westview Press.

Harff, Barbara. 1994. "A Theoretical Model of Genocides and Politicides." *The Journal of Ethno-Development* 4 (1): 25–30.

_____. 1995. "Rescuing Endangered Peoples: Missed Opportunities." *Social Research* 62 (1): 23–40.

_____. 2003. "No Lessons Learned from the Holocaust: Assessing the Risks of Genocide and Political Mass Murder since 1955." *American Political Science Review* 97 (1): 57–74.

Hartzell, Caroline. 1999. "Explaining the Stability of Negotiated Settlements to Intrastate Wars." *Journal of Conflict Resolution* 43 (1): 3–22.

Hartzell, Caroline, Matthew Hoddie, and Donald Rothchild. 2001. "Stabilizing the Peace after Civil War: An Investigation of Some Key Variables." *International Organization* 55 (1): 183–208.

Hegre, Havard, et al. 2001. "Toward a Democratic Civil Peace? Democracy, Political Change, and Civil War, 1816–1992." *American Political Science Review* 95 (1): 33–48.

Henderson, Errol A., and J. David Singer. 2000. "Civil War in the Post-Colonial World, 1946–92." *Journal of Peace Research* 37 (3): 275–299.

_____. 2002. "'New Wars' and Rumors of 'New Wars.'" *International Interactions* 28 (2): 165–190.

Hoge, Warren. 11 December 2007. "Serbia Accused of Failure to Catch Massacre Suspects." *New York Times*, sec. A, p. 18.

Holsti, Ole R. 1972. *Crisis, Escalation, War.* Montreal: McGill-Queen's University Press.

Human Rights Watch. 18 September 2004. "UN: Darfur Resolution a Historic Failure." <http://www.hrw.org/english/docs/2004/09/18/darfur9355.htm> (accessed 16 May 2008).

Hunter, Amanda Marie. 2007. "The New Policy Regime of Civil Society." Course paper, Detroit: Wayne State University.

Huntington, Samuel P. 1993. "The Clash of Civilization?" *Foreign Affairs* 72 (3): 22–34.

Immerman, Richard H. 1982. *The CIA in Guatemala: The Foreign Policy of Intervention.* Austin, TX: The U of Texas P.

Institute de Droit International. 1975. "The Principle of Non-Intervention in Civil Wars." Session of Wiesbaden.

Inter-Governmental Authority on Development (IGAD). 20 July 2002. Machakos Protocol, "Secretariat on Peace in the Sudan."

International Conference on the Great Lakes Region. 30 November 2006. "Protocol on Non-Aggression and Mutual Defence in the Great Lakes Region." Second Summit of the International Conference on the Great Lakes Region. <http://www.icglr.org/common/docs/docs_repository/protocol_nonaggression.pdf>.

International Conflict Research (INCORE). "Peace Agreements." <http://www.incore.ulst.ac.uk/services/cds/agreements/> (accessed 20 May 2008).

International Monetary Fund. *International Financial Statistics*. Washington, DC: 1958-.

Janis, Irving L. 1972. *Victims of Groupthink*. Boston, MA: Houghton Mifflin Company.

Jett, Dennis C. 1999. *Why Peacekeeping Fails*. New York: St. Martin's Press.

Jones, Bruce D. June 2001. "The Challenges of Strategic Coordination: Containing Opposition and Sustaining Implementation of Peace Agreements in Civil Wars." IPA Policy Paper Series on Peace Implementation, CISAC-IPA, Project on Peace Implementation.

Kaldor, Mary. 1999. *New and Old Wars: Organised Violence in a Global Era*. Cambridge, UK: Polity Press.

———. 2006. *New and Old Wars: Organized Violence in a Global Era*, 2nd ed. Cambridge, UK: Polity Press.

Kalyvas, Stathis N. 2001. "'New' and 'Old' Civil Wars: A Valid Distinction?" *World Politics* 54 (1): 99–118.

———. 2006. *The Logic of Violence in Civil War*. New York, NY: Cambridge UP.

Kaufmann, Chaim. 1996. "Possible and Impossible Solutions to Ethnic Civil Wars." *International Security* 20 (4): 136–175.

Kaufman, Stuart J. 1996. "Spiraling to Ethnic War: Elites, Masses, and Moscow in Moldova's Civil War." *International Security* 21 (2): 108–138.

———. 2001. *Modern Hatreds: The Symbolic Politics of Ethnic War*. Ithaca, NY: Cornell UP.

Keesing's Worldwide. 1960-2000 *Keesing's Contemporary Archives*. London, UK: Keesing's Worldwide.

Khan, Ismail, and Carlotta Gall. 25 April 2008. "Pakistan Asserts It Is Near a Deal with Militants." *New York Times*, sec. A, p. 1.

King, Charles. 1997. *Ending Civil Wars*. Aldephi Papers. London, UK: Routledge.

Kira, Ibrahim A., et al. 2006. "The Mental Health Effects of Retributive Justice: The Case of Iraqi Refugees." *Journal of Muslim Mental Health* 1 (2): 145–169.

Krause, Volker, and Susumu Suzuki. 2005. "Causes of Civil War in Asia and Sub-Saharan Africa: A Comparison." *Social Science Quarterly* 86 (1): 160–177.

Kresock, David M. 1994. "Ethnic Cleansing in the Balkans: The Legal Foundations of Foreign Intervention." *Cornell International Law Journal* 27 (1): 203-239.

Kriesberg, Louis M. 1998. *Constructive Conflicts: From Escalation to Resolution.* Lanham, MA: Rowman and Littlefield.

LaFeber, Walter. 1994. *The American Age: US Foreign Policy at Home and Abroad, 1750 to the Present*, 2nd ed. New York, NY: W.W. Norton and Company.

Laufer, R.S., M.S. Gallops, and E. Frey-Wouters. 1984. "War Stress and Trauma: The Vietnam Veteran Experience." *Journal of Health and Social Behavior* 25 (1): 65-85.

Lawson, Alistair. 6 June 2005. "Who are the Maoist Rebels?" BBC News online. <http://news.bbc.co.uk/2/hi/south_asia/3573402.stm>.

Leites, Nathan, and Charles Wolfe, Jr. 1970. *Rebellion and Authority: An Analytic Essay on Insurgent Conflicts.* Chicago: Markham Publishing.

Lichbach, Mark. 1994. "Rethinking Rationality and Rebellion." *Rationality and Society* 6 (1): 8-39.

_____. 1998. *The Rebel's Dilemma.* Ann Arbor, MI: U of Michigan P.

Licklider, Roy. 1995. "The Consequences of Negotiated Settlements in Civil Wars, 1945-1993." *American Political Science Review* 89 (3) (September): 681-90.

Long, Jeffrey Scott. 1997. *Regression Models for Categorical and Limited Dependent Variables.* Thousand Oaks, CA: Sage Publications.

Lorenz, Konrad. 1967. *On Aggression.* New York, NY: Bantam.

Mansfield, Edward D., and Jack Snyder. 2005. *Electing to Fight: Why Emerging Democracies Go to War.* Cambridge, MA: MIT Press.

Marker, Sandra. August 2003. "Unmet Human Needs." In *Beyond Intractability.* Edited by Guy Burgess and Heidi Burgess. Boulder, CO: Conflict Resolution Consortium, University of Colorado. <http://www.beyondintractability. org/essay/human_needs/>.

Mason, T. David. 2004. *Caught in the Crossfire: Revolutions, Repression, and the Rational Peasant.* Lanham, MD: Rowman and Littlefield.

Mason, T. David, et al. December 2005. "When and Why Civil Wars Recur: Conditions for a Durable Peace after Civil Wars?" Denton, TX: U of North Texas P.

Mason, T. David, and James D. Meernik, eds. 2006. *Conflict Prevention and Peacebuilding in Post-war Societies: Sustaining the Peace.* New York, NY: Routledge.

Mason, T. David, and Jason Quinn. August 2003. *"Sustaining the Peace: Determinants of Civil War Recurrence."* Presented at the Annual Meeting of the American Political Science Association, Philadelphia, PA.

Mason, T. David, Joseph P. Weingarten, Jr., and Patrick J. Fett. 1999. "Win, Lose or Draw: Predicting the Outcome of Civil Wars." *Political Research Quarterly* 52 (2): 239-68.

Mason, T. David, and Patrick J. Fett. 1996. "How Civil Wars End: A Rational Choice Approach." *Journal of Conflict Resolution* 40 (4): 546–68.

Mattler, Michael J. 1994. "The Distinction Between Civil Wars and International Wars and Its Legal Implications." *Journal of International Law and Politics* 26: 655–700.

May, R.J. 2003. "Ethnicity in the Philippines." In *Ethnicity in Asia*. Edited by Colin Mackerra. London, UK: Routledge.

Melander, Erik. 2005. "Gender Equality and Intrastate Armed Conflict." *International Studies Quarterly* 49 (4): 695–714.

Mendelsohn, Daniel. 2006. *The Lost: A Search for Six of Six Million*. New York, NY: Harper Collins.

Miall, Hugh. 1992. *The Peacemakers: Peaceful Settlement of Disputes since 1945*. London: Macmillan Academic and Professional LTD.

Moore, Barrington, Jr. 1966. *Social Origins of Dictatorship and Democracy: Lord and Peasant in the Making of the Modern World*. Boston, MA: Beacon Press.

Moore, Will H., Ronny Lindstrom, and Valerie O'Reagan. 1996. "Land Reform, Political Violence and the Economic Inequality-Political Conflict Nexus: A Longitudinal Analysis." *International Interactions* 21 (4): 353–363.

Most, Benjamin A., and Harvey Starr. 1989. *Inquiry, Logic and International Politics*. Columbia, SC: U of South Carolina P.

Mukherjee, Bumba. 2006. "Why Political Power-Sharing Agreements Lead to Enduring Peaceful Resolution of Some Civil Wars, but Not Others?" *International Studies Quarterly* 50 (2): 479–504.

Murdoch, James C., and Todd Sandler. 2002. "Economic Growth, Civil Wars, and Spatial Spillovers." *Journal of Conflict Resolution* 46 (1): 91–110.

Murphy, Sean D. 1996. *Humanitarian Intervention: The United Nations in an Evolving World Order, Volume 21*. Philadelphia: University of Pennsylvania Press.

Nagel, Jack. 1974. "Inequality and Discontent: A Nonlinear Hypothesis." *World Politics* 26 (4): 453–472.

National Public Radio. 29 December 2006. "Morning Edition." *All Things Considered* program.

New York Times Online. 26 January 1994. "State of the Union: Excerpts from President Clinton's Message on the State of the Union." <http://query.nytimes.com/gst/fullpage.html?res=9C00E4DA1E30F935A15752C0A962958260> (accessed 20 May 2008).

Nguyen, Van. Windows on Asia Website. Asian Studies Center, Michigan State University. "History of Vietnam." <http://asia.msu.edu/seasia/Vietnam/History/Civil%20War.html> (accessed 16 May 2008).

O'Brien, Connor Cruise. June 1986. "Thinking About Terrorism." *Atlantic Monthly*: 63.

O'Connell, James. 1993. "The Ending of the Nigerian Civil War: Victory, Defeat, and the Changing of Coalitions." In *Stopping the Killing: How Civil Wars End*. Edited by Roy Licklider. New York, NY: New York UP.

Ofodile, Anthony Chukwuka. 1994. "The Legality of the ECOWAS Intervention in Liberia." *Columbia Journal of Transnational Law* 32: 381–418.

Olson, Marie, and Frederic S. Pearson. 2002. "Civil War Characteristics, Mediators and Resolution." *Conflict Resolution Quarterly* 19 (4): 421–445.

Olson Lounsbery, Marie. 2003. "Discriminatory Policy Change and Ethnopolitical Violence: A Cross National Analysis." Doctoral Dissertation. Detroit: Wayne State University.

_____. September 2005. "Enduring Intrastate Rivalries in Southeast Asia: A New Direction in Intrastate Conflict Exploration." Presented at the Annual Meeting of the American Political Science Association, Washington DC.

Olson Lounsbery, Marie, and Frederic S. Pearson. 2003. "Policy Making and Connections to Violence: A Case Study of India." *Peace and Conflict Studies* 10 (2): 20–45.

Olsson, Ola, and Heather Congdon Fors. 2004. "Congo: The Prize of Predation." *Journal of Peace Research* 41 (3): 321–336.

Onwar.com. "Wars of the World." <http://www.onwar.com/aced/index.htm> (accessed 16 May 2008).

O'Toole, Kathleen. 19 November 1997. "Why Peace Agreements Often Fail to End Civil Wars." Stanford Online Report. <http://newsservice.stanford.edu/news/1997/november19/civilwar.html> (accessed 20 May 2008).

Owen, John M. 1996. "How Liberalism Produces Democratic Peace." In *Debating the Democratic Peace*. Edited by Michael E. Brown, Sean M. Lynn-Jones, and Steven E. Miller. Boston, MA: MIT Press.

Pearson, Frederic S. 1974. "Foreign Military Interventions in Domestic Disputes." *International Studies Quarterly* 18 (3): 259–290.

Pearson, Frederic S., et al. 2006. "Replicating and Extending Theories of Civil War Settlement." *International Interactions* 32 (2): 109–128.

Pearson, Frederic S., and J. Martin Rochester. 1998. *International Relations: The Global Condition in the Twenty-First Century*, 4th ed. New York, NY: McGraw-Hill.

Pearson, Frederic S., John Sislin, and Marie Olson. 1998. "Arms Trade: Economics of." In *The Encyclopedia of Violence, Peace, and Conflict*. Edited by Lester Kurtz. San Diego, SA: Academic Press.

Pearson, Frederic S., and Marie Olson. August 2001. "Policy-Making and Connections to Violence: A Case Study of India." Presented at the American Political Science Association Annual Meeting, San Francisco, CA.

Pearson, Frederic S., Marie Olson Lounsbery, and Suzette R. Grillot. 28 February–3 March 2007. "Controlling the Flow of Small Arms and Light Weapons: The Role of Official and NGO Sanctions." Presented at the International Studies Association Annual Meeting, Washington, DC.

Penn World Tables. Center for International Comparisons at the University of Pennsylvania. <http://pwt.econ.upenn.edu/> (accessed 1 March 2003).

Pickering, Paula M. 2007. *Peace Building in the Balkans: The View from the Ground Floor*. Ithaca, NY: Cornell UP.

Pike, John. 2001. "Moro National Liberation Front." Federation of American Scientists. <http://www.fas.org/irp/world/para/mnlf.htm> (accessed 16 May 2008).

Polity IV Project. *Political Regime Characteristics and Transitions, 1800–2006*. Center for Systemic Peace, University of Maryland.

Preston, Matthew. 2004. *Ending Civil War: Rhodesia and Lebanon*. International Library of War Studies #02. London, UK: Tauris and Co.

Prezeworski, Adam, et al. 2005. *Democracy and Development: Political Institutions and Material Well-Being in the World, 1950–1990*. Cambridge, UK: Cambridge UP.

Project Ploughshares. "Armed Conflict Reports: Tajikistan." <http://www.ploughshares.ca/libraries/ACRText/ACR-Tajikistan.html> (accessed 20 May 2008).

Pruitt, Dean G., Jeffrey Z. Rubin, and Sung Hee Kim. 1994. "Conflict Escalation." In *Social Conflict: Escalation, Stalemate, and Settlement, 2nd Edition*. New York, NY: McGraw Hill College Division.

Public Broadcasting Service. 1999. *Frontline: War in Europe*. WGBH Educational Foundation.

Public Broadcast System. "Judgment Day, 1831–1865." *Africans in America*. Resource Bank, Part IV. Boston, MA: WGBH. 1998–1999. <http://www.pbs.org/wgbh/aia/part4/narrative_txt.html>.

Queen, William. 2005. *Under and Alone: The True Story of the Undercover Agent Who Infiltrated America's Most Violent Outlaw Motorcycle Gang*. New York, NY: Ballantine Books.

Rapoport, Anatol, and Albert M. Chammah. 1965. *Prisoner's Dilemma*. Ann Arbor, MI: U of Michigan P.

Reeder, Brett. "Book Summary of *Ending Civil Wars: the Implementation of Peace Agreements* by Stephen John Stedman, Donald Rothchild, and Elizabeth M. Cousens." Conflict Resolution Consortium. 2006. <http://www.beyondintractability.org/booksummary/10649/> (accessed 20 May 2008).

Regan, Patrick M. 2000. "Users Manual for Pat Regan's Data on Intervention in Civil Conflicts." <http://bingweb.binghamton.edu/~pregan/>.

_____. 18–20 May 2001. "Data on Third Party Interventions in Intrastate Conflicts." Paper prepared for the UC Irvine/World Bank workshop on the Economics of Political Violence, University of California Irvine.

_____. 2002. "Third-Party Interventions and the Duration of Intrastate Conflicts." *Journal of Conflict Resolution* 46 (1): 55–73.

Regan, Patrick M., and Allan C. Stam. 2000. "In the Nick of Time: Conflict Management, Mediation Timing, and the Duration of Interstate Disputes." *International Studies Quarterly* 44 (2): 239–260.

Regan, Patrick M., and Aysegul Aydin. 2006. "Diplomacy and Other Forms of Intervention in Civil Wars." *Journal of Conflict Resolution* 50 (5): 736–756.

Regan, Patrick M., and Daniel Norton. 2005. "Greed, Grievance, and Mobilization in Civil Wars." *Journal of Conflict Resolution* 49 (3): 319–336.

Reisman, Michael. 1990. "Sovereignty and Human Rights in Contemporary International Law." *American Journal of International Law* 84 (4): 866.

_____. 1995. "Haiti and the Validity of International Action." *American Journal of International Law* 89: 82–84.

Rosenau, James. 1971. *The Scientific Study of Foreign Policy.* New York, NY: The Free Press.

Ross, Marc Howard. 1993. *The Culture of Conflict: Interpretations and Interests in Communities.* New Haven, CT: Yale UP.

Ross, Michael L. 2004. "What Do We Know About Natural Resources and Civil War?" *Journal of Peace Research* 41 (3): 337–356.

Roth, Brad R. 1999. *Governmental Illegitimacy and International Law.* Oxford, UK: Oxford UP.

_____. September 2005. "State Sovereignty, International Legality, and Moral Disagreement." Presented at the American Political Science Association Annual Meeting, Washington, DC; updated, Detroit: Wayne State University. <http://www.law.uga.edu/intl/roth.pdf>.

Rothchild, Donald S. 2002. "Settlement Terms and Post-Agreement Stability." In *Ending Civil Wars: The Implementation of Peace Agreements.* Edited by Stephen John Stedman, Donald Rothchild, and Elizabeth M. Cousens. Boulder, CO: Lynne Reinner.

Rummel, R.J. 1979. *Understanding Conflict and War, Vol. 4: War, Power and Peace.* Beverly Hills, CA: Sage.

Russett, Bruce M. 1964. *Inequality and Instability: The Relation of Land Tenure to Politics.* Baltimore, MA: Johns Hopkins UP.

Saideman, Stephen M. 2001. *The Ties that Divide: Ethnic Politics, Foreign Policy, and International Conflict.* New York, NY: Columbia UP.

Saideman, Stephen M., and Marie-Joëlle Zahar, eds. 2008. *Insecurity in Intra-State Conflicts: Governments, Rebels, and Outsiders.* London, UK: Routledge.

Saideman, Stephen M., and R. William Ayres. 2008. *For Kin or Country: Xenophobia, Nationalism, and War*. New York, NY: Columbia UP.

Sambanis, Nicholas. 2001. "Do Ethnic and Non-Ethnic Civil Wars Have the Same Causes? A Theoretical and Empirical Inquiry (Part 1)." *Journal of Conflict Resolution* 45 (3): 259–282.

Sandole, Dennis J.D. 1999. *Capturing the Complexity of Ethnic Conflict: Dealing with Violent Ethnic Conflicts of the Post-Cold War Era*. London: Routledge.

Saperstein, Alvin M. 1996. "The Prediction of Unpredictability: Applications of the New Paradigm of Chaos in Dynamic Systems to the Old Problem of the Stability of a System of Hostile Nations." In *Chaos Theory in the Social Sciences*. Edited by Euel Elliott and Douglas L. Kiel. Ann Arbor, MI: U of Michigan P.

Sarkees, Meredith Reid, Frank Whelon Wayman, and J. David Singer. 2003. "Inter-State, Intra-State, and Extra-State Wars: A Comprehensive Look at Their Distribution over Time, 1816–1997." *International Studies Quarterly* 47: 49–70.

Singer, J. David, Stuart Bremer, and John Stuckey. 1972. "Capability Distribution, Uncertainty, and Major Power War, 1820–1965." In *Peace, War, and Numbers*. Edited by Bruce Russett. Beverly Hills, CA: Sage.

Sisk, Timothy D. 1996. *Powersharing and International Mediation in Ethnic Conflicts*. Washington, DC: United States Institute of Peace.

Sislin, John, and Frederic S. Pearson. 2001. *Arms and Ethnic Conflict*. Lanham, MD: Rowman and Littlefield.

———. 2006. "Arms and Escalation in Ethnic Conflicts: The Case of Sri Lanka." *International Studies Perspectives* 7 (2): 137–158.

Slater, Jerome, and Terry Nardin. 1986. "Nonintervention and Human Rights." *Journal of Politics* 48 (1): 86–95.

Small, Melvin, and J. David Singer. 1982. *Resort to Arms: International and Civil Wars, 1816–1980*. Beverly Hills, CA: Sage Publications.

Smith, M. Shane. April 2004. "Sanctions: Diplomatic Tool, or Warfare by Other Means?" *Beyond Intractability*. <http://www.beyondintractability.org/essay/sanctions/>.

Snyder, Jack. 2000. *From Voting to Violence: Democratization and Nationalist Conflict*. New York, NY: W.W. Norton.

Stedman, Stephen John. 1997. "Spoiler Problems in Peace Processes." *International Security* 22 (2): 5–53.

———. 1 May 2001. "Implementing Peace Agreements in Civil Wars: Lessons and Recommendations for Policymakers." <http://www.ipacademy.org/pdfs/Pdf_Report_Implementing.pdf>.

Stedman, Stephen John, Donald Rothchild, and Elizabeth M. Cousens, eds. 2002. *Ending Civil Wars: The Implementation of Peace Agreements*. Boulder, CO: Lynne Rienner Publishers.

Strakhovsky, Leonid, I. 1944. *Intervention at Archangel: The Story of Allied Interven-tion and Russian Counter Revolution in North Russia, 1918–1920.* Princeton, NJ: Princeton UP.

Sutton, Malcolm. 2002. *An Index of Deaths from the Conflict in Ireland.* CAIN Web Service. <http://cain.ulst.ac.uk/sutton/book/index.html>.

Suzuki, Susumu. 2006. "All Armed Internal Conflicts Must End: Rethinking the Empirical Models of Internal Armed Conflict Outcomes." Preliminary draft. Detroit: Wayne State University.

———. 2007. "Explaining Internal Conflict Outcomes: An Empirical Test." Working paper. Version 05-19-07. Detroit: Wayne State University.

Talentino, Andrea Kathryn. 2006. *Military Intervention After the Cold War.* Athens, OH: Ohio UP.

Taylor, Telford. 1970. *Nuremburg and Vietnam: An American Tragedy.* New York, NY: Quadrangle Books.

Theis, Cameron G. 2005. "War, Rivalry, and State Building in Latin America." *American Journal of Political Science* 49 (3): 451–465.

Toft, Monica Duffy. 14 August 2006. "Iraq's Civil War What Next?" *Nieman Watch-dog.* Cambridge, MA: Nieman Foundation for Journalism, Harvard Univer-sity. <http://www.niemanwatchdog.org/index.cfm?fuseaction=ask_this.view&askthisid=00228>.

Trel, Lisa. 24 September 2002. "Causes of the World's Civil Wars Misunderstood, Researchers Say." News Release, Stanford University. <http://news-service.stanford.edu/pr/02/civilwar925.html>.

Tuchman, Barbara. 1962. *The Guns of August.* New York, NY: Macmillan.

United Nations. 2000. "Agreement on a Comprehensive Political Settlement of the Cambodia Conflict." Peace Agreements Digital Collection: Cambodia. United States Institute of Peace. <http://www.usip.org/library/pa/cambo-dia/comppol_10231991_annex1.html>.

———. "Facts and Figures." <http://www.un.org/Depts/dpko/dpko/co_mission/onusalfacts.html> (accessed 20 May 2008).

———. "United Nations Peacekeeping: List of Operations." <http://www.un.org/Depts/dpko/list/list.pdf> (accessed 15 May 2008).

United Nations High Commissioner for Refugees. 2005. UNHCR Statistical Yearbook.

United Nations News Centre. 2004. "Tajikistan: Rising from the Ashes of Civil War." Ten Stories the World Should Hear More About, Department of Public Affairs, and Development Programme. <http://www.un.org/events/tensto-ries/story.asp?storyID=600> (accessed 20 May 2008).

———. 2005. "Sierra Leone: Building on a Hard Won Peace." Ten Stories the World Should Hear More About, Department of Public Affairs, and

Development Programme. <http://www.un.org/events/tenstories/06/story.asp?storyID=600>.

———. 2006. "Liberia: Development Challenges Top Agenda as the Nation Recovers from Years of Civil Strife." Ten Stories the World Should Hear More About, Department of Public Affairs, and Development Programme. <http://www.un.org/events/tenstories/story.asp?storyID=2100>.

———. 15 December 2006. "At UN Meeting, 11 African Countries from Great Lakes Region Sign New Stability Pact." <http://www.un.org/apps/news/story.asp?NewsID=21000&Cr=great&Cr1=lakes> (accessed 20 May 2008).

United Nations Security Council. Press Release. 30 July 2004. "Security Council Demand Sudan Disarm Militias in Darfur, Adopting Resolution 1556 (2004) by Vote of 13-0-2." <http://www.un.org/News/Press/docs/2004/sc8160.doc.htm> (accessed 16 May 2008).

United States Department of State. December 2007. Background Note: Yemen. <http://www.state.gov/r/pa/ei/bgn/35836.htm> (accessed 16 May 2008).

United States Institute of Peace. December 1996. "Why Peace Agreements Succeed or Fail." Peace Watch Online. <http://www.usip.org/peacewatch/1996/1296/peace.html>.

University of Maryland. 2004. "Assessment for the Mossi-Dagomba in Ghana." Minorities at Risk Project (MAR). <http://www.cidcm.umd.edu/mar/assessment.asp?groupId=45203>.

Uppsala Conflict Data Program and International Peace Research Institute, Oslo. 2007. UCDP/PRIO Armed Conflict Dataset Codebook, Version 4-2007. <http://www.prio.no/sptrans/2119005713/UCDP_PRIO_Codebook_v4-2007.pdf>.

———. Sudan Conflict Summary. <http://www.pcr.uu.se/database/conflictSummary.php?bcID=233> (accessed 16 May 2008).

Van Evera, Stephen. 2001. "Primordialism Lives!" *APSA-CP: Newsletter of the Organized Section in Comparative Politics of the American Political Science Association* 12 (1): 20–22.

Vanhanen, Tatu. 1999. "Domestic Ethnic Conflict and Ethnic Nepotism: A Comparative Analysis." *Journal of Peace Research* 36 (1): 55–74.

Vasquez, John A. 1993. *The War Puzzle*. Cambridge, UK: Cambridge University Press.

Victor, Barbara. 2003. *Army of Roses: Inside the World of Palestinian Women Suicide Bombers*. New York, NY: Rodale Press.

Volkan, Vamik. 1998. "Ethnicity and Nationalism: A Psychoanalytic Perspective." *Applied Psychology: An International Review* 47: 45–57.

Walter, Barbara. 1997. "The Critical Barrier to Civil War Settlement." *International Organization* 51 (3): 334–335.

_____. 2002. *Committing to Peace: The Successful Settlement of Civil Wars*. Princeton, NJ: Princeton UP.

Waltz, Kenneth N. 1979. *Theory of International Politics*. New York, NY: McGraw Hill.

Waltzer, Michael. 1995. "The Politics of Rescue." *Social Research* 62 (1): 53–65.

Watson Institute for International Studies. March 2007. "No War, No Peace: Coping with the Aftermath of Wars." Conference sponsored by Brown University and the University of Lisbon. <http://www.watsoninstitute.org/events_detail.cfm?id=894> (accessed 20 May 2008).

Weede, Erich. 1978. "U.S. Support for Foreign Governments or Domestic Disorder and Imperial Intervention 1958–1965." *Comparative Political Studies* 10 (1): 497–527.

Weede, Erich, and Edward N. Mueller. 1998. "Rebellion Violence and Revolution: A Rational Choice Perspective." *Journal of Peace Research* 35 (1): 43–59.

Wehr, P., and J.P. Lederach. 1996. "Mediating Conflict in Central America." In *Resolving International Conflicts: The Theory and Practice of Mediation*. Edited by Jacob Bercovitch. Boulder, CO: Lynne Rienner Publishers.

Weiner, Myron. 1996. "Bad Neighbors, Bad Neighborhoods: An Inquiry into the Causes of Refugee Flows." *International Security* 21 (1): 5–42.

Wood, Gordon S. 2008. *The Purpose of the Past: Reflections on the Uses of History*. New York, NY: Penguin.

World Bank. "Measuring Inequality." <http://go.worldbank.org/3SLYUTVY00> (accessed 17 May 2008).

Wright, Quincy. 1942. *A Study of War*, 2 vols. Chicago, IL: U of Chicago P.

Yawanarajah, Nita, and Julian Ouellet. September 2003. "Peace Agreements." Beyond Intractability.org. <http://www.beyondintractability.org/essay/structuring_peace_agree/>.

Yongo-Bure, B. April 2007. "Human Capital Policy in Southern Sudan in the Post-Second War Period." Policy Brief #53. Ann Arbor, MI: The William Davidson Institute, University of Michigan.

Zartman, William I., and Saadia Touval. 1996. "International Mediation in the Post-Cold War Era." In *Managing Global Chaos*. Edited by Chester Crocker, Fen Hampson, and Pamela Aall. Washington, DC: United States Institute of Peace Press.

INDEX

A

Abu Sayyaf group (ASG), 144
action-reaction cycles. *See under* conflict
    processes
actors and warriors in civil conflicts, 6–11
Afghanistan, 2, 98, 110, 172, 204
    civil war, 95–96, 135
    NATO involvement, 89, 95, 113, 135, 212
    opium trade, 133
    Soviet forces, 49, 94, 96, 115
    Soviet military intervention, 94, 96
    terrorists and, 220
    US intervention, 128, 151
Africa, 21, 186. *See also* names of
    individual countries
    artificial boundaries, 64–65, 97
    black markets and smuggling, 99
    children recruited as soldiers, 42, 124
    civil wars following decolonization,
        20 (*See also* post-colonial states)
    control of natural resources, 79, 172,
        187 (*See also* diamonds; oil)
    framework for ending Central
        African civil wars, 180–81
    outside economic forces, 99
    war-proneness, 186
African National Congress, 9, 66
African Union (AU), 84, 98, 111–12, 174.
    See also Organization of African
    Unity (AU)
aftermath of civil war, 198, 202, 213
    arms surpluses, 200
    environmental degradation, 201, 204
    foreign debt, 209, 211
    post-traumatic stress disorder
        (PTSD), 199, 203
    refugees, 199–200, 202
Agent Orange, 117
agrarian-type societies, 77, 80–81

Al-Jazeera, 102
al-Qaeda, 13, 89, 95, 99, 220
Algeria, 17
American Abraham Lincoln Brigade, 115
American Civil War, 6, 10, 14, 79, 130, 163
    background conditions, 27–29
    Britain's nonintervention, 33, 58,
        97, 156
    causes and precipitants, 25, 27, 29, 31
    (*See also* slavery)
    chaos and corruption of
        reconstruction, 198
    death toll, 161
    democratic peace thesis and, 58
    development of communications and, 28
    economic issues, 48
    election of Lincoln, 31
    feared loss of "way of life," 48
    first laws of war and treatment of
        prisoners, 90
    governmental "reforms" and, 120
    military victory, 155
    nationalism, 29, 42
    "one-off" affair, 138
    party system breakdown, 28
    uprisings by abolitionists (US), 29
American Revolution, 35
American "war on terror." *See* "war on
    terror"
Angola, 93, 97, 116, 134, 172, 204
    failed agreement (1991), 184
    Soviet involvement, 115
Annan, Kofi, 191
anocracies, 59
Anstee, Margaret, 184
anticolonial struggles, 61. *See also* post-
    colonial states
Arbenz Guzman, Jacobo, 78, 93
Arias, Oscar, 111

arms. *See* weaponry
Asia. *See also* names of individual Asian
    countries
    insurgency peak (1960s and '70s), 20
Atlanta Olympic bombings, 7
AU. *See* African Union (AU); Organization
    of African Unity (AU)
Australia, 188
Austria, 26–27
autocratic regimes, 56–57, 147, 206
    fewer civil wars, 58
    success of negotiated settlements, 170
autonomy movements. *See* secession or
    local autonomy
Axis powers, 84
Ayers, Edward, 25, 27–28, 47

B
al-Badr, Muhammad, 135
Baghdad, 11, 33
"balance of power" or "hegemonic"
    systems, 33
Balkan wars, 1, 113
Baltic region, 14, 107
Bangladesh war, 200
Basque country, 39
Batista regime, 13
Belgian Congo, 92–93
belligerents. *See* actors and warriors
Bengali nationalism, 188
Bercovitch, Jacob
    "internationalized civil war," 4, 6
"Beyond Intractability" (website), 50
Biafra region of Nigeria, 15, 156, 163
Bin Laden, Osama, 49, 96, 165
black markets and smuggling, 137, 145,
    148, 172, 210. *See also* crime;
    weaponry
Black September, 154
bombings. *See* terrorism
Bosnia, 2, 11, 88, 103, 108, 110, 136
    Dayton Peace Accords, 113, 173
    example of the "new wars," 100
    identifying the enemy, 123
    mass rape, 199
    NATO, 113–14
    partition question, 189
boundaries and cross-border kindred
    groups, 64, 97

cross-border raids and sanctuaries, 115–16
    porous borders, 98
Boutros-Ghali, Boutros, 104, 201
Brezhnev Doctrine, 112, 116
Britain, 15, 26–27, 90, 209
    nonintervention in American Civil
        War, 33, 58, 97, 156
    support for Nigeria, 156
    unilateral interventions, 115
    veto power in UN, 110
Brown, John, 29, 31
Burma, 172
Burton, John, 49–50
Burundi, 52, 134
Bush, George H. W., 103
Bush, George W., 11, 57, 182, 186
    invasion of Afghanistan, 220
    push to spread democracy, 58
    "you're either with us, or against us," 125

C
Cambodia, 20, 115, 183–84, 205
    reconstruction, 211
    US invasion, 41
Camp David negotiations, 189
Canada, 20, 58, 72
Castro, Fidel, 7, 13, 38, 94, 146
casualty rates. *See* intensity
causation, theories of, 25–26
    deep contingency, 26, 30
ceasefire agreements, 62, 106, 156, 159–60,
    181, 183, 203
Central African Republic, 115
Chad, 106, 115–16, 134
Chechnya, 17, 39
Chiang Kai-shek, 14, 204
children and young people, 205
    aftermath of civil war, 198, 213
    post-traumatic stress disorder
        (PTSD), 124–25
    "re-education" abductions, 64
    recruited as soldiers, 42–43, 202, 204
    socializing, 39
    in wartorn society, 34
Chile, 94
China, 39, 152
    aid to Vietnam, 165
    civil war, 147, 204
    intervention in Angolan civil war, 97

Japanese invasion, 147
oil interests, 99, 180
as outside guarantor, 185
potential for political uprising, 60
veto power in UN, 110
CIA, 78, 93
"civil society" organizations, 193
civil violence, 3, 18, 21
   categories of, 4
   underlying motives, 16
civil war
   See also "new wars," 3–5
   actors and warriors, 6–11
   aftermath (See aftermath of civil war)
   categories, 4, 19
   causes contributing to, 16, 26–27, 37, 210
   challenges for international
      community, 21, 85
   change over time, 2
   definitions, 3–5, 7, 9–10, 18
   duration, 121, 149–50, 168–69, 174, 187
   "early warning," 111, 117, 119
   economic motivations intertwined
      with identity, justice, and honor
      issues, 48
   "enabling conditions" for, 124
   foreign intervention (See outside
      intervention)
   human rights (See human rights
      violations)
   increase in numbers, 18, 103, 145
   instilling civil violence, 43
   international remedies and responses
      to, 33, 103, 110 (See also
      international; UN)
   involvement of international actors, 33
   long-term consequences, 200–201
   motivation, 16, 35, 48, 52–53
   origins of, 27
   precipitants or triggers, 16, 26–27
   predictors of (See predictors of civil war)
   prevalence in post-Cold War period, 2
   prevalence throughout history, 18
   proliferated post Cold War, 2, 16–17, 20
   spillover effects, 2, 22, 98, 134
   successful settlement of, 167–74,
      184–85, 191
   threat to international peace and
      security, 17, 85

thresholds and criteria, 3–5
training grounds for terrorist
   organizations, 220
underlying factors, 164
civil war duration
   international factors affecting, 150–52
   negotiated outcomes and, 159
   presence of other wars and, 152
   state factors and, 145–49
civil war onsets, 18
civil war onsets per region, 20
civil war onsets per region (table), 19
civil war outcomes (tables), 176–79
civil war settlements
   coerced settlements, 165
   military victory vs. negotiation, 157–
      63, 168, 172, 180
   nature of the conflict and, 161–63
   state characteristics and, 163–64
   third party pressure and, 156
Clinton, Bill, 186
   bombing of Afghanistan and the
      Sudan, 220
   proposal for Palestine state, 189
   push to spread democracy, 57
"codetermination," 101
"cognitive dissonance," 142
Cold War, 61, 112–13, 128
   human rights issues and, 93
   kept lid on various animosities, 17
   limited UN peacekeeping, 110
   post-colonial states as pawns in,
      92–93, 135
   power struggle, 93
   small countries as pawns, 94, 135
   unilateral interventions during, 114
   US Cold War strategy, 78, 128
Colombo, 68
colonialism, 15
   arbitrary boundaries, 64–65
   no longer the accepted norm, 83
Colombia, 17, 133, 172
   criminal syndicates, 9–10
communal violence, 8
communal violence/criminal offenses
   distinction, 9–10
conciliatory overtures, 128, 130–31
Confederate States of America. See
   American Civil War

conflict dynamics, 119, 121–25
conflict expansion, 151
conflict intensity, 4–5, 121, 161, 168, 174
conflict processes, 119
    action-reaction cycles, 29, 75, 121, 128,
        139, 171
Congo, 98, 133
Congolese civil war, 92
Congress Party (India), 73
Correlates of War (COW), 4–5, 10, 18, 119
corruption (leaders and state apparatus),
        65, 79, 102, 122, 172, 216
coups, 14, 150
crime, 6, 10, 99
    criminal syndicates, 9
    drug trade, 10, 133
    "hate crime," 9
    illegal trade, 153
    need for international agreements, 187
crimes against humanity, 9, 85. See also
        genocide; human rights violations
Croatia, 88
cross-border raids. See boundaries
Cuba, 91, 94, 97–98, 146
Cuban Revolution, 7, 13, 48, 62
Cyprus, 16, 189
    UN peacekeeping mission, 136
    unilateral Turkish intervention, 136
Czechoslovakia, 91, 96, 112
    Prague Spring, 113
    Soviet military interventions, 94

D
Darfur, 98, 106, 111, 156, 165, 198
    human rights violations, 106–7
    outside humanitarian intervention, 157
Darfur peace negotiations
    AU as guarantor, 174
    factional disputes, 166
    marginalization of rebel groups, 167
Dayton Peace Accords for Bosnia, 113, 173
decentralization. See devolution or
        decentralization
decolonization, 64–65. See also post-
        colonial states
democratic peace thesis, 32, 57–59, 84, 170
democratic regimes, 56–57, 120, 147
    economic growth and, 206
    "guided" or strongman democracy, 60

majoritarian democracies, 65–67
mature democracies, 58
success of negotiated settlements, 170, 174
Democratic Republic of the Congo, 115, 203
democratization process, 57, 65. See also
        transitional states
    volatility, 60
demographic structure of states, 75–76,
        143–44, 147
dependence on natural resources, 186
devolution or decentralization, 72–73. See
        also power-sharing provisions
diamonds, 79, 99, 133, 146, 148, 187, 208–10
diplomatic efforts, 137, 219
diplomatic recognition, 97, 205
diplomatic sanctions, 136
"divided societies," 67
Doe, Samuel, 210
domestic regime type. See regime type
domestic violence, 124–25
Dominican Republic, 94, 128
    US unilateral intervention, 114
Doss, Alan, 210
Douglas, Stephen A., 31
Doyle, Michael, 191
drug trade, 10, 133

E
East Germany, 94
East Timor, 98
Economic Community of West African
        States (ECOWAS), 209
economic development, 206–7
    importance in avoiding civil war, 186
    settlement success and, 171
economic equality, 77
economic inequality, 78, 94, 146
economic or class-based civil violence, 77
ECOWAS (Economic Community of
        West African States), 112
Egypt, 102, 135
El Salvador, 111, 184, 186
elite motivation, 37–38. See also leaders
    altruistic sense of obligation, 37
    exploitable resources (greed), 133
elites
    role in facilitating or preventing civil
        war, 38
    smart sanctions, 137

elites and masses
  interest divergence, 59, 183
Ending Civil Wars (Stedman), 191
enduring and persistent rivalries, 138, 141–42
Entente Cordiale, 26
"entrapment," 171
environmental degradation, 2, 62, 94, 117
  aftermath of civil war, 201, 204
Eritrea, 106, 175–76
Estonia, 20
Ethiopia, 175, 185
ethnic and religious diversity, 75, 164
ethnic cleansing, 11, 99, 213. *See also* genocide
ethnic conflict, 1, 147, 150, 214. *See also* identity-based groups
  fear of group extinction, 42
  military victories and, 172
  negotiation success and, 8, 162, 169–70
  partition question, 188
  territorial autonomy provisions, 168, 173–74
  underlying causes, 47
ethnic nationalism, 26, 103, 105
ethnic nepotism, 76
ethnic symbols and myths, 42
ethnicity, 35
  most prevalent struggle in the 1970s, 19
  not the cause of war, 47
ethno-political conflicts, 8, 19, 68–72, 74, 141, 172
ethnocentrism, 75
evolving rivalries, 138–42
  action-reaction sequences, 139
  constructive leadership and, 138

F
failed states, 10, 155, 183, 204
  breeding grounds for terrorists, 185
federalism. *See* power-sharing provisions
feminist peace theory, 73–74
Ferdinand, Franz, 27
Ferguson, Niall, 170
fertility rate, 74
financial assistance, 97
fiscal federalism, 146
foreign debt, 209, 211
foreign direct investment, 80

foreign interveners. *See* outside intervention
former Eastern bloc states, 20
  insurgency of subordinate populations, 107
France, 15, 26, 39, 90, 96, 156
  as outside guarantor, 185
  outside pressure on Lebanon, 101
  unilateral interventions, 115
  veto power in UN, 110
Franco, Francisco, 202
Frank, Anne, 43
"free riding" problem, 31
"freedom fighters," 6, 15, 128
freedom of the press, 59
French Revolution, 58, 90
Freud, Sigmund, 34
Frontline: War in Europe, 87

G
Gandhi, Indira, 73
gender inequality, 80
genocide, 91–92, 98, 104, 134, 172, 183, 199
  Rwanda, 52
Genocide Convention (1948), 84, 92
Georgia, 17
Germany, 26–27, 88, 90, 113
  Nazi Germany, 9, 115, 174, 185
  "Reassurance Treaty" with Russia, 26
  rise in power, 26
Ghana, 8
glasnost, 60
globalization, 80, 95
  effect on rural economies, 81
  fueling arms and contraband trade, 145
  instantaneous international communications, 100, 102
  goals of civic violence, 13–14, 16. *See also* motivation
  success of negotiation and, 162
gold, 214
Gone with the Wind (Mitchell), 198
"good governance," 182
Gorbachev, Mikhail, 14, 60, 163
Gore, Al, 57
government, 9, 88. *See also* state
  composition, 73
  as tool of politically dominant group, 67
Great Britain. *See* Britain
Greece, 16, 114

greed, 53
greed vs. grievance argument, 36–37, 172
Grenada, 94, 114
grievance, 172
   addressed through political process, 58
   necessary for mass mobilization, 36–37
group dynamics, 31
   little room for neutrality, 125
   miscommunication, 126–27
group identity, 39, 65
   attempts to shape, 46
   honor and service, 47
   in "new wars," 99
   selective perception, 142
   symbols, 42
   use of scapegoating, 36, 45–46, 51, 124
group insecurity, 45
group-level analysis, 32
group level motivation, 46, 52
group security and survival, 45, 127
group splintering, 131–32, 134, 144, 166
Guatemala, 128, 191
   economic or class-based civil violence, 77
   land reform, 78
   military coup, 93
   US intervention, 94, 114
guerrilla tactics, 5, 7, 63, 100–101, 146
Guevara, Che, 7, 13
Guyana, 140

H
Habre, Hissene, 115
Hague Conference (1907), 90–91
Hague war crimes tribunals, 9
Haiphong, 41
Haiti, 91
Halmahera, 213–14
Hamas, 102
Hanoi, 41
Hashim, Salamat, 144
"hate crime," 9
Hazara, 95
"hearts and minds," 49, 217
Hezbollah, 11, 100–102
Hindu Nationalist Bharatiya Janata Party, 73
Hitler, Adolf, 34, 44, 199
Ho Chi Minh, 7, 40–41
Holocaust, 43, 84
Honduras, 94

human needs theory, 49–51
human rights, 21, 85–86, 91, 117, 184
   during Cold War, 93
   legislation, 90–92, 107
   prevailing global standards, 102
   second string in larger game, 94
human rights violations, 98–99, 104, 106, 208
   Darfur region, 106–7
   Somalia, 104
human rights vs. state sovereignty
      contradiction, 84–89, 92, 103
humanitarian intervention, 84, 86–89,
      103–5, 112, 114, 136, 157, 212
   legalities of, 116
Hungary, 91, 94, 115
Hussein, King of Jordan, 126
Hussein, Saddam, 11, 33, 77, 95
   poison-gas attacks on ethnic Kurds,
      89, 132, 173

I
Ibrahim, Khalil, 166
identification of enemy as "irrational,"
   127–28
identification with state, 217–18. See also
   nationalism
identity, 19, 53
   cards or symbols, 124
   hardening during political crisis, 46
identity-based groups, 15. See also ethnicity
   rivalries, 141
   shifts in power, 140
identity-based political parties, 73, 76
identity wars, 8, 150
   motivation, 35
   settlement success, 169
"ideological violence," 10
ideological war, 10, 141
   motivation, 35
   negotiation success and, 162
   settlement success, 170
IGO. See intergovernmental
   organizations
imperialism, 83
India, 72–73, 102, 147, 200
individual level of analysis, 31, 122–25. See
   also leaders
individual level of leadership and
   participation, 21, 30–31

individual motivation, 46
individual survival and security, 122
    recognizing the enemy, 123
Indo-Pakistani partition, 188
Indonesia, 141, 213
inequality, 53, 78, 94, 146
"instrumentalist" process, 36
insurgencies, 5–7, 11, 13
    require toleration of the majority, 31
intensity of fighting, 4–5, 18, 121, 161–62, 174
    settlement success and, 169
Inter-Governmental Authority on
    Development (IGAD), 106
intergovernmental organizations (IGOs),
    103, 114, 116
internally displaced persons (IDPs),
    213–15. See also refugees
International Court, 87–89
International Covenant of Civil and
    Political Rights (ICCPR), 91
International Covenant on Economic,
    Social and Cultural Rights
    (ICESCR), 91
International Criminal Court, 9, 85, 107, 219
international factors affecting civil war
    duration, 150–52
international law, 9, 88, 114
    adaptable over time, 86
    barring expansion through warfare, 90
    human rights field, 90
    post-colonial states, 84
    sovereignty-human rights debate, 89
    on unilateral interventions, 116
International Military and Training
    Team, 209
international or "system" level of
    analysis, 30, 32–33
International Peace Research Institute
    Oslo. See PRIO
international relations, 84
international sanctions, threats of, 153
international security organization, 112–14
international system, 15, 133
    caught off guard post Cold War, 104–5
    emphasis on state sovereignty, 83–84
    increased multilateral intervention
        (See multilateral interventions)
    lesson learned in Somalia, 107
    nation state as primary actor, 89–90

non-interventionist norms, 85–87, 89,
    94, 112, 116, 156, 186
    reluctance to recognize the new (post
        Cold War) violence, 104
    willingness to uphold peace
        agreements, 192
international wars, 2, 11, 15, 26, 30, 32,
    73, 104, 157, 199, 219
"internationalized civil war," 4, 6, 99, 135.
    See also "new wars"
interstate rivalry
    literature on, 139–41
interstate wars, 2, 11, 13, 74, 124, 134, 152,
    157, 171, 182
    decline, 17
intrastate rivalry, 139–41. See also civil war
intrastate violence, 3, 21
    onsets post World War II, 18
    prevalence in post-Cold War period, 16
Iran, 11, 95, 106, 132, 135
    fall of Shah Pahlavi government, 33
    forced replacement of Mohammed
        Mossadeq's government, 93
    Islamic revolution, 57
    oil-rich, 103
    pressure on Lebanon, 101
    "Sony revolution," 102
    US intervention, 103
Iran-Iraq War, 89
Iraq, 2, 5, 39, 102, 132, 193, 204
    American intervention, 32, 66, 77,
        95, 140
    "Coalition of the Willing," 112
    ethnic divisions, 64
    insurgency phase, 11, 32, 95
    international war criteria and, 11
    interstate phase of war, 11
    Kurds' secession attempts, 15, 33
    majoritarianism, 66
    oil, 95
    partition possibility, 217
    sectarian violence, 13
Iraqi civil war, 11–13, 32, 58, 95, 184
    caused by US intervention, 135
irredentist movements, 15–16
Islamic Court forces (Somali), 175
Islamic law, 107, 156, 175
isolated rivalries, 141
Israel, 3, 11, 133

American partisanship for, 102
children, 34
intervention against Hezbollah, 100
Israeli-Palestinian conflict, 3, 17, 138, 213
cultural and historical similarities, 126
miscommunication, 126–27
partition question, 189
Israeli settlement policy, 134
Italy, 90, 115, 156

J
Jabidah massacre, 143
Janis, Irving, 31–32
"groupthink" analysis of crisis
decision-making, 32
Janjaweed militias, 106–7, 157, 165
Japan, 13, 26, 90, 96
Jews, 43–44
Star of David, 124, 126
Johnson, Lyndon B., 40–41
Johnson-Sirleaf, Ellen, 209–10
Jordan, 101, 126, 135
Juba (Sudan), 198
economic boom, 197, 206
justice, 53
Justice and Equality Movement (JEM), 166

K
Kabila, Laurent, 134
Kant, Immanuel, 57
Karadzic, Radovan, 220
Kashmir, 17, 73, 102, 188
Kayibanda, Gregoire, 52
Kellogg-Brand Pact (1928), 91
Kennedy, John F., 40
Kenya, 106, 156, 176
Khartoum, 99, 105
Khomenei, Ruhollah, 102
King, Rodney, 189
Kissinger, Henry, 41
Korea, 114
Korean War, 96
Kosovo, 30, 108, 110, 190
ethnic Albanians, 15–16, 87
NATO, 113
Kosovo Liberation Army (KLA), 15, 114
Kruschev, Nikita, 93
"Kurdistan," 16

L
Lakar Jihad, 214
landmines, 201–2
Laos, 20, 115
Latvia, 20
law and order. See police and law and order
leaders, 146. See also elites
ability to retain leadership, 129–31
ambitious leaders, 78
corruption, 79, 99, 122
economic incentives, 36
enlightened leadership, 37, 138, 209
motivation, 36
portrayed as exploiters, 37
risk acceptance in, 36
use of religion to mobilize masses, 45
League of Nations, 85, 91
Lebanon, 2, 11, 170, 172, 218
"codetermination," 101
democracy, 101
economic or class-based civil violence, 77
ethnic divisions, 64
Israeli occupation, 100
penetrated society, 100
periodic recovery, 101
refugees, 100
religious cleavages, 100–101
legalities of intervention in civil wars,
86–87
Lenin, Vladimir I., 96
liberal model of peace, 80
Liberia, 99, 112, 210–12
Libya, 106, 144
Lincoln, Abraham, 27, 29–30, 97, 129–30,
146, 156
Lithuania, 20
Lomé Peace Agreement, 208
Lord's Resistance Army, 43
Lounsbery, Olson, 142
Lumumba, Patrice, 93

M
Macedonia, 190
Machakos Protocol, 106
Machel-Mandela, Graça, 209
majoritarian democracy, 65–67, 72
Malaysia, 141
Mandela, Nelson, 37, 66, 137–38
Mao Zedong, 14, 204

Maoist guerrilla tactics, 63–64
Marcos, Ferdinand, 143
Marker, Sandra, 50
Maslow, Abraham, 50
mass-based industrial states, 90
mass motivation, 32, 36, 51
  grievance, 36–37
  use of hatred and blame, 36
mass participation
  critical to civil war, 31, 38, 47
Matalam, Udtog, 144
McClellan, George, 130
McVey, Timothy, 7
media, 102, 214
  freedom of the press, 59
  instantaneous communications, 100, 102
  role in highlighting human rights
    abuses, 104, 124, 193
  use in motivating masses, 36
mediation, 153
Meir, Golda, 73
mercenaries, 2
Mexico, 90, 98
militarization of society, 74
militarized competitiveness, 142
military coups, 149
military intervention, 13–14, 97, 128, 151
  chances for rebel victories and, 165
  negotiated outcomes and, 165
  resource plunder and, 172
military victories, 157–58, 168
  genocide or politicide, 159, 199
  political and economic civil wars, 172
  settlement success, 169
military victories *vs.* negotiated
  outcomes, 157–63, 168, 172, 180
Milosevic, Slobodan, 15, 30, 34, 87, 114, 220
  use of outside threats, 36
Mindanao insurgency, 143–44
Mindanao Muslim communities, 131
minority rights, 67, 72
  Cold War and, 93
  "fit" concept and, 87
minority-ruled governments, 67. *See also*
  majoritarian democracy
  ethno-political conflict, 68
mirror imaging (in civil war opponents),
  126, 128
miscommunication, 126–27, 145

Misuari, Nur, 144
Mitchell, Margaret, *Gone with the Wind*, 198
Mladic, Ratko, 220
Mobutu, Joseph, 93, 98, 134
Molotov-Ribbentrop Pact, 44
Monroe Doctrine, 116
Montenegro, 190
Moro Islamic Liberation Front (MILF),
  131–32, 144
Moro National Liberation Front (MNLF),
  131–32, 144
Mossadeq, Mohammed, 93
motivation. *See also* goals
  elite, 35–36
  honor and service, 47
  individual, 35, 46
  mass, 36–37, 47, 51
  use of hatred and blame, 36
mountainous terrain, 146
  higher rates of civil war, 56
Mozambique, 116, 134, 172, 187, 204
Mugabe, Robert, 66
multi-ethnic states, 76
multilateral interventions, 135–36, 170, 186
  rebel victories and, 165
multilateralism, 103–4, 183
multinational corporations, 99, 192
Musharaf, Pervez, 103
Muslim Shari'a law, 105
"mutually hurting stalemate" (MHS), 130

N
Namibia, 134, 184
Nasser, Gammal Abdul, 101
nation-state
  party to and setting of civil war, 55
  as primary actor in international
    system, 89–90
  Westphalian system, 85, 90–91
national characteristics level of analysis, 32
"national defense" claims, 116
national identity, 65
national liberation struggles, 14
  difficulty defining, 91
nationalism, 29, 39, 45, 90, 218
  American Civil War, 42
NATO, 87, 108, 112
  Afghanistan, 95, 110, 113
  Bosnian civil war, 113–14

Kosovo, 113–14
 neutrality questions, 114
 used to bypass Security Council, 113
natural resource plunder, 99, 146, 148,
  172, 210
 diamonds, 99, 133, 146, 148, 187,
  208–10
Nazi Germany, 9, 115
negotiated agreements
 interim or preliminary agreements, 181
negotiated settlements, 157–58, 170, 184
 and civil war duration, 159
 conciliatory overtures, 128, 130–31
 framework and comprehensive
  agreements, 180–82
 implementation agreements, 182
 outside persuasion and, 164
 power-sharing formulas, 184
 Protocol on Non-Agression and
  Mutual Defence in the Great
  Lakes Region, 180–82
 resembling formal treaties, 180
 third party security guarantees and,
  159–61, 174 (See also third party
  guarantors)
 timeliness of concessions, 163
negotiated settlements vs. military
  victories, 168, 172, 180
negotiation, 127–28, 130, 141
Nepal, 62–64, 77
Netherlands, 90
"new Soviet man," 46
"new wars," 10–11, 22n2
 civilian victims, 99–101, 124
 guerrilla or terrorist struggles, 101
 instantaneous communications, 100, 102
 international supply, 101
 resource plunder, 99
 smuggling and crime networks, 99, 101
"new world order" prediction, 103
Ngo Dinh Diem, 40
Nicaragua civil war, 48, 77, 111, 128
 socio-political overtones, 62
 US intervention, 94, 114
Nigeria, 185
Nixon, Richard, 41, 97
Nkomo, Joshua, 66
nongovernmental organizations, 192,
  211, 215

nongovernmental armed groups. See
  private militia groups
North Atlantic Treaty Organization. See
  NATO
North Maluku conflict, 213–16
 deaths, 215
 gold, 214
 internally displaced persons (IDPs),
  213–15
 reconciliation, 215–16
 religious war, 214
Northern Ireland, 3, 141, 213
 about political dominance and
  subservience, 61
 British "occupation," 62
 EU membership, 136, 202
 "hegemonic masculinity," 125
 religion used as proxy for political
  affiliation, 8
 "Troubles," 61–62
Nuremberg war crimes tribunal, 9, 107, 219
"nurture" as opposed to "nature" school
  of thought, 34, 39, 45
"nurture" explanations for civil war, 34–35

O
oil, 79, 95–97, 99, 102–4, 106, 146, 148,
  180, 185, 197
Oklahoma City bombing, 7
opium trade, 96, 133
opportunism, 139
opportunity (or odds of successful
  revolt), 37–38, 42
 "death watch," 38
Organization of African Unity (AU), 84,
  97–98. See also African Union (AU)
Organization of American States (OAS), 111
Oueddi, Goukouni, 115
outside intervention, 10, 13, 65, 94, 99,
  134, 156
 counter-intervention, 97–98, 165
 multilateral, 135–46, 165, 170 (See also
  UN peacekeeping; unilateral
  intervention)
 antiterrorist concerns, 98
 forms of, 97
 humanitarian (See humanitarian
  intervention)
 legality, 87

power-related and self-interested
    motives, 89
support for a "peace process," 156
unilateral, 114–17

P
Pahlavi, Reza, 33, 93
Pakistan, 2, 95, 102, 188, 220
Palestinian-Israeli conflict, 3
    miscommunication, 126–27
    partition question, 189
Palestinian Liberation Organization, 154
Palestinian territories, 17
    proposal for Palestinian state, 189
Palestinians, 100–101, 133–34, 138
parenting. *See* "nurture"
partition question, 188–90, 216–17
pawns and proxies, 92–94, 98, 135, 175
    religion as proxy for political
        affiliation, 8
"peace," 193, 207. *See also* negotiated
        settlements; settlement success;
        UN peacekeeping
    "constituency for peace," 172
    contexts for, 191
    definitions of, 190–91
peace agreement implementation, 184.
        See also settlement success
Peace Research Institute (PRIO), 4, 119
peacebuilding, 183, 202–3
percentage of women in labor force, 74
perestroika, 60
personal ambition, 19
personality, role of, 21, 36. *See also* leaders
Peruvian Shining Path guerrillas, 63
Philippines, 91, 128, 131–32, 143–44
    Japanese military crimes, 219
    Muslim minority, 143
    self-rule, 143
Pol Pot, 183
Poland, 11, 91
    Soviet military interventions, 94
polarization, 125
police and law and order functions, 62,
        66, 160, 187–88, 193, 205, 207–8,
        210
"policy coherence" strategy, 187
political autonomy, 14
political economic power, 35

political freedoms, 59
political instability, 164
political nature of the state, 62
political openness, 56
political opportunism, 53
Political Quality of Life Index (PQLI), 77
political rights, 35, 51, 59
Popular Movement for the Liberation of
        Angola (MPLA), 97
popular revolutions, 149–50
popular sovereignty, 88
population and power shifts, 143–44
population size, 76, 147
Portugal, 90, 115, 184
post-colonial states, 74, 97
    artificial boundaries, 92
    civil war outbreaks, 103
    dissatisfied minority groups, 107
    pawns in Cold War, 92–93, 135
post-traumatic stress disorder (PTSD),
        122, 124
    aftermath of civil war, 199, 203
post-war political and human rights
        observance, 207
poverty, 164, 171
power or control, 16
    fear of losing, 29
power-sharing provisions, 158, 173.
        See also "codetermination";
        devolution or decentralization;
        partition question
power vacuums, 38
Prague Spring, 113
predictors of civil war, 38, 67–70, 75–76,
        164, 177, 218
    greed, 36
    national wealth and, 79
private militia groups, 217
    government use of, 98
    Janjaweed, 106–7, 157, 165
Protocol on Non-Agression and Mutual
        Defence in the Great Lakes
        Region, 180–82
protorivalries, 141–42
psychological damage, 122. *See also*
        post-traumatic stress disorder
        (PTSD)
Puerto Rico, 91
Putin, Vladimir, 60

Q
Qaddafi, Mu'ammer, 144
Quebec, 20

R
Rabin, Yitzhak, 132
racism, 185
Ramos, Fidel, 144
"rational choice," 48
rebel victories, 162, 165
    ability to survive first few months, 145
rebels, 6–7
    economic incentives, 36
rebel's dilemma, 31
recognizing "the enemy," 123–24
reconciliation process, 142, 204, 213, 215
    role of government in, 216
recovery. See successful reconstruction
refugees, 85, 98, 101, 197, 204
    aftermath of civil war, 199–200, 202
    Bengali refugees, 188
    from Darfur region, 106
    post-traumatic stress disorder
        (PTSD), 124–25
Regan, Patrick, 37, 161, 165
    civil war definition, 4, 19
regime type (or political regime), 56, 217
    influence on conflict duration, 147
    mobilization of opposition and, 57
    settlement success and, 170
regimes that have seized or claimed power
    legitimacy question, 88
regional actors
    price for cooperation, 193
regional intervention, 111–12
    neutrality questions, 112
rejectionists, 132, 165, 172
religion, 100–101, 189
    as convenient marker, 45
religious conflicts, 35, 188, 214. See also
    sectarian violence
representation, 35
repression, 58, 60, 74, 105, 107, 120–21
resource pillaging. See natural resource
    plunder
reversal of power. See status reversal
revolution, 13, 60. See also names of
    individual revolutions
"revolution of rising expectations," 102

Revolutionary United Front (RUF), 208
Rhodesia (now Zimbabwe) anticolonial war
    rebel bases in Zambia and
        Mozambique, 134
risk acceptance, 36
rivalry patterns, 142–44
Rudolph, Robert, 7
rural economies, 80–81. See also agrarian-
    type societies
Russia, 26–27, 90, 184. See also Soviet Union
Russian Civil War, 13, 96, 202
Russian Revolution
    foreign intervention attempt, 13, 112
Rwanda, 2, 17, 105, 107, 134, 184, 203–4
    genocide, 1, 98, 115, 184
    Hutu Interhamwe militia chiefs, 35
    identifying the enemy, 123
    international community and, 192
    status-reversal leading to civil war, 52
    war crimes tribunal, 220
Rwanda agreement
    failure to negotiate power sharing, 184
Rwandan Patriotic Front, 52

S
Saigon, 41–42
sanctions, 136–37, 153
Sandinista National Liberation Front, 48
Saudi Arabia, 96, 101–2, 135
Scandinavia, 77
scapegoating, 36, 45–46, 51, 124
secession or local autonomy, 14–15, 133,
    158, 163, 190, 216
sectarian violence, 8, 13, 19, 35. See also
    religious conflicts
security. See international security
    organization
"self-defense," 83
self-determination
    ethnic nationalism and, 105
    right of states to, 91
    UN Charter intentions, 107
self-rule, 105, 143
semidemocracies, 59
separatist wars, 133, 149
September 11, 2001, 7, 95, 110
Serbia, 15, 27, 87, 114, 220
settlement success, 167–73
    outside interference and, 171

peace agreement implementation, 184
political-economic motives and, 169
readiness and, 164
state corruption and, 172
third party guarantors, 168, 173–74,
    185, 188, 190–91
Sherman, William Tecumseh, 7
Siam. See Thailand
Sierra Leone, 99, 208–9
    diamond mines, 208–9
    illicit natural resource extraction, 208
    maintaining the peace, 209
    third party enforcement, 209
    truth and reconciliation committee,
        208
slavery, 27, 29, 48, 130, 156
    economic lynchpin, 80
    "unfinished business," 141
Slovenia, 88
"smart sanctions," 221
    aimed at ruling elites, 137
smuggling and crime networks. See crime
social violence. See crimes against
        humanity; genocide; human
        rights violations
Solomon Islands, 188
Somalia, 1–2, 6, 204
    clan warfare, 105
    Ethiopian troops sent to, 175
    lesson to international community,
        104–5, 107, 175, 191–92
    terrorists and, 220
Somoza regime, 48
"sons of the soil" wars, 150
South Africa, 66, 204
    economic sanctions, 137
    ethnic identity groups, 9
    intervention in Angolan civil war, 97
    minority-rule, 66–67
    racial violence, 10
    transition away from war, 3
    white community, 9, 67
"sovereignty of a people," 88
Soviet Union, 91, 115, 135. See also Russia
    assistance to North Vietnam, 151, 165
    disintegration (See Soviet Union
        collapse)
    expansionism, 115
    identity formation, 46

intervention in Angolan civil war, 97
military interventions, 94
protested UN intervention in Belgian
    Congo, 92
support for Nigeria, 156
in UN Security Council, 87, 93
unilateral interventions, 114
use of post-colonial states as pawns in
    Cold War, 93
veto power in UN, 110
Soviet Union collapse, 103. See also Cold War
    emergence of old grievances, 47
Spain, 11, 90, 143
Spanish Civil War, 115, 202
"spoilers" or "rejectionists," 132, 165, 172
Sri Lanka, 3, 17, 63, 148–49, 170
    desire for secession, 163
    "entrapment" (prior "sunken costs"), 171
    ethnic nationalism and repression,
        105, 138
    India's military intervention, 213
    politicized ethnic dominance pattern,
        67–68
"stability," 93
Stalin, Joseph, 44, 46
state capabilities, 160
state coherence, 218
state level of analysis, 21, 30, 33, 55, 62, 140
    economic state, 77–80
    political state, 56–75
    social state, 75–77
state monopoly on use of force, 120
state policy or role, 52
state repression, 74, 105, 107, 120–21
state reprisals, 163
state role in civil war, 9, 13, 79, 120
state sovereignty, 21, 83–84, 86–88
    colonial expansion and, 90
    post Westphalia, 90
    propping up dictators, 93
    as sovereignty of the people, 88
state sovereignty/human rights
        contradiction, 84–89, 92, 103
"state terrorism," 7
states dependent on primary
        commodities, 80, 186
state's refusal to negotiate with
        terrorists, 127
status reversal, 52, 65, 140

Stedman, Stephen John, *Ending Civil Wars*, 191
strategic interests, 107–8, 110, 135, 185, 192
structural changes, 49, 129–37
Study of War, A (Wright), 32
successful reconstruction, 203–18
   individual level, 203–4
   international level, 205
   partition, 216–17
   reconciliation, 216
   state level, 204–5
   targeting aid, 188
Sudan, 17, 98, 146, 202, 206
   arms and military training aid
     (intervention), 105–6
   ethnic nationalism and repression, 105
   fiscal federalism, 79
   international response, 105–7
   Machakos Protocol, 106
   oil, 180, 197
   outside encouragement for peace
     process, 156
   religious cleavages, 106
   resistance to UN peacekeeping troops,
     99, 174
   self-rule, 105
   target and refuge for extremist
     groups, 180
   terrorists and, 220
Sudan Liberation Movement/Army
   (SLM/A), 105–6, 166
Sudan negotiated settlement, 180
   aftermath, 197–98
suicide bombers, 3, 7, 45, 126, 220
   motivated by sense of honor, 49
Sula Archipelago, 213
Sulu Archipelago, 143
superpowers. *See also* Cold War; Soviet
   Union; US
   aid to fanatics, 128
   other powers as proxies, 98
Syria, 11, 101
system level of analysis, 32

T
Taiwan-China dispute, 88
Tajikistan, 205–6
Taliban, 95, 212
Tamil Tigers, 63
Taylor, Charles, 208, 210

territorial autonomy provisions
   effect on settlement success, 174
   importance to settlement success, 168,
     173–74
territory, 16, 141
   key issue leading states to war, 163
terrorism, 3, 7, 11, 132, 180, 207
   "al-Qaeda-linked" terrorists, 128
   connection to civil war states, 220
   counterterrorism, 7
   "new wars," 100
terrorists, 2, 6–7, 10, 101, 181, 186
   states' refusal to negotiate with, 127
   well-educated and well-to-do, 49
Tet Offensive, 40–41
Texas, 90
Thailand, 38, 90
Thaksin, Shinawatra, 38
Thatcher, Margaret, 73
third party guarantors, 173–74, 188, 191
   importance in negotiated
     settlements, 159–61, 168
   strategic interests and, 185
   Western powers as, 185
third party peacekeeping, 142. *See also*
   NATO; UN
Third World countries, 64
thresholds and criteria of civil violence, 3
   battle-related deaths per year, 4–5
   COW threshold level, 4–5
   intensity of fighting, 4
   PRIO, 4–5
Tiananmen Square, 60
Tito, Josip, 17, 38
topography, 164
Torture Convention (1984), 92
"transitional authorities," 211
transitional states, 56, 59, 64–65, 120
Treaty of Westphalia, 84, 186
Trent Affair, 97
Triple Alliance, 26
"truth and reconciliation," 204, 208
Turkey, 17, 26, 88

U
Uganda, 17, 43, 106, 134
UK. *See* Britain
Ukraine, 43
Ukrainian holocaust, 44–45

Ulster Unionist Party (UUP), 61
UN, 87–89, 91, 98
   civil war "early warning," 111
   commitment to state sovereignty, 94
   designated to enforce Angolan
      agreement, 184
   embargoes on Liberia's exports
      (diamonds and timber), 210
   interventions for humanitarian
      reasons, 136 (See also
      humanitarian intervention)
   multilateral interventions, 165
   overextended and overburdened post
      Cold War, 108, 111
   reliant on willingness of member
      states, 111
   reluctance to recognize the new (post
      Cold War) violence, 104
   role in human rights crises, 89
UN Charter, 83, 85, 91, 104
   principle of state sovereignty, 21
   on self-determination, 15, 107
UN Integrated Office in Sierra Leone
   (UNIOSIL), 209
UN Mission in Liberia (UNMIL), 211
UN Mission in Sierra Leone
   (UNAMSIL), 209
UN Mission of Observers of Tajikistan
   (UNMOT), 206
UN peacekeeping, 170, 191
   Belgian Congo, 92
   Cyprus, 136
   democratic peace thesis and, 84
   Somalia, 104
   Sudan, 99
   transformed nature of, 206
UN peacekeeping missions in civil wars
   (table), 108–10
UN Security Council, 83, 87, 166, 180
   check against expansionist regional
      powers, 112
   mechanisms for human rights
      enforcement, 91
   resolution on Sudan, 107
   special war crimes tribunals, 220
   US-Soviet rivalries, 111
   veto powers, 94, 110
underlying basic needs. See human needs
   theory; unmet human needs

unilateral intervention, 114–16
   "compelling interests," 116
   international law on, 116
   legitimacy questions, 115
   "national defense" claims, 116
   negative impact on human rights, 117
   rationalizations for, 116
   requested by governments or rebels, 115
United Fruit Company, 78
United Kingdom. See Britain
United Nations. See UN
United State. See US
United Tajik Opposition (UTO), 205
Universal Declaration of Human Rights, 92
unmet human needs, 53, 127
   violence potential, 50–51
uranium, 115
US, 13, 90, 96, 99, 112, 135, 143
   in Arabian Peninsula, 49
   broker for Angolan agreement, 184
   Central Intelligence Agency, 78, 93
   colonialism, 91
   Darfur struggle and, 98
   democracy, 57
   federal system, 72
   "first new nation," 91
   interest in Sudan, 180
   intervention in Angolan civil war, 97
   invasion of Cambodia, 41
   as outside guarantor, 185
   outside pressure on Lebanon, 101
   policy of anti-Soviet containment, 114
   support for Ethiopian invasion of
      Somalia, 175–76
   terrorist attacks, 7
   unilateral interventions, 103, 114, 116
   use of post-colonial states as pawns in
      Cold War, 93
   veto power in UN, 110
   Vietnam War, 39–41, 220
   war in Iraq, 12–13
   war with Mexico, 90
US/Soviet Union power struggle, 32, 135
US civil war. See American Civil War
US Cold War strategy, 78
US oil corporations, 97
US Roadmap principles for Israeli-
   Palestinian negotiations, 182
US Supreme Court, 57, 219

US/UN defense of Kuwait against Iraqi "aggression," 104
US "war between the states." *See* American Civil War
US "war on terror." *See* "war on terror"
USS Maddox, 40
USSR. *See* Soviet Union

V
Vietnam War, 14, 20
    American atrocities, 220
    American participation, 39–41
    anti-war sentiment, 41
    Chinese aid, 165
    economic issues, 48
    economic or class-based civil violence, 77
    guerrilla tactics, 7
    "internationalized civil war," 5–6
    nationalism, 39
    socio-political overtones, 62
    Soviet assistance, 151, 165
    spread to Laos and Cambodia, 115
Vietnamese civil war, 40–42
Vietnamese revolt, 7

W
Wahid el-Nur, Abder, 166
"walling off" or "cleansing" enemies, 123
war
    definition, 3
    struggle over political power, 61
    upper end of a violence continuum, 4
war crimes
    difficulties assessing and punishing, 124, 219–20 (*See also* genocide; human rights violations)
War Crimes Tribunals, 85, 219
"war on terror," 125, 220
    antiterrorism arrests, 58
    delegitimizing opponents, 128
Warsaw Pact, 112
weaponry, 2, 75, 165
    availability and access to armament, 22, 148, 200
    black market, 137, 145
    control and sales (or resales), 133
    international arms sources, 94

mutual arms races and weapons-spending, 142
    restricting arms flows, 137, 153, 221
    smuggling, 210
    type of weapons, 149
    weapons stockpiles, 146
West Africa, 133
Westphalian nation-state system, 85, 90–91
Wilson, Woodrow, 96
withdrawal of support by key foreign powers, 158
women
    aftermath of civil war, 198, 213
    leaders and role in government, 73
    percentage in parliament, 74
    post-traumatic stress disorder (PTSD), 125
    victims of rape, 124–25
women's suffrage, 74
World Bank, 187
World Trade Center, 7, 95, 110
World War I
    background conditions, 26
    triggering event, 27
World War II, 84
    genocide, 199
Wright, Quincy, *Study of War, A,* 32

Y
Yamashita, Tomoyuki, 219
Yemen, 135, 138
young people. *See* children and young people
Yugoslavia (former), 17, 30, 88, 190
    state sovereignty issue, 88
    war crimes tribunal, 220
    young people forced into armies, 42

Z
Zaire, 97–98. *See also* Democratic Republic of the Congo
Zambia, 134
Zapatista guerrillas, 98
Zimbabwe, 65, 134, 184. *See also* Rhodesia
    economic or class-based civil violence, 77
    effect of minority-rule discrimination, 66